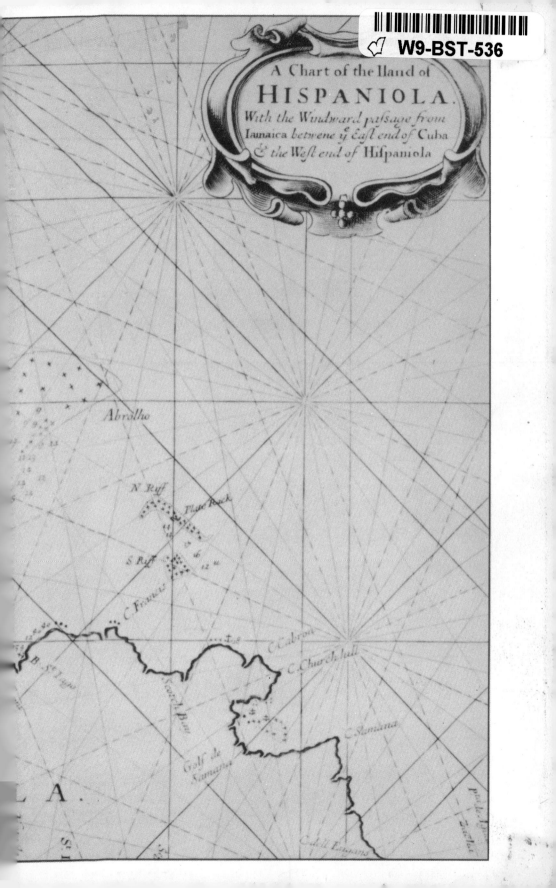

A Chart of the Iland of
HISPANIOLA.
With the Windward passage from
Iamaica betwene ye East end of Cuba
& the West end of Hispaniola

Abrolho

N Reef

Flatt Rock

S Reef

C Frances

C Cabron

C Church Jull

B St Iago

French Bau

Golf de
Samana

C Samana

L A.

Cabell Engano

THE WRECK OF THE ALMIRANTA

THE
TREASURE
OF THE
CONCEPCIÓN

PETER EARLE

THE VIKING PRESS   NEW YORK

972.9
E

First published in England under the title
The Wreck of the Almiranta

Copyright © Peter Earle, 1979, 1980
All rights reserved
Published in 1980 by the Viking Press
625 Madison Avenue, New York, N.Y. 10022

LIBRARY OF CONGRESS CATALOGING IN PUBLICATION DATA
Earle, Peter, 1937-
The treasure of the Concepcion =
The wreck of the Almiranta.
Bibliography: p.
Includes index.
1. Treasure-trove—West Indies. 2. Shipwrecks—
West Indies. 3. Salvage--West Indies. 4. West Indies
—History. 5. Phips, William, Sir, 1651-1695.
I. Title.
F1621.E2 1980   972.9'03   79-26510
ISBN 0-670-72558-7

Printed in the United States of America
Set in Monotype Bembo

Contents

List of Illustrations

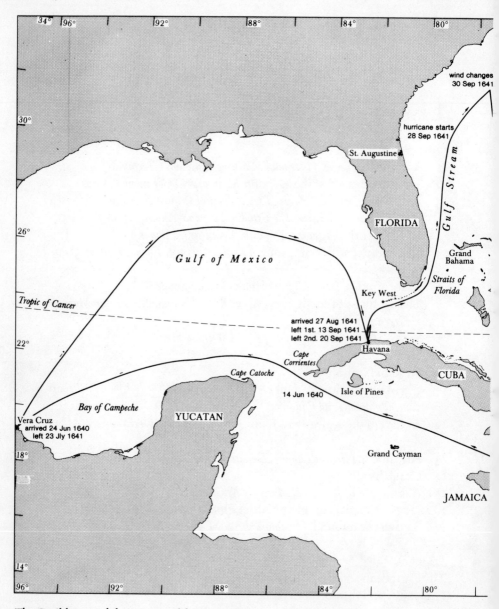

The Caribbean and the voyage of the *Concepción*.

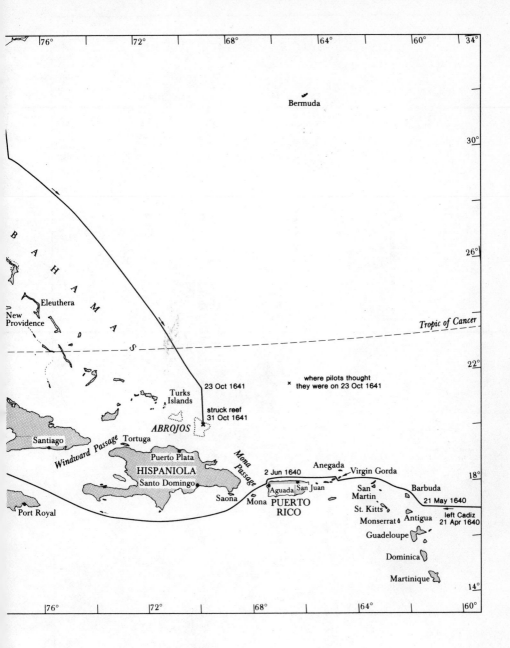

76° 72° 68° 64° 60° 34°

30°

Bermuda

B

A

26°

H

Eleuthera

New
Providence

Tropic of Cancer

A

22°

M

A

Turks
Islands

23 Oct 1641

where pilots thought
× *they were on 23 Oct 1641*

S

struck reef
31 Oct 1641

ABROJOS

Santiago

Tortuga

Windward Passage

Puerto Plata

18°

HISPANIOLA

*Mona
Passage*

2 Jun 1640

Anegada

Virgin Gorda

Santo Domingo

Aguada San Juan

San
Martin

Barbuda

21 May 1640

Saona

Mona

PUERTO

St. Kitts

Port Royal

RICO

Monserrat

Antigua

left Cadiz
21 Apr 1640

Guadeloupe

Dominica

Martinique

14°

76° 72° 68° 64° 60°

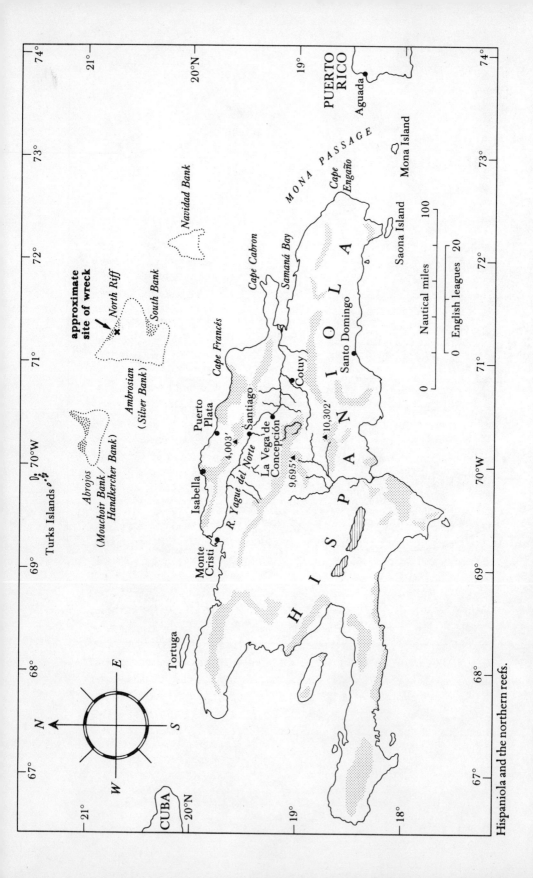

Hispaniola and the northern reefs.

Introduction

Witness *Sir William Phip's* Voyage to the Wreck; 'twas a mere Project, a Lottery of a Hundred Thousand to One odds; a hazard, which if it had fail'd, every body wou'd have been asham'd to have own'd themselves concern'd in; a Voyage that wou'd have been as much ridicul'd as *Don Quixot's Adventure upon the Windmill:* Bless us! that Folks should go Three thousand Miles to Angle in the open sea for Pieces of Eight! Why, they wou'd have made Ballads of it; and the Merchants wou'd have said of every unlikely Adventure, 'Twas like *Phips* his Wreck-Voyage; but it had Success, and who reflects upon the Project?

I first became interested in the subject of this book when I read this passage in Daniel Defoe's *Essay upon Projects* published in 1697. It seemed such a marvellous story, a story which conjured up the very essence of the late seventeenth century, a mixture of romance, adventure, greed and hard-headed business sense. I began to read a little more about Sir William Phips and his treasure and soon found that my first instinct was right. It is a marvellous story, and one that is quite superbly documented, so I decided to write this book.

The story is very little known in England, even amongst historians with a professional interest in the seventeenth century, but it forms part of American folklore and has attracted much more attention on that side of the Atlantic. Even so, there has been no book written on the subject since *The Hispaniola Treasure* by Cyrus H. Karraker, which was published in Philadelphia in 1934. Karraker's book and Robert H. George's article, 'The Treasure Trove of William Phips', which was published in the *New England Quarterly* in 1933, have been very valuable to me, but there have been many important documents discovered since they were written and my book breaks much fresh ground. In particular, I have been able to tell the Spanish end of the story. Neither Karraker nor George identified the wreck, a task which is made much easier for a modern author who can make use of the detailed documentation contained in Huguette and Pierre Chaunu's massive *Séville et l'Atlantique*. Even Phips himself did not know the name of the wreck that he discovered, so this is the first time that the full story has been told, from the time when the *Nuestra Señora de la Concepción* was chosen as the Capitana of the Mexican plate fleet of 1640 to her shipwreck in 1641 and so eventually to her rediscovery and salvage by an expedition led by William Phips in 1687.

Another advantage of writing a book on this subject in 1978 rather than in 1934 is that I have been able to benefit from the literature produced as a result of the modern treasure-hunting boom which started in the 1950s. It is in fact treasure-hunters, and not historians, who know most about Phips's wreck, for they look on him as their most successful forebear and many have tried to emulate him by discovering the wreck of the *Concepción* for a second time. Little did I know when I started writing this book that my research would play a crucial role in their realizing this ambition. My congratulations to Burt Webber and his colleagues for their sensational achievement, which is described in my final chapter. My thanks, too, for sharing with me their vast knowledge of the wreck and for their very generous invitation to visit the wreck-site. Nothing has made Phips more real to me than meeting his successors.

I owe another great debt to Victoria Stapells-Johnson, my research assistant in Seville, who has been responsible for reading, taking notes from and translating nearly all the Spanish documents used in the preparation of this book. This was a difficult task, even for someone as experienced as she is in reading seventeenth-century Spanish documents, and I must congratulate her on doing a superb job. The handwriting was often very difficult to read, particularly in the marvellous 'Jesuit letter' which contains an eye-witness account of the shipwreck and the adventures of the survivors. But, even when the documents were quite easy to read, they were full of archaisms and forgotten maritime terminology which made them very difficult to interpret.

I would also like to thank the staff of the Archivo General de Indias in Seville who drew our attention to documents which we would otherwise have missed. Closer home, I would like to thank the staffs of the various record depositories which I have used and, especially, A. W. H. Pearsall of the National Maritime Museum at Greenwich, who was particularly helpful to me. One thing that was very encouraging in the preparation of this book was the fact that I never met anyone who helped me who did not become fascinated by the story. This was certainly true of Victoria Stapells-Johnson in Seville, and it was also true of the last two people whom I would like to thank, Janet Baker who drew the maps, and Joan Lynas who typed the manuscript. It is always nice to know that people are actually enjoying working for you.

All the translations from foreign languages, mainly Spanish, but also a little French and Italian, have been made by Victoria Stapells-Johnson or myself. We have not attempted to make the translations completely literal, trying instead to make quotations readable while retaining the sense of the original. Dates in Chapters 1–6, which are based mainly on Spanish documents, are New Style, and in Chapters 7–17, which are based mainly on English documents, are Old Style, which was ten days behind New Style. Throughout the book the year has been taken as beginning on 1 January. One last problem which needs to be considered is the interpretation of Spanish moneys and measures. The main difficulty arises from the fact that the same word, *peso,* was used for two different units of value and it is often impossible to distinguish which is meant in any given context. The *peso ensayado* (assayed peso) was normally used as a measure of bullion and had a value varying from 425 to 450 *maravedís*, the basic unit of account. But the word peso could also mean the *real de a ocho*, or piece of eight, which was worth only 272 maravedís. Bearing this in mind, the relative values of the Spanish coins and units of account mentioned in this book were as follows:

Real: A silver coin = 34 maravedís
Real de a ocho: Silver coin = 272 maravedís. This was the famous piece of eight or dollar. It was worth around 5s. sterling.
Escudo: A gold coin of equal weight and fineness to the silver real. Its value therefore varied depending on gold/silver ratios. These became fixed at 16 to 1 in the eighteenth century, and so the *escudo* became equal to two pieces of eight.
Ducat: A unit of account = 375 maravedís.

There are also a few problems with weights. The English used both the pound troy and the pound avoirdupois to weigh silver, so it should be remembered that the pound troy contains 5,760 grains and is divided into 12 ounces, while the pound avoirdupois contains 7,000 grains and is divided into 16 ounces, and so is considerably heavier. The Spanish used the libra, roughly equivalent to the pound avoirdupois, and the quintal, which was 100 libras.

Finally, as this is a book on maritime history, we have to worry about the league and the fathom. The Spanish divided a degree of latitude into $17\frac{1}{2}$ leagues of 4 miles each, while the English divided it, as we do now, into 60 nautical miles or 20 leagues of 3 miles each. The Spanish league was thus a little longer than an English one, and the mile a little shorter. For shorter measurements the Spanish used the *dedo*, the *palmo*, the *vara* and the *braza* which had the following relationship:

12 dedos = 1 palmo
4 palmos = 1 vara
2 varas = 1 braza

The two commonest in the documents used were the palmo (21 cm. = $8\frac{1}{4}$ in.), which I have translated in feet and inches, and the braza (1.67 m. = 5 ft. 6 in.), which I have translated as 'fathom', though it is a little shorter than the English fathom of six feet.

London. 6 June 1978   PETER EARLE

14

CHAPTER ONE

A Capitana for New Spain

'There was about this time brought into the Downs a vast treasure, which was sunk in a Spanish galleon about 45 years ago, somewhere near Hispaniola, or the Bahama Islands, and was weighed up by some gentlemen, who were at the charge of divers etc., to the enriching them beyond expectation.'[1]

This entry in the diary of John Evelyn for 6 June 1687 sums up the story of this book, the story of the shipwreck of a Spanish galleon on a coral reef and the story of the many futile and frustrating attempts by men of many nations to locate the wreck, leading up to the day in January 1687 when an excited Englishman could record in his log-book 'the happy and joyfull news of ye cannew's findeing the wrecke [of] . . . ye richest ship that ever went out of ye West Indies'.[2] The story travels round the Atlantic, from Cadiz to Vera Cruz, from Havana to Santo Domingo, from Port Royal in Jamaica to New Providence in the Bahamas and from Boston to London, but it starts in Seville, the great commercial centre in southern Spain which was the home of the Casa de la Contratación, or House of Trade, the department of the Spanish government responsible for the organization of the fleets which connected Spain with her far-flung empire in America.

By 1639, the year when this book starts, Spain had been sending fleets to America for over a century, and the whole business was controlled by an elaborate system of rules and regulations administered by an ever-growing bureaucracy.[3] Rules laid down in minute detail the equipment, armament, provisioning and manning of every ship that sailed in the fleets. All goods carried in the ships had to be registered and inspected to prevent contraband and to provide the basis for the allocation of the taxation that paid for the defence of the fleets. Every passenger had to be registered in a book, so that the officers of the Crown would be able to control the quality of emigration and prevent the settling of heretics, foreigners, vagabonds and other undesirables in the American colonies. Any infringement of these rules carried very heavy penalties, and an enormous amount of time and effort was expended by the officers of the Casa de la Contratación in at least appearing to be trying to implement them. Each ship in the fleets received three different inspections, the last taking place shortly before she set sail. Even this was not the end since, following this last inspection, guards were posted on board until the ships were out at sea. Despite all these efforts, corruption was rife, and every ship that sailed to or from America carried large quantities of unregistered goods and many illegal passengers.

Two fleets were normally despatched each year. One was supposed to sail in the spring for Vera Cruz, the port of Mexico, or New Spain as it was then called; the other in August for Tierra Firme, the mainland of South America, with its terminus in Porto Bello. Both fleets were escorted by warships, normally eight galleons for the Tierra Firme fleet and two for New Spain. Both fleets normally spent the winter in America, unloading and selling their European cargoes and waiting for the arrival of the silver, which made up over ninety per cent by value of their return cargoes. Some of the silver was the property of the King, the product of royal taxation in the Indies. The rest belonged to individuals, the profits of the merchants and shipowners who had freighted goods to America, the wages and perquisites of the officers and crews of the fleets, and the remittances and savings of the latest batch of returning emigrants who had made their pile in America and were now planning to return to Spain to spend it. When the silver had been loaded, the two fleets sailed to Havana in Cuba, the best defended port and the main shipbuilding centre of the West Indies. Here the ships were, if necessary, refitted and revictualled before sailing together for Spain in the summer, preferably before the beginning of the hurricane season. The return of the combined silver fleets was awaited anxiously in Spain, where both the King and his subjects relied very heavily on this constant flow of precious metal to retain their solvency and their credit. Any delay or disaster could rapidly bring the whole of the ailing Spanish economy to a grinding halt, with repercussions throughout Europe. The effect was even worse for the King, whose resources were always at full stretch in a desperate and never-ending effort to preserve his enormous empire. No silver meant no cash to pay his troops, and unpaid Spanish troops refused to fight, a fact which naturally jeopardized the progress of the many campaigns all over Europe in which the Spanish military machine was constantly engaged.[4]

In recent years the cost of disaster had become even greater, for as military expenditure rose, the quantity of silver being shipped back to Spain had declined.[5] The mines, affected by rising costs, were producing less silver,[6] and more of what they did produce was being retained by the colonial economies which were becoming increasingly independent of Spain. The fact that the colonists could now produce for themselves many of the European goods previously exported to them also discouraged the great merchants of Seville from freighting as many ships as they had done in the past, and naturally, if less goods were sent out, less silver was returned in payment. But this was not the only problem. Since the 1620s there had been an almost continuous increase in the cost of defending the fleets from the attacks of the numerous predators who tried to short-circuit the flow of silver to Spain. This was reflected in the increased rate of the *avería*, the tax on imports and exports which paid for defence of the fleets. The merchants' reaction was to ship more goods clandestinely, a fact which meant that those which actually appeared on the registers of the Casa de la Contratación were taxed at an even higher rate, so reducing the legitimate profits to be made from the trade to virtually nothing. In the early 1630s the rate rose from 6 to 35 per cent and, although it was to fall again, the level of fraud had risen to an all-time maximum.

The problems of the merchants were compounded by the behaviour of the King, who, desperate for ready cash, had got into the habit of taking not only the silver that was his of right, but also all that private silver which represented the capital and profits of the merchants of Seville, giving them in return miserable debased copper currency or the equally miserable *juros*, a form of irredeemable government stock which could only be turned into cash at a high discount. Naturally the King's confiscations encouraged the merchants to conceal more and more of the silver which was remitted from America. If this were to go on much longer there would be no registered goods to load on the ships, no registered private silver to send home, no tax on such goods to pay for the defence of the fleets from marauding foreigners and so ultimately no fleet and no silver.

Things had not yet reached this pass, but the 1630s had seen a rapid decline in the shipments of silver from America, even allowing for the fact that a far greater proportion was now being shipped illegally. Such a decline made little difference to the reputation acquired by Spanish America as an inexhaustible reservoir of riches. Nor did it make any difference to the anxiety with which the King of Spain waited for the return of the fleets from America. The fact that there was less silver shipped simply meant that what was shipped acquired an even greater significance for those who waited desperately for its arrival. A ship lost in the late sixteenth century was certainly bad for business, but it could be written off in the confident expectation that future gains would amply make up for past losses. But a ship lost now would be an absolute disaster, with armies to pay all over Europe and no money in the royal coffers.

However, the very decline of the trade made disaster more likely. With fewer ships engaged in the trade each year, it was clear that there was little commercial incentive to build or buy new ships, even had there been sufficient money to do so. As a result the stock of ships engaged in the American trade became older and older and thus less able to withstand the strains of the eight-thousand-mile round trip. The danger of shipwreck was increased by the fact that the general difficulties had seriously dislocated the tidy organization and timetable of the fleets, whose departure from Spain and return from America was now often delayed by commercial and financial pressures. Fleets left Spain late because there was not sufficient money to fit them out. Fleets left America late because it often took a very long time to get rid of the cargo in the overstocked markets. A slow turn-round obviously reduced merchants' profits still further. It also tempted the Captains-General of the fleets to leave directly all the ships under their command had made up their lading, even when the time of year was extremely dangerous for shipping, a temptation which was increased by peremptory demands from the King for the rapid return of his silver.

Such facts were well known to the officials of the Casa de la Contratación, who, early in the summer of 1639, were instructed by the King's Council of the Indies to arrange for a fleet to sail to Mexico. The fleet was originally supposed to sail at the beginning of July, but shortage of money led to a series of postponements, and it was eventually decided that the fleet should sail in the spring of the following year. The first task of the officials was to select the two ships which would serve as escort to the fleet, the Capitana, or flagship, and the Almiranta, or vice-admiral. It would have been nice to have chosen two brand-new, purpose-built galleons for the job but, as we have seen, the economic circumstances of the day prohibited such a luxury and the officials were forced to compromise. Their final choice fell on two elderly merchant ships which would be converted to fulfil the requirements and regulations of the Casa de la Contratación.[7]

The ship we are interested in was the *Nuestra Señora de la pura y limpia Concepción*, commonly known as the *Concepción*, which was selected as the Capitana of the fleet. She was described as a *nao*, a generic term for a large merchant ship, and had been built in the shipyard at Havana in Cuba in 1620.[8] On 1 June 1639 a contract was signed between the officials of the Casa de la Contratación and the ship's owner, Don Tomas Manito of Seville. He agreed to hire his ship to the King to serve as Capitana for the voyage to Vera Cruz in Mexico, and to make all the preparations necessary for such a voyage, which would include very considerable alterations to the structure of the ship to enable her to take the forty bronze cannon which would be supplied from the royal arsenal. Don Tomas was to be paid 9,785 ducats for the hire of his ship, but he could expect to make considerably more on the side. The owner of the Capitana of a plate fleet was in a very privileged position.

The preparation of the *Concepción* was carried out during the winter of 1639–40 under the supervision of her mate, Francisco Granillo. The ship had only recently returned from her last voyage to New Spain and had in fact still been at sea when the contract was signed. She therefore needed a complete overhaul and refitting. She was hauled down and her bottom cleaned and, where necessary, resheathed with lead, to try to protect her from the ravages of the shipworm which throve in the trop- ical waters of the West Indies. All her planking and decking was scraped down and recaulked. Altogether 50 quintals of tar, 18 of black oakum, 12 of hemp, 16 of lead and two barrels of grease were used in an effort to make the twenty-year-old ship sufficiently watertight to cover the four thousand miles of sea that lay between Cadiz and Vera Cruz. New masts, sails, rigging, cables and anchors were fitted as necessary and the decks reinforced to take the much greater weight of artillery required of a Capitana. On 1 March 1640 the ship was inspected, and it was noted in the margin of the copy of the contract kept by the Casa de la Cont- ratación that Don Tomas had complied with the stiff conditions laid down by the officials.[9]

Most of this book will be concerned with the fate of the *Concepción*, above and below the water, and it is necessary to have some idea of what she looked like. We do not have a painting or even an inventory of the ship, but there is little doubt that she conformed to the general speci- fications for ships of her size built in Spanish and West Indian yards.[10] She was referred to in the contract as a *nao* of 600 tons, but, by the time she had been refitted, she had been transformed into a galleon, and it is as a

19

galleon that she is normally described. She would have been about 140 feet long, with three masts, the foremast and mainmast carrying three square sails and the mizzen a large lateen sail with a square topsail. Into this comparatively small space, apart from the guns, the gear and the spare tackle necessary to make the ship a reasonably efficient sailing and fighting unit, were crammed two hundred tons of official cargo, many more tons of unofficial cargo, over five hundred men, women and children, and the general clutter of penned animals, cooped-up fowls, crates, chests, casks and barrels, which were the normal complement of a ship sailing to America.

Shipbuilding had been revolutionized by the Dutch in the previous half-century, but this had affected the Spaniards very little. Much to the scorn of foreigners, they continued to build large ships of the galleon type to very much the same design as in the late sixteenth century.[11] Their most strikingly archaic characteristic was their enormous, lavishly decorated poops, up to forty-five feet high, with four decks of beautifully appointed cabins, topped by the privileged poop deck from which the great could look down at the activity in the waist of the ship far below. On the poop deck of the *Concepción* there was a magnificent statue of the Virgin, the patroness of the ship. Spanish ships also continued to have built-up forecastles and very high bulwarks, which, coupled with their shallow draughts, made them extremely top-heavy and appallingly uncomfortable in a heavy sea. They were powerful, and they could carry a considerable amount of cargo, but they were very slow, very difficult to manoeuvre, liable to drift a long way off course, and unable to sail anywhere near the wind. When they were as old as the *Concepción* they were a recipe for disaster.

When the *Concepción* had passed the inspection of the officials of the Casa de la Contratación she was taken the sixty miles down the winding Guadalquivir river to the sea and so to the bay of Cadiz, some twenty miles down the coast, to join the ships of the fleet which she was to escort and to complete her lading. Meanwhile, all over Spain, those planning to travel with the fleet were making their final preparations before setting off on their separate journeys to the sea. There were many great men among them, but it is unlikely that anyone travelled in quite such style as Don Diego López Pacheco y Bobadilla, Marquis of Villena and Duke of Escalona, the newly appointed Viceroy of New Spain, who left his family estates near Madrid on 10 March 1640 to set forth on the long overland journey to the bay of Cadiz.[12]

The duke was accompanied by a magnificent concourse of mounted noblemen and their families, many eagerly looking forward to the lucrative jobs which the new viceroy's patronage would ensure them in America. In their wake followed a small army of servants and two hundred mules to carry the baggage and a supply of luxurious foodstuffs to sustain them through the long voyage. The Spanish populace was suitably impressed by the grandeur of the duke's suite. Crowds gathered everywhere to stare and applaud as the long procession slowly made its way across New Castile and then down to Andalusia and the sea. Great cities threw open their gates to allow the assembled nobility and clergy to greet the duke in the countryside outside. At Toledo, the duke's chaplain assures us, not a single man of quality failed to ride out to meet his master. Such welcomes were warmly received and well rewarded. For the great there were fine presents, while the lesser fry could scramble for the showers of money distributed by the duke's treasurers. Here was a fine show of liberality befitting a grandee. Four thousand ducats were handed out in Cordoba alone, fourteen thousand altogether on the long, slow journey, not counting the three thousand distributed among the sailors of the fleet when the duke at last reached his immediate destination at Puerto Santa Maria in the bay of Cadiz. Here he settled down with his family and servants, entertained the local aristocracy and spent six or seven hundred ducats each day, 'with the *grandeza* accustomed in his House', as he waited for the day of departure.

We must hope that the duke was too haughty to bother himself with such sordid details but, if he ever did feel qualms at the extent of his generosity, he could comfort himself with the thought that such sums were but trifles to what he could hope to lay up for himself as Viceroy of New Spain. For the duke, like the members of his family and suite, like the hundreds of other passengers now assembling in the local inns and hostels, like the officers and crews of the twenty ships of the fleet which lay at anchor in the bay, was going to Mexico with the firm intention of improving his fortune, of acquiring for himself some of the fabled silver won from the mountains and hills of the King of Spain's possessions in the New World. This dream of silver would sustain them all through the tedium and possible dangers of the four-thousand-mile voyage that lay before them.

In faraway Mexico, in places whose names have that romantic appeal associated with bonanza mining camps throughout world history, in Zacatecas and Durango, in Parral and San Luis Potósi, Indian miners hacked away with crowbar and pickaxe deep under the ground to make the dream of silver come true.[13] Porters staggered along honeycombed cuttings and up hundreds of feet of ladders carrying leather bags with loads of over three hundred pounds of ore on their shoulders. Thousands of mules trod their slow way round in endless circles to turn the mills which ground the ore to dust. Technicians and labourers spread the ore on the ground and amalgamated it with mercury to separate the silver from the dross. Stokers fed furnaces with charcoal to free the silver from the mercury with which it had been combined. Carriers brought the resulting fine silver bars hundreds of miles, often having to fight their way through wild Indian country, to Mexico City, where much of the silver was minted and transformed into the famous pieces of eight, whose very name made men dream of wealth throughout Europe. And then the chests and sacks of coin and the unminted bars of silver were carried down to the sea, ready to be taken across the ocean to Spain by the ships of the silver fleet. Few men in Spain gave much thought to anyone quite so insignificant as Indian miners and Indian porters, but it was as a result of their labours that in April 1640, as so often before, there was a fleet waiting in Cadiz Bay to sail to Vera Cruz and men and women waiting on the shore for the signal to go aboard and sail with it.

At last the warning gun rang out across the crowded bay of Cadiz. Passengers and crews sailing with the 1640 fleet to New Spain must embark the following morning. They had waited many months for the signal, but this did not prevent the usual flurry of last-minute activity. As we have seen, there were pressing economic and fiscal reasons for much of the lading of the fleet to be done in the last few hours before departure, after the royal officers had made their final inspection of the cargo. This, too, was the time for barefoot, ragged stowaways who dreamed of a fortune in America to smuggle themselves aboard and pay out their last few coppers for the privilege of being regarded as invisible. Barges and lighters shuttled between the twenty ships of the fleet and the mass of Flemish, English, German and Scandinavian shipping that had freighted the rich textiles and furniture, the glass, the paper and the other desirable products of northern Europe for the delectation of the Mexican colonists. Such goods were carefully stowed away under the supervision of the ships' officers who may well have reflected, as they pocketed their bribes, that, for them at least, the Carrera de Indias, that maritime lifeline that linked Spain with her American colonies, remained a profitable business to be engaged in. No doubt similar thoughts passed through the minds of the guards placed on board by the Casa de la Contratación.

Other boats were shuttling between the ships and the shore, bringing aboard the more perishable provisions, left till the last moment so as to retain their freshness as long as possible during the two- or three-month voyage that lay ahead. The diet on Spanish ships naturally varied with the quality of the recipient. The ordinary soldiers and sailors had to make do with a daily ration of one and a half pounds of black bread and half a pound of salt pork or cod washed down with a couple of pints of wine.[14] Officers did rather better: white bread or biscuit instead of black, ham instead of salt pork, fine sherry in place of the rough, unpalatable wine that was provided for the common seamen. And they were able to vary their rations with what would seem to be luxuries in the weeks ahead – raisins, almonds and sugar, eggs from the cooped-up hens, fresh meat from the cattle, sheep and pigs that were being ferried aboard. The many important passengers planning to sail with the fleet organized their own supplies of delicacies. Thomas Gage, an English Dominican friar who travelled with the fleet of 1625, tells us how his Superior tempted him to make the journey by reciting an inventory of the dainties which he had provided for the voyage. 'What varieties of fish and flesh, how many sheep, how many gammons of bacon, how many fat hens, how many hogs, how many barrels of white biscuit, how many jars of wine of Casalla, what store of rice, figs, olives, capers, raisins, lemons, sweet and sour oranges, pomegranates, comfits, preserves, conserves, and all sort of Portugal sweetmeats.'[15] All this and more was loaded in 1640 on behalf of the new viceroy, enough indeed, according to his chaplain, to have lasted for two voyages, but so great was his generosity that before he reached Vera Cruz all had been consumed and he was reduced to eating salt dried beef like any other mortal.[16]

On Sunday 8 April the passengers went aboard the waiting fleet. Since there had been virtually no shipping to Mexico for two years there were more passengers than usual this year, but their composition would have occasioned little surprise to those who watched them as they were rowed out to the ships. As usual there were a large number of friars eager to reap a harvest of Indian souls in the Mexican and Philippine missions. But such godly passengers were easily outnumbered by the worldly. Here were young Basques travelling out to take up a position in their uncle's merchant house in Mexico City, fortune-hunters seeking a creole bride with a fabulous dowry, traders and commission merchants travelling with their goods, wide-eyed innocents quite certain that there was more

chance for a poor man in a wealthy country where privilege went with a
white skin than there was in hungry, overtaxed Spain. Here, too, were
many going out to fill posts in the teeming colonial bureaucracy, a sure
way to a quick sufficiency, if not a fortune. Many had already paid well
in Spain for such a right to mulct the colonial economy. As these people
went aboard they viewed with alarm the extremely cramped quarters
that they would have to live in for the next three months and heard with
amazement the exorbitant price that the ships' officers declared they
would have to pay for them. Passengers were crammed in regardless of
safety. In 1646, when Friar Domingo Navarrete sailed to Mexico, his
party was given the gunroom cabin for 2,000 pieces of eight, while the
gunners were forced to find their quarters elsewhere, far from the guns
they were supposed to serve.[17] The Spanish ships were nearly always
dangerously overcrowded and overloaded with passengers in every hole
where you could swing a hammock, and the decks littered with crates
and casks and pens full of livestock and poultry for the officers and important passengers. There were, of course, no problems of cramp for
great men who travelled with the fleet. They found their quarters in the
magnificent cabins in the towering poops of the ships. Among the great
this year were no less than three bishops making their way to their Mexican sees, including a man who was to make a great name for himself in
Mexico, Don Juan de Palafox, Bishop of Puebla de los Angeles, second
city of New Spain.[18]

And here finally was the greatest man of all, the Duke of Escalona,
who, after taking communion for the last time ashore, was escorted to a
brilliantly decorated launch which carried him past the rest of the fleet to
the *Concepción*, where he was received on board with pipes and a salvo of
guns by the Captain-General of the fleet, Roque Centeno y Ordonez.

The Viceroy had distributed his family and suite throughout the fleet
to minimize the risk of loss on the voyage. This was just one of many precautions that he had taken to ensure their safety. We have seen that he
had made the obvious precaution of giving the sailors a hand-out and
making sure that he had an adequate supply of provisions. He had also
arranged to carry at his own expense an extra pilot of his own choice, in
addition to the normal complement of the Capitana. This might have
caused jealousy and confusion in the ship's councils, but, in view of what
we shall later discover about the competence of Spanish pilots, it was a
sensible precaution. Finally, and probably most important for the
Viceroy's peace of mind, he carried in his baggage some exceedingly

powerful relics, including a thorn from Christ's crown and one of St Andrew's fingers. Few men can ever have sailed to Mexico so well prepared and so well protected.

And yet, when the fleet set sail the next day, the voyage nearly ended in disaster before it had even fairly begun. No sooner had they left the shelter of the bay of Cadiz than an onshore gale threatened to fling them back and dash them to pieces on the coast that they had just left. It was only with the very greatest good luck that they managed to get back into the bay and re-anchor in safety.[19] A bad omen? Possibly; the fleet was to get to Mexico all right, but none of these twenty ships was to return safely to Spain in the following year.

CHAPTER TWO

A Passage to Mexico

The Viceroy was taking no chances when the fleet set sail again on 21 April 1640. Shortly after leaving Cadiz they were becalmed, and Don Diego took this opportunity to give orders that everyone in the fleet should take communion and fulfil their religious obligations.[1] The service on the *Concepción* was followed by a sermon given by the Viceroy's chaplain, in which he emphasized the penalties of mortal sin and the story of Jonah. Almost immediately the men and women in the fleet were made to feel the benefits of such devotion, 'since within five hours of the calm there came a pleasant north-east wind with which we continued our voyage'.

Religion seems to have played as important a part as good navigation and seamanship in ensuring the safety of the ships that sailed in the Carrera de Indias. Twentieth-century sceptics may find Friar Domingo Navarrete's account of his voyage in 1646 difficult to credit. 'Our method was, at break of day we sang the *Te Deum*. After sun-rising, having first consulted the Master, four or five masses were said, and all the crew resorted to them; in the afternoon the *Salve Regina* and Litany of our Lady was sung, then the Rosary was said by Gangs, some miraculous stories were read, and there was some discourse of religious matters. On Sundays and Holidays there was a sermon.'[2] Nearly all accounts of voyages have similar descriptions to make, and the book written by the Viceroy's chaplain about his master's voyage to Mexico in 1640, which is the main source for this chapter, is no exception. Much of what the chaplain writes relates to the Viceroy himself, the object of the exercise being an extended panegyric of his master's devotion, courage, self-sacrifice and *grandeza*. We learn, therefore, that the Viceroy's great cabin in the poop was 'more like a monastery than a palace' where his master, accompanied by three friars who were in constant attendance on him, spent the best part of every day in a long series of religious exercises. Such private devotions were interrupted every now and then by the great festivals of the Church which were celebrated by the fleet as a whole.

While the Viceroy remained on his knees in his cabin the fleet sailed south-west towards the Canaries, the ships in the sailing order which had long been laid down by order of the Casa de la Contratación.[3] In the van, and slightly to windward of the fleet, the Capitana, the *Concepción*, made an impressive show of force. The merchant ships which made up the fleet sailed in two lines in the wake of the Capitana. Most of these were described as *naos*, ranging from 220 to 650 tons.[4] They were less heavily armed and manned than the Capitana, but, except for those built in foreign yards, conformed to the same general type. Finally, bringing up the rear of the fleet was the Almiranta, the vice-admiral, a 550-ton *nao* called the *San Pedro y San Pablo*. Communications between the ships and with the shore were ensured by two fast advice-boats, a *petachio* and a *saettia*. These shallow-draught ships were also available to scout ahead in dangerous waters.

Elaborate instructions governed the efficient shepherding of the fleet. The Capitana must adjust its speed to that of the slowest sailor in the convoy, so that none of the merchant ships could fail to keep the flagship's standard in sight by day, or its splendidly ornamented poop lanterns by night. Every day the Almiranta sailed right through the fleet to check that all the ships were in good order and report to the Capitana. Every day both the Capitana and the Almiranta had to count all the ships and it was the Almiranta's task to look after any laggards. Such instructions seem to have been efficiently carried out, and it was rare for a ship to be seized from within a Spanish convoy.

Until the very end of this particular voyage there was no need for the escorting warships to demonstrate their strength. The Tierra Firme fleet which sailed in late July ran into a strong Franco-Dutch war fleet, and the galleons had to fight a long battle before they were able to shepherd the merchantmen back into harbour. But in April there were no problems, and the Mexican fleet hardly saw another ship before they reached the West Indies. At dawn on 27 April, six days out, they sighted Alegranza and Lanzarote, the first islands of the Canaries. This was good going, considering a whole day had been lost while repairs were done to one of the merchant ships, whose bowsprit and stem had been smashed after a night collision in a storm. The Canaries, although Spanish, formed a potentially serious loophole in the system of monopoly which governed the Spanish trade with America, providing almost unlimited opportunities for shipping contraband and unregistered goods. The islands were also potentially dangerous, being regularly frequented not

27

only by foreign merchant ships but also by corsairs belonging to the enemies of Spain. As a result the fleets were forbidden to call at the islands, except in dire need. This regulation was much disliked by passengers and crew alike, who regretted losing this opportunity to stretch their legs on dry land and do a little clandestine business, but our fleet, unlike many, obeyed these instructions and sailed on, past Fuerteventura and Grand Canary, past Tenerife with its great volcano which Christopher Columbus had thought so 'remarkably lofty', past Hierro, and so west-south-west into the region of the regular north-east trade winds which blew them, like so many Spaniards before them, happily along towards the West Indies, 'one day as pleasant as the next'.

Boredom was the main problem for passengers and crews in the three or four weeks of empty ocean which lay between the disappearance of the last of the Canaries over the eastern horizon and the first landfall in the West Indies. Enemy attack was not likely so far from land, and the weather in May was not likely to turn sour, but one could soon tire of watching the porpoises or fishing for *dorado*, however pleasant the sailing conditions. This was where the many festivals in the Catholic year became a real blessing. The big day on this voyage was 3 May, the day of Santa Cruz, when the Viceroy arranged to celebrate the festival with the same disdain of expense as he would have done on land. The whole of the waist of the *Concepción* was cleared, fine carpets were laid down, and a rich altar, complete with hangings, was erected close to the foot of the mainmast. Nearby on a raised platform was a great cross, covered with jewels and other decorations in honour of the day. More than four hundred people took communion, which was followed by a sung mass with music provided by pipes, dulcimers, bassoons and trumpets. Then, to the accompaniment of salvoes from the guns, there was a solemn procession round the ship. The rest of the day was one long party presided over by the Viceroy and the Captain-General, who sat in ceremonial chairs high up on the poop deck to watch the proceedings. This was one side of life where no one could compete with the Spaniards. There was music and dancing, mock bull-fights and jousting, various kinds of competition and charade, and, as night fell, magnificent fireworks displays punctuated by the roar of the guns and the rattle of musket fire. And all this as the fleet made its steady way with soft trade winds and clear skies across the mid-Atlantic.

Even on days when there was no *fiesta* there was usually something to keep the passengers amused, to take their minds off their cramped conditions and enable them 'to cheat the penal servitude of the voyage'. Great interest was taken in the progress of a baby girl born to the wife of one of the Viceroy's servants. Shortly after giving birth the mother had an accident and injured her breasts so badly that she could not feed her baby. The child was kept alive for eight days on a mixture of lemon and almond juice, but then broke into a terrible fever and would drink no more. Despair – the doctors gave up and the baby was quickly baptized by one of the bishops. But then a miracle – a little bitch dog who had lost her puppy waddled into the cabin and was pressed into service by the baby's father. The bitch was still suckling the baby when the ship reached Puerto Rico twenty-two days later and a more conventional foster-mother could be found.

Much more serious was the sad state of one of the most heavily laden ships in the fleet, the *Serena*. Despite the fine weather, she began to leak so badly that she was in grave danger of sinking, a damning indictment of the sort of ships that were pressed into the service of the Carrera de Indias. The Viceroy, 'seeing that some of his own servants were aboard her, as well as so much property and eighteen Franciscan friars', gave orders for the fleet to heave to while repairs were carried out. Divers were a normal part of the complement of both the Capitana and the Almiranta and these, mostly Indians or Negroes, were sent over together with carpenters and caulkers, oakum and sheets of lead, to patch up the sinking ship. It took two days to do the repairs, but they were successful. The *Serena* was pumped out and was to reach Vera Cruz in safety.

The fleet continued to sail west-south-west until their noon sighting of the sun showed the pilots that they were in the latitude of 17° north, the approximate latitude of Antigua and Barbuda, where they hoped to make their landfall. They then changed course due west to run along the line of latitude. Such was the normal practice of navigators before the invention of a reliable chronometer in the eighteenth century made the accurate calculation of longitude possible.

Navigation was subject to a host of errors. It was difficult to estimate latitude with open-sight instruments on a moving deck. Most sailors were happy if they could get the degree of latitude roughly right. One rarely sees the mention of a sub-division of a degree in contemporary log-books. The distance between two degrees of latitude is sixty nautical miles. The horizon for the look-out at the top of a hundred-foot mast is about twelve and a half miles on a clear day, so that it is obvious that fairly small errors by the pilots could have very serious consequences. It was even harder to calculate the distance travelled once one had reached the desired latitude. Currents and variable winds could soon make a mockery of dead reckoning as a means of plotting one's position, especially in deep waters where the almost uncanny knowledge of the sea bottom acquired by pilots working in coastal and shoal waters could not be brought into play. Despite all these problems some ocean pilots were astonishingly skilful, but, judging by the almost universal contemporary condemnation of the navigational standards of the Carrera de Indias, there were few Spanish pilots to be found in this class.

From the early years of their American adventure the Spaniards had naturally taken a great interest in improving their standard of navigation. A famous school was established in Seville, and all pilots serving in the silver fleets were supposed to have had at least six years' experience of sailing to America and to have passed a stiff examination.[5] But, as in so many other walks of life, both the apparent experience and the knowledge required to pass the examination could be bought with money rather than time, and there is no doubt that corruption allowed many incompetent pilots to be in charge of Spanish ships. Sailing in fleets reduced the danger, since knowledge and judgement could be pooled, but the results of such sharing of professional expertise must have been alarming to the laymen who sailed in the fleets. In his account of the Mexican fleet of 1625, Thomas Gage described a council of

all the pilots of the ships, to know their opinions concerning our present being and the nearness of the land. . . . Here was cause of laughter enough for the passengers to hear the wise pilots' skill; one saying we were three hundred miles, another two hundred, another one hundred, another fifty, another more, another less, all erring much from the truth (as afterward appeared) save only one old pilot of the smallest vessel of all, who affirmed resolutely that with that small gale wherewith we then sailed we should come to Guadeloupe the next morning.[6]

Thomas Gage was concerned in his book to denigrate his former Spanish friends on all possible occasions, so that we can assume he exaggerated, but the same general point is made by too many other contemporaries to be ignored.

One result of Spanish navigational practices was that the ships rarely sailed at night once the pilots had estimated that they were anywhere

near their landfall, a fact reported with scorn by another English writer of the period. 'When they expect to fall with the windward or Cariby Islands it is ordinary with them to lye short in the nights sometimes three, four and five nights before they make them, which is occasioned by their badd keeping of their reckoninge and not understanding either variation or longitude. . . . They have noe other helpe but the latitude and looking out.'[7] This practice naturally delayed the fleets considerably. It also gave their enemies plenty of time to learn of their whereabouts and then strike at them at night from the windward so as to drive them on to the islands.

The Spanish were, of course, aware of these dangers, which became more and more serious from the 1620s, as the English, French and Dutch began to settle many of the islands in the long chain of the Lesser Antilles. These islands, all claimed by the Spaniards, were formerly inhabited only by the fierce Carib Indians and had been ignored by the Spaniards who annually had to pass this strategic barrier before making their way to their destinations on the mainland. They had little attraction for the Spaniards, whose destiny drew them ever westwards to exploit the silver and gold of the larger islands and the mainland, and who were hardly to know that such islands as Guadeloupe and Martinique would be among the richest places in the world in the eighteenth century. The natives did nothing to make the Lesser Antilles any more attractive. Indeed, it was to take the English and the French longer to subdue the Caribs, with their poisoned arrows and their war canoes, than it took the Spaniards to conquer either Mexico or Peru. Nevertheless, one would have expected some of the small islands to have been powerfully fortified to receive the American fleets and to provide a windward* base to control the eastern Caribbean. Even after the foreign incursion the Spanish did little to retrieve the situation. The infant foreign settlements were occasionally destroyed, but the usual policy was simply to avoid the more obviously dangerous of the islands, such as Guadeloupe, for long a corsair base and from 1635 a French settlement. Otherwise the only precautions taken were to try and conceal the landfalls of the fleets by varying them from year to year and by not allowing Captains-General to open their detailed orders until they were out to sea. The net result of the new situation was to push the first landfall of the Mexican fleets further north, where, although there were foreign settlements at St Christopher and Nevis, these were somewhat to leeward of the outer chain of islands and so pre-

---

* Note that in writing about the West Indies the term 'windward' always means eastern or north-eastern, because of the constancy of the trade winds.

sented less danger to the incoming fleet.

There were, then, complex strategic and navigational reasons for the fleet commanded by Roque Centeno in 1640 to turn west along the latitude of 17° north towards the islands of Antigua and Barbuda. Barbuda was a particularly dangerous landfall, a very flat island with reefs on the windward side, so it can be imagined that the fleet approached the island with the usual caution. The whole fleet hove to on three successive nights before Antigua was at last sighted on 21 May, a month out from Cadiz, and they knew exactly where they were. The first landfall in the West Indies was naturally a happy time for the passengers and crew, but the celebrations must have been somewhat clouded by the thought that there was as long a voyage still to come before they could hope to arrive at Vera Cruz. Voyages had in fact become longer than in the past, since the danger from enemies now forced the fleet to sail round the outer rim of the Lesser Antilles and along the north coast of Puerto Rico, instead of using the direct passage along the south coast. This route was much farther in miles and was studded with islands which necessitated frequent halts at night.

From Antigua the fleet sailed past Barbuda and St Bartholomew towards 'our island of San Martín', the one island in the Lesser Antilles where there was a fort and a Spanish garrison, who received the fleet with an eighteen-gun salute. No one was allowed ashore here. News of Spain and corsairs was exchanged with the officers of the garrison, who took the opportunity to complain to the new Viceroy of their shortage of manpower, munitions and provisions. Gifts were also exchanged, and passengers took much delight in their first taste of West Indian fruit, the water-melons in particular 'being no little pleasant in such a hot place'.

From San Martín the fleet sailed through the Virgin Islands, carefully avoiding the dangerous passage between Virgin Gorda and the low-lying Anegada, 'the drowned island', and so made their way towards San Juan de Puerto Rico, as usual heaving to at night so as not to overrun it. San Juan was the windward bastion of the Spanish Empire in the Indies, second only to Havana as a powerfully fortified port. The long-suffering passengers were not allowed ashore even here, though their frustration was somewhat allayed by the fact that their arrival off San Juan coincided with the feast of Corpus Christi, which was celebrated with all the trimmings that they must have come to expect. The highlight of the day was when the Almiranta, dressed overall and with her guns run out, sailed up to the Capitana and, after giving her the *buen viaje* on the hornpipes, sent over a boarding-party who challenged the flag-ship to a poetry competition.

On the following afternoon the fleet anchored at Aguada, the 'water-ing place' at the north-west corner of Puerto Rico. After forty-three days at sea the passengers and crew were allowed ashore, although they were first carefully disarmed, lest they take this opportunity to desert or start fighting, 'which had occurred on other occasions'. It was, however, a happy crowd who were rowed ashore, eager to embrace their friends from other ships and describe in detail everything that had happened to them. Everyone found the island delightful, very fertile and full of exotic animals and birds, fruits and plants. Everywhere could be seen little knots of people playing music, dancing, splashing themselves with de-licious fresh water and generally having a lovely time. Meanwhile, all the ships' barrels and casks were swung out into the boats and refilled with water and the crew went to cut firewood, while the servants washed the salt and sweat out of their own and their masters' clothes.

They were allowed only two days in paradise. On 4 June everyone returned to the ships, the *Concepción* fired the starting gun and the voyage continued, through the Mona Passage, along the south coast of Hispani-ola, past Jamaica and the Cayman Islands to Cape Corrientes on the south-west coast of Cuba, which was sighted on 14 June. For the last part of this leg of the voyage the fleet was shadowed by an enemy ship, the first sight that they had had of corsairs. Fears were confirmed when the *saettia* was sent ashore to the garrison. Some of the soldiers came out in a canoe to kiss the Viceroy's hands and report that there were four or five other corsairs along the coast. Not much could be done about this, except to get on towards their destination, and the fleet set a course towards Cape Catoche, the north-eastern point of the Yucatan penin-sula.

Between Yucatan and Cuba the wind blew up from the south-west, and the fleet was struck by a savage tropical storm. 'So great were the waves that they crashed on to the deck and extinguished the galley fires, so that no more cooking could be done ... the sea roared, the wood creaked, the masts trembled, and so did the crew, seeing the confusion of the other ships; although the strength of our Capitana gave us security, and the fact that we were carrying in our ship such great relics.' The relics and constant prayers were effective; the storm abated as rapidly as it had arisen, and, although a count of sails showed three ships missing, they were later discovered safe and sound.

33

The storm was not sufficient to shake off the corsairs. Six enemy ships were sighted astern of the fleet, waiting for a chance to snap up a straggler or a ship damaged by the bad weather. The Viceroy ignored the standing orders of the fleet and the advice of the Captain-General that the warships should stay in position, and ordered the *Concepción* to break away from the van of the fleet and run down on to the corsairs. This was successful, and the enemy was chased away, but it was a dangerous move, leaving the leading ships of the fleet unprotected. The corsairs might well have been decoys. In any case they were almost certainly capable of outsailing the clumsy Capitana and doing much damage in the fleet before her return. Standing orders are not always stupid, and the Viceroy seems to have been rather vainglorious, much to the delight of his chaplain.

The last few days of the voyage, as the fleet made its way round the Yucatan peninsula and so into the Gulf of Mexico and the bay of Campeche, were dreary and unpleasant, as was so often the case. Navigation was very tricky, with several reefs to avoid; the ships were often becalmed; the mid-June sun pounded down, and the crowded cabins became unbearable, while the water and fresh provisions picked up in San Martín and Puerto Rico were becoming extremely unpleasant. Many fell sick and some died, especially in the Almiranta.

Relief was at hand. On the morning of 24 June, Midsummer Day, the Viceroy's chaplain heard the sailors at the masthead cry out the long awaited words, '*Tierra, tierra!*' and everyone embraced each other, weeping for pleasure at the thought of the end of their long ordeal. 'Oh Lord, if only men would long for Heaven as people at sea long for land!' And now from the deck they could see for themselves the vast mountains that rose behind the swampy coastal strip of Vera Cruz. At three in the afternoon they sighted the fort of San Juan de Ulloa on its little rocky island, only a musket shot from the shore.

The fleet anchored half a league from the fort and waited for boats to come and place buoys and marker flags to show the difficult channel through the reefs, which were the port's main protection from the sea. Next day the fleet carefully passed through the channel and round the corner of the island fort, where they moored in a line, fastening the stems of the ships to the great bronze rings which had been set into the four-hundred-foot wall below the guns. The fort saluted the new Viceroy with twenty-three guns and the people in the ships gave thanks to God that the whole fleet had reached safety with much music and a *Te Deum*.

The *armada y flota* of New Spain for 1640, Captain-General Roque Centeno y Ordonez, had arrived.

All in all this was a pretty average voyage. The fleet had made good time and had had few problems – a couple of ships requiring running repairs in the Atlantic, one bad storm, one clash with corsairs and fairly heavy mortality in the Gulf of Mexico. Still there were rarely many problems on the way out. The real trouble only started when the fleets set sail from Vera Cruz to return home.

CHAPTER THREE

Too Long in Vera Cruz

The clash with the corsairs off Yucatan had been a sharp reminder of the insolent manner in which foreigners ignored the fact that the Caribbean was a Spanish sea. Something must be done about it. When something had to be done in seventeenth-century Spain the first step was to set up a committee to discuss it. The new Viceroy decided to postpone the pleasures of the shore for a while and summoned a junta, sending out papers for the members of the committee to study before they offered their opinions or advice. On the last day of June the Captain-General and the Almirante of the fleet, the castellan of the fort and many leading local officials, captains and people experienced in the ways of war sat down with the Viceroy in the fort of San Juan de Ulloa to discuss the problem.[1]

It was a big problem. Spain was at war with both France and Holland at this moment, and was soon to be at war with her own province of Portugal. But it was not necessary for there to be war in Europe for there to be war in the West Indies. The leading maritime nations of Europe recognized existing Spanish colonies in America and the West Indies and accepted the right of Spain to declare trade between these colonies and between the colonies and Europe as a Spanish monopoly which might be defended by force. But they were not prepared to recognize rights in unoccupied territory, and, in any case, had no control over those of their subjects who chose to sail to the West Indies to engage in contraband trade or a little raiding. The Spaniards naturally regarded such people as enemies, and the result was that the West Indies were in a continuous state of war, the concept of 'No peace beyond the line' being generally accepted till near the end of the century.

The Dutch, the greatest seamen and merchants of the early seventeenth century, were by far the most persistent interlopers in the West Indies. Great fleets of Dutch merchantmen sailed west, regardless of peace or war in Europe, to sell cloth and slaves to the colonists on the Spanish Main or to collect salt from Araya on the coast of Venezuela. Bases were established on the mainland and in some of the islands, such as

Curaçao or San Martín, and attempts by the Spaniards to disturb their business were usually successfully fought off. The expiration of the Twelve Years' Truce with Spain in 1621 increased the scale and persistence of the Dutch incursion. The Dutch West India Company, which was founded in the same year, was specifically designed as a privateering organization whose object was to make money by doing the maximum damage to the maritime interests of Spain and Portugal in the Atlantic and the South Seas. The Company's major effort was concentrated on the long-term attempt to conquer the Portuguese overseas possessions in Brazil and West Africa. But the Dutch were well aware of the vital importance of the arrival of the silver fleets to the Spanish and Portuguese war efforts and made regular sweeps of the West Indies in an attempt to capture them. Only once were they successful, when Piet Heyn captured the homecoming Mexican silver fleet in 1628, but in the late 1630s the summer campaigns of the one-legged Admiral Joll (*pie de palo* or 'wooden-leg' to the Spaniards) had been so effective as to bring the trade between the various colonies virtually to a standstill.[2]

The English and the French were able to infiltrate the West Indies under the shadow and protection of the mighty Dutch. Settlements were begun in many of the islands of the Lesser Antilles in the 1620s. These relied very heavily on Dutch ships to bring in provisions and slaves and to carry out the tobacco, ginger and indigo which Dutch and other experts had taught the early planters how to grow. The numbers of colonists grew, as impoverished or adventurous Frenchmen, Englishmen and particularly Irishmen realized the possibilities of the good life in the tropics. Many, if not most, of these white immigrants failed to succeed as planters and provided the potential manpower for the settlement of further colonies or the manning of the many corsair ships, whose captains saw the raiding or ransoming of Spanish ships and settlements as a quicker way of making money than the laborious routine of managing a plantation. Meanwhile, with more money and more men, the colonies were slowly able to shake off the tutelage of the Dutch and to emerge as fairly powerful units in their own right. In 1640, unknown to the junta in Vera Cruz, the Dutch were giving the English their last and most important lesson in the art of making money in America. It was in this year that the techniques of sugar cultivation and refining were introduced into the islands by Dutchmen from Brazil, and the beginnings were made of that phenomenal rise of small islands, such as Barbados, Guadeloupe and Martinique, which was to make them such valuable prizes and valuable pawns in the wars and peace conferences of the future.

The Spaniards naturally did not like the activities of these foreign colonists, but, with a world empire to protect, they must have seemed pretty small beer. Strategic and financial possibilities dictated just what could and could not be maintained. Small islands, uninhabited by Spaniards and not lying on the homeward routes of the silver fleets, could largely be ignored, as indeed could most of the eastern coast of the Spanish Main. Far more serious to Spanish pride and, potentially, to Spanish greatness were the incursions made by foreigners further to the west.

These were particularly serious in the great island of Hispaniola, the first Spanish colony in America where Columbus had established the first attempt at a permanent settlement at Isabella on the north coast in 1494. Nowhere were the demographic effects of Spanish settlement so terrible as in Hispaniola. 'At the time of its discovery it contained 1,800,000 Indians, not counting old people, women and children', wrote Antonio Vázquez de Espinosa in the 1620s. 'Today there is not one Indian in all the island; it was a just judgment of God.'[3] While the Indians died of overwork and strange European diseases, the population of Spaniards and Negro and mulatto slaves grew; so, much faster, did the numbers of cattle, horses, goats, pigs and sheep who escaped from Spanish farms and ranches to form great wild herds and flocks roaming the island and living well off its luxuriant vegetation. By the late sixteenth century it was estimated that there were forty cows for every man on the island, beef in the city of Santo Domingo fetched only three per cent of the Spanish price and it had no price at all in the interior. Animals belonged to whoever killed them.[4]

From an early stage foreign corsairs and smugglers began to use the many ports on the sparsely populated north coast of the island to refit their ships, pick up provisions and extra hands and to trade with the Spanish settlers. Among the trade goods introduced were 'heretical' books which were widely distributed through the island. The reaction of the government at Santo Domingo was desperate. In 1605 and 1606 the three north-coast settlements at Puerto Plata, Monte Cristi and Yaguana were abandoned.[5] Soldiers were sent over the mountains, and the settlers were forced to move to the south coast, closer to Santo Domingo, closer to government control and protection. Many settlers fled the island; others remained in hiding to lead a wild, lawless life in which they were soon joined by escaped Negro slaves and by foreigners

– corsairs, deserters and other adventurers – who supplemented what they could get by petty raiding in canoes and other small craft, by living off the wild herds and flocks that roamed the mountains and dense forests of the empty island. Such men began to acquire the name of *boucanier* from the *boucan*, the place where they dried strips of their captured meat in the Indian fashion, but in the early days these mainly land-bound, half-wild men dressed in skins were a long way from the dashing pirates who were to give the world its image of a buccaneer later in the century. They were, however, an embarrassment to the Spanish government of the island, who punctuated the normal boredom of colonial life by organizing large-scale man hunts, or who occasionally made rather half-hearted attempts to starve them to death by rounding up and killing the herds of animals which provided their main livelihood.

The government of Santo Domingo learned to live with the wild men beyond the mountains to the north of the city. Most of the time they simply pretended that they were not there. Much more irritating at this time were the activities of a strange institution called the 'Governor and Company of Adventurers for the Plantation of the Islands of Providence, Henrietta and adjacent islands'.[6] This company had been founded by a group of Englishmen, mainly puritans, led by the Earl of Warwick, a well-known figure in the business of privateering and founding colonies, a famous privateer himself who was to command the parliamentary navy during the English Civil War. In 1630 the Company settled colonists from England and Bermuda on the uninhabited island of Santa Catalina, off the coast of Nicaragua, renaming the island Providence. The nearby island of Andres (Henrietta) was also settled, and the Company likewise claimed control over the island of Tortuga (Association) off the north-west coast of Hispaniola. Tortuga was regularly frequented by buccaneers from northern Hispaniola and was already a corsair base of some importance. The Company's ostensible plans were to develop the islands as plantations and trading posts, but it is clear that from the beginning the main object of the enterprise was 'to annoy the King of Spain in the Indies'.[7]

Providence Island was ideal for this purpose, only 450 miles from Cartagena, and sufficiently fertile to maintain a large garrison and several privateering ships. A contemporary description gives some idea of the strength of the island.

This island, for the greatness of it, may be termed rather a rock than an island, not exceeding ten or eleven miles in length and five in breadth . . . the island has these particular benefits in it: a port containing eighteen feet in depth with good ground to ride in; it is environed with huge rocks and cliffs . . . there is only one place to land in; for that excepted, it is encompassed about with such rocks that a boat cannot come near the shore. If a ship put but one mile to leeward of the harbour she cannot recover it by reason of the current.[8]

When the harbour had been fortified it was nearly impregnable, as the governor of Cartagena was to discover when the expedition he led against the island in 1635 retired with the loss of many men, 'being much torn and battered by the ordnance from the forts'.[9] The Spanish attack was taken as sufficient cause to issue large numbers of privateering licences and, for the next six years, Providence was to be the very worst enemy of Spain in the West Indies, attracting Dutch privateers with commissions from the Prince of Orange or the Dutch West India Company in addition to the many English privateers and freebooters who used its facilities.

The somewhat uneasy co-existence of puritans, privateers and planters, not to mention pirates, which was to be typical of many early English colonies, provides an entertaining background to the island's principal business. Shareholders in London envisaged an ideal type of settler who was rarely, if ever, realized, a pious man who would work hard to raise crops and exotic plants on his land in the intervals of going to church and sailing out to fight the Spaniards. In fact the plantations tended to be neglected, and the island naturally attracted men who were more interested in quick money and gambling than in God. A sad indication of the state of affairs was a letter from the shareholders to the Governor of the island reporting that they had heard that the islanders had ordered a supply of dice, cards and backgammon boards. The Governor was told to burn them on arrival and to encourage the colonists to engage in lawful recreations, such as chess and shooting.[10] But even pious settlers found the practices of the puritan ministers who were sent out to the island a bit much to take. On 25 December 1639 the Governor, Captain Nathaniel Butler, wrote in his diary: 'I stirred not from my house all this daye, though I wished an invitement to goe to Church; but our Ministers held it superstitious to preache on Christmas Day.'[11]

Butler's diary also provides conclusive evidence of the effectiveness of the stranglehold imposed by the foreign corsairs. It was, indeed, too effective; the goose that laid the golden eggs had been killed, and there was not much profit in privateering. In 1639, Butler led an expedition of four ships round the waters of the Central American coast and the south coast of Cuba and Jamaica. The journal of this voyage demonstrates incidentally that Spanish pilots had no monopoly of poor seamanship; it also shows what had happened to Spanish local shipping. In fifteen weeks out of the island, 'a tedious and dangerous voyage', Butler hardly saw a Spanish ship of any type. And this was the heartland of the Spanish Indies.

It would be wrong to think that the Spanish made no attempt to counter the foreign incursion into their sea.[12] Several successful attacks were made on the infant foreign colonies. The English and French were driven out of Nevis and St Kitts by the galleons of the plate fleet in 1629. Four years later the governor of Margarita cleared Trinidad of Englishmen and then went on to Tobago where he slaughtered the entire Dutch population. In the same year, 1633, San Martín was also recovered from the Dutch. Two years later an expedition of 250 men from Santo Domingo had no trouble in recapturing the corsair island of Tortuga, following the cowardly flight of the governor appointed by the Providence Company, Christopher Wormeley. The Spanish could clear the islands of people and demolish the fortifications, but nothing permanent could be achieved unless a Spanish garrison was left behind. There were too few Spaniards and too little money for this, and so, shortly after every Spanish success, the foreigners began to trickle back, rebuild their forts and settle down to their old lives. The only recaptured island which had been provided with a garrison was San Martín and this exception simply served to prove the truth of the rule. Men for the garrison were hard to find and often hungry, as ships attempting to provision the island from Puerto Rico and Santo Domingo had to run a gauntlet of corsairs.

Spain's main maritime effort in the West Indies continued to be the protection of the silver fleets and, as we have seen, except for one year this was done successfully. Once the silver fleets had left the Caribbean the nearest Spanish warships were on the Brazil station, so the corsairs were free to do as they liked. Spain had no spare ships and no spare money to maintain a West Indian squadron, especially in 1640, when money had never been scarcer and the Spanish navy had just suffered two terrible defeats at the hands of the Dutch, in October 1639 at the Battle of the Downs off the English coast and in January 1640 in the Bay of All Saints off the coast of Brazil. Two such defeats, so far apart, merely served to emphasize the fact that Spanish resources were at full stretch in a desperate effort to maintain the enormous empire against all comers.

Such facts were known only too well to the members of the junta who sat in the fort of San Juan de Ulloa on the last day of June 1640. So indeed was the solution that the Viceroy proposed, a permanent West Indian squadron, based on Puerto Rico, victualled and stored from Vera Cruz and Santo Domingo, and financed by taxes drawn from the Caribbean and Mexico.[13] The same solution had in fact been proposed in 1636. It was estimated that a fleet of twelve fairly light galleons and a few support craft would be sufficient to sweep the coast clean of impudent foreigners. It was further estimated that this would cost half a million pesos a year, and Mexico City had agreed to pay 200,000 pesos of this out of an increased sales tax, in return for various privileges, a serious consideration of the city's many grievances and a promise of more than a fair share of the lucrative contracts that could be expected for the building and maintenance of the armada. Orders had been placed in the shipyards of Havana and Campeche and arrangements had been made for the acquisition of guns, gear and gunpowder from all over the Spanish empire, from Flanders to the Philippines. But, despite such apparent enterprise, very little had been achieved four years later. The shipyards had not yet completed the galleons, and indeed had not even started to make enough to fill the squadron. The gunpowder manufacturers had had a row with the Duke of Escalona's predecessor as Viceroy of New Spain. There was said to be not a grain of gunpowder in the kingdom and no raw materials with which to make any. Worst of all, much of the money sent to Europe for equipment had been seized by the hard-up Spanish government for its own purposes. The members of the junta knew about all this as well and may have agreed with a certain scepticism when the new Viceroy said that he was absolutely determined to get the Armada de Barlovento, the Windward Squadron, built and a minimum of seven galleons and two advice boats ready to sail in the following spring.

The Viceroy, eager no doubt to make an early mark in his new post, was to surprise everyone. His very first decision was to condemn the fleet which had brought him to Mexico to a long and dreary wait in Vera Cruz. He ordered that all the ships be distrained of their arms, munitions and other war material for the service of the King.[14] He then went to work to organize the building and fitting-out of the Armada. The shipyards in Havana and Campeche were chased up, other ships were bought or hired, including one of the incoming fleet, the *Santissimo Sacramento* of 350 tons, which was taken into the new fleet as its Capitana.[15] New dockyards were established in Vera Cruz itself and in the nearby Alvarado river for the fitting-out of the squadron. Heavy guns were moved from Acapulco to Vera Cruz, and a satisfactory contract was made with a local businessman to provide bronze for more guns. Even the gunpowder manufacturers were sorted out. The city had never seen such energy. Nor had the corsairs. Three alarmed corsair ships sailed in to try and destroy the new dockyards before they could turn out a squadron to spoil their business. They were too late. There were already three galleons ready to receive them, who chased the two biggest corsairs away and captured the third after a stiff fight in which twenty-three of the corsair crew were killed. The prize was immediately taken into the new fleet as its *petachio* or advice boat and the successful Spanish commander, Don Antonio de la Plaza, was promoted to be the Almirante of the new squadron.[16]

When the Viceroy had set this important business in progress, he felt ready to leave the island fort of San Juan de Ulloa. A launch with an awning of crimson damask carried him to the quay of Vera Cruz, where the city received him in suitable style. He then rode through the city on a magnificent horse to the cathedral, where he gave rather belated thanks for his safe arrival. After several days of fiesta and bull-fights the Viceroy rode out of Vera Cruz and out of this book on the first stage of his triumphal two-hundred-mile journey to Mexico City, nearly eight thousand feet above the steaming heat of Vera Cruz. Here we will leave him to enjoy what was sadly, after such a promising start, to be one of the shortest and least successful vicereigns in Mexican history.[17]

The fiesta continued in Vera Cruz as the ships were unloaded and the passengers disembarked. The arrival of the fleet from Spain was a big moment for the port, where the normal population of a thousand whites and five thousand blacks and mulattos could double or treble, as traders and sightseers came to see the ships and haggle for the best of the goods from Europe. But gradually the strangers dispersed, to return to their homes, leaving the business of bargaining for the bulk of the cargoes to the representatives of the big companies in Mexico City, men who had control of the ready silver money which the importers demanded, men who were prepared to haggle for ever until they got the price they wanted. There was no hurry. The longer the Mexican market waited for the goods, the more it would pay. And it had been decided that the ships would not return to Spain until the Armada de Barlovento had been completed. Months passed, as the goods were slowly sold and the silver began to pile up for the return voyage, to be added to the treasure which had already been accumulated in royal taxation since the departure of the last fleet to leave Vera Cruz in April 1639.

Summer and winter passed, while the ships of the fleet remained tied to their bronze rings, burned up by the sun which melted the pitch in their joints, saturated by tropical rainstorms which were followed by steaming hot days which rotted their rigging and cordage, bashed together at their moorings by the terrifying 'northers' which crashed into the bay, eaten by the *broma*, the greedy shipworm which throve so happily in the lukewarm water that washed around them. No effort was made to careen the ships and give them the complete overhaul that they needed. Time enough for that nearer to the date of departure. The new galleons for the Armada de Barlovento were not ready in the spring. The return home was therefore postponed till February 1642, after the hurricane season, when the Mexican fleet would be able to sail from Havana together with the Tierra Firme fleet. At last, some time in the middle of the summer of 1641, the Capitana and the Almiranta which now had not been overhauled for eighteen months were hauled down on their sides ready for inspection and repair. But nobody was in any hurry, there were constant arguments about the cost of repairs, and the work went on very slowly. It was still a long, long time till they were due to sail.[18]

Vera Cruz was a horrible place in which to spend any time, a town of sleazy bars and brothels and wooden shacks rotting in the sun and rain, a town built on sand and surrounded by swamps and pools of stagnant water. Vázquez de Espinosa liked to have a good word for everywhere, but the best he could say for the climate of Vera Cruz was that it was 'hot, damp and somewhat unhealthy'.[19] Most visitors left out the 'somewhat' and would have agreed with a modern writer that the city had 'a humid dank atmosphere that was almost suffocating', in which 'every sort of pest and repulsive creature seemed to proliferate'.[20]

Soon, many of those members of the crews from the fleet who had not taken the first chance to desert fell sick, and several died. Among the deaths was one which was to have an important influence on the story we are telling. This was Roque Centeno y Ordonez, the well-respected Captain-General of the fleet. Many commanders died abroad, and the King's orders covered all such contingencies. The Almirante Juan de

Campos was promoted to Captain-General, and the senior captain in the fleet, Don Juan de Villavicencio, became Almirante in his place. These two men seemed to have disliked each other from the start. Juan de Campos was getting on in years. He was a haughty, domineering and impatient man who had been serving in high positions in the Carrera de Indias since 1620,[21] but he was much more of a businessman than a sailor. He was a shipowner, merchant and dealer in silver, a man who bought his post with the clear intention of making money out of it. This was not unusual, but there could be few men with such experience of the ocean and placed in such a position of responsibility who could openly say: 'I know nothing about shipbuilding and the affairs of the sea.'[22] Such an admission did not bode well for a fleet which depended ultimately on the good sense of the Captain-General's decisions on maritime affairs. Juan de Villavicencio, the new Almirante, was a much younger man of only thirty-seven,[23] whose good birth had enabled him to rise fast in the service of the Carrera. Unlike Campos, he was a real sailor, a man who knew his way around the sea and around charts. He was not unused to responsibility. In 1635 he had already been senior captain (*capitan más antigua*) in the Mexican fleet, when both the Captain-General and the Almirante died in Vera Cruz, and he had successfully commanded the fleet on the return home.[24] So this promotion was nothing very new to him, and he shifted his gear from the Capitana to the Almiranta, the smaller *San Pedro y San Pablo*.

Early in July 1641, after the fleet had spent more than a year rotting in idleness in the Mexican port, things began to happen rather more urgently. The financial situation in Spain was now desperate, and the new Captain-General, Juan de Campos, received orders to return home that year and not to spend another winter in the Indies.[25] The fleet would have to depart in a hurry if there was to be a chance to sail before the hurricane season. Ancient wisdom had decreed that the last safe date to sail from Havana in Cuba for the Bahama Channel and home was 20 August,[26] and Havana was a thousand miles straight into the wind from Vera Cruz. The arrangements necessary for departure were rapidly made. The Capitana and the Almiranta of the fleet, still not repaired, were hauled upright once again and brought from the careening place to load for the return voyage. Provisions and water were laid in. Hides, sugar, drugs and dyestuffs, the produce of Mexico and Central America, were loaded on to the merchant ships travelling with the fleet.

Meanwhile the really important business, the object of the whole exercise, was in hand as black slaves and mules sweated and struggled to bring down the treasure from royal and private warehouses ready to be ferried across to the waiting ships. There were some jewels and some gold, but practically all the treasure was silver; coined silver, pieces of eight and lesser denominations, from the Royal Mint at Mexico City; stacks of silver ingots of various sizes; silver beaten out into pieces of plate. All this was hauled aboard and stowed away under the careful eye of royal officials, the most valuable items in registered chests in the cabins of senior officers in the poop, money and worked silver belonging to private individuals in strong-rooms deep down in the ship, while some of the heaviest pieces lay right down in the hold on top of the ballast to give the ship extra stability.[27]

Single ships sometimes carried up to two hundred tons of silver. How much was there this time? This, unfortunately, is a question which it is impossible to answer with any precision. According to the Royal Officers at Vera Cruz the King's treasure sent in the fleet commanded by Juan de Campos totalled just under two and a half million pesos, representing royal revenue for two and sometimes three years from Mexico, Guatemala and Campeche, together with four registered chests containing gold, silver, precious jewels, pearls and gold dust, the property of the former Viceroy and Archbishop of Mexico. The Royal Officers apologized that it was not more, but 350,000 pesos of colonial taxation had been set aside to finance the construction and manning of the Armada de Barlovento and further sums had been spent in paying off old debts. The King's silver was distributed half-and-half between just two ships, the *Concepción* and the *San Pedro y San Pablo*, the Capitana and the Almiranta of the fleet. A letter with full information on the weight of every bar and piece of silver was delivered to the silver-master (*maestre de plata*) of each ship, the official who was responsible for the safe delivery of the silver in Spain and who received one per cent of all coin and three quarters per cent of all bullion as a reward for his demanding and nerve-racking office. On the basis of this document one would assume that there was more than a million pesos of the King's silver on each of the two ships.[28] However, the silver-master of the *Concepción*, Pedro de Medina, was later to claim that there was only 550,000 pesos of silver belonging to the King on the ship and, since the actual register has been lost, it is impossible to be sure what the true figure was.[29]

It is even harder to estimate how much silver was loaded on the *Concepción* by private individuals. Pedro de Medina said that there was

500,000 pesos, but this seems quite absurdly small. Private remittances were nearly always much greater than royal remittances, and, since there had been no fleet home to Spain in 1640, one would expect the return in 1641 to be particularly high. It is also clear that the rewards of concealment, which were always great, were greater than usual this year when the threat of confiscation by the nearly bankrupt King must have seemed a very real one. Some idea of the scale of fraud can be had from a later statement made by Antonio Petri y Arce. This was based on information from the mate, Francisco Granillo, who, being in charge of the stowage of the silver, should have had some idea of the truth. 'The quantity [of silver] belonging to the King was large and an even greater quantity belonged to individuals who had not registered it, as there was no time and, as the masters preferred the risk to the registration, it was known that it [silver] was brought without the necessary formalities.' Granillo's estimate of the total silver loaded on the *Concepción* was four million pesos, four times as great as that made by the official silver-master. This is a very wide discrepancy, and there is little the historian can do at this remove but say that there was between one and four million pesos of silver loaded on the *Concepción*, a sum then worth between £250,000 and £1,000,000 sterling and weighing between thirty-five and 140 tons. It seems probable that the sum was nearer the upper than the lower bound. One million pesos would have been rather a small cargo in the circumstances, and those people who travelled on the ship who later discussed the treasure nearly all emphasized that it was very large. In addition to the silver and the small amount of gold and jewels there was a cargo consisting mainly of 1,200 chests and bags of cochineal and indigo, two valuable dyestuffs much in demand by the European textile industry.[30]

On 23 July 1641 the ships were loaded and ready to sail. There were thirty ships in all. The Viceroy's energy had eventually paid off, and the Armada de Barlovento had been fitted out and was ready to escort the silver fleet, although suitable men for so many new ships had been difficult to find on the sparsely populated coast, and it was unkindly remarked that there was 'not one ship with four seafaring men'. The Armada was commanded by a crusty and very awkward veteran of the Carrera de Indias called Don Fernando de Sosa Suarez and comprised eight small galleons ranging in size from 170 to 350 tons and the *petachio* which had been captured from the corsairs. Then there was the silver fleet itself, the two escorting warships and nineteen merchant vessels.

Just when everyone was ready to sail, the Captain-General, Juan de Campos, made an extraordinary decision and ordered the Almirante, Juan de Villavicencio, to shift his flag into the *Nuestra Señora de la Concepción*, while he made the smaller *San Pedro y San Pablo* his flagship. The object of this move is not clear. The official reason was that it was done 'in order to safeguard the treasure', but this makes little sense, since both ships were supposed to be carrying an equal quantity of treasure. Maybe Campos simply wanted to travel home in the same ship as he had come out in. Maybe there was a more sinister motive. For Villavicencio was soon to find out that the *Concepción* was barely seaworthy. Whatever the reason for the change of flags, it was likely to cause a lot of trouble, as was pointed out by Antonio de Volumbozcar, the Vedor of the fleet, a very senior official directly appointed by the King to keep an eye on everyone else from the Captain-General downwards, 'a sort of royal watchdog for all occasions'.[31] The main problem that Volumbozcar foresaw was that the change of flags would give rise to much litigation, as all documents such as bills of lading which referred to goods in the Capitana would now be inaccurate, since the Capitana had become the Almiranta after the ships were fully laden.* It is easy for the historian to sympathize with the Vedor's complaint, since the same confusion has crept into historical documents. So it will be as well to make it clear that, from now onwards, the ship which will be referred to as the Almiranta is the *Nuestra Señora de la Concepción*, the flagship on the outward voyage, and the ship referred to as the Capitana is the *San Pedro y San Pablo*, the vice-admiral on the outward voyage.

The switch of flags had one incidental result which was to have a very important bearing on the outcome of our story. The pilot-major of the fleet always travelled on the Capitana, and so Juan de la Feria, the experienced man who held this position, had to change ships. His place as senior pilot of the *Concepción* was taken by Bartolomé Guillen who had piloted the *San Pedro* on the way out and was considered satisfactory by Captain-General Juan de Campos. But no one else considered him satisfactory. Guillen was in fact, like Campos, much more of a businessman than an experienced sailor. He was one of two men who had bid successfully for the right to freight the two hundred tons of cargo space which private individuals were allowed to load on each of the royal ships, and this was the sort of thing which chiefly interested him.[32] The fact that he

---

* Documents nearly always refer to the 'Capitana', 'Almiranta' etc., rather than giving the actual name of the ship.

was an accredited pilot was simply a reflection of the general corruption that ruled in the Carrera de Indias. A senior pilot's salary of a thousand ducats a year was not to be sniffed at, and there were many perks which went with the post. Volumbozcar summed up the general opinion of this man whose decisions would legally outweigh those of the Almirante himself on all matters concerning the navigation of the ship. 'It is well known that Bartolomé Guillen knows more about business and management than to take charge of such an important ship.'[33]

Few other people seem to have bothered to switch ships. The senior officials of the fleet, such as the Vedor, Volumbozcar, and the Gobernador, Don Bernardo de Tejada, the commander of the two companies of marines assigned to the fleet, remained in the larger and more comfortable Almiranta, despite its drop in status. Altogether the *Nuestra Señora de la Concepción* was to carry over five hundred people,[34] including many important passengers such as Don Diego Centeno, the son of the dead Captain-General, officials, merchants, priests and friars returning from Mexico, many of whom travelled with several servants or slaves, a company of marines and the officers and crew of the ship. Of the last we need mention only two, Eugenio Delgado, master and co-owner of the ship, and the first mate,* Francisco Granillo, a tough, brave and experienced seaman of forty-eight whom we first met supervising the outfitting of the *Concepción* back in Spain and who plays a considerable part in the story.

Don Juan de Villavicencio was not at all happy when he was commanded to fly his flag in the *Concepción*. The ship was twenty years old, had not been careened properly or re-sheathed with lead for eighteen months, and her seams were wide open. The first thing he did when he went aboard was to call a meeting consisting of the mate, Francisco Granillo, the master caulker and the carpenter. Was the ship fit to sail to Havana? All three men said that, as it was summer, they would get to Havana all right, but that it was absolutely imperative for the ship to be completely overhauled if she was to get back to Spain. 'If this was not done, safe arrival could not be assured at all.'

It was then, with a certain trepidation, that Villavicencio took up his position in the rear of the fleet when they set sail that same day. The voyage from Vera Cruz to Havana was generally considered to be the very worst part of the whole round-trip, a thousand ship-shaking miles

* *Contramaestre*. 'First mate' seems to describe this officer's duties and status more accurately than the dictionary translation, 'boatswain', or 'quartermaster'.

due east into the prevailing wind, liable to be struck suddenly by the vicious 'northers' which blew up with very little notice, and subject the whole time to the appalling July sun of the Gulf of Mexico. The fleet normally sailed north-east to the latitude of the south of Florida or even till they sighted the coast of modern Louisiana before steering east and then south for the run into Havana. Juan de Campos's fleet had the normal run of difficulties, a storm which forced one of the new galleons in the Armada de Barlovento back to Vera Cruz and several clashes with corsairs, but nothing serious except the fact that the journey took thirty-five days, and it was not till 27 August, a week after the last safe date to leave for Spain, that the *Nuestra Señora de la Concepción* entered the massively fortified harbour of Havana, 'one of the best, roomiest, and deepest known [where] ships of no matter what size are practically moored to the houses of the city'.[35] Havana was traditionally the place where the crews of the silver fleets had a wild fling before the long, dangerous voyage home, a fling which often went on for months while the Mexican fleet waited for the Tierra Firme fleet, or *vice versa*, and the ships stocked up with provisions or refitted in the well-equipped dockyard. But the fling was not to last very long this time. Juan de Campos was determined to obey his orders and get back to Spain. Villavicencio reported the condition of the Almiranta, a condition which had almost certainly deteriorated after over a month spent beating into the wind across the Gulf of Mexico, and demanded that time be found for the ship to be careened and fully repaired. Campos would have none of it. There must be no delay. Villavicencio, supported by the Vedor, Antonio de Volumbozcar, tried another tack. Would it not be more sensible and safer to wait in Havana until the arrival of the Tierra Firme fleet under Admiral Francisco Diaz Pimienta? Then all the ships could be refitted, and the two fleets could sail together back to Spain, after the hurricane season had ended.

The last thing that Juan de Campos wanted to do was to wait for Francisco Diaz Pimienta. Campos was proud to be Captain-General of the fleet and was keen to obey His Majesty's orders. In particular, he wanted the honour, and no doubt the reward, of returning to Spain in command of a fleet carrying so much silver for his impecunious King. He did not want to share his glory with anyone, least of all Pimienta. For Pimienta was a hero, having achieved what two previous expeditions had failed to do, the capture of the English corsair base at Providence Island. Pimienta had landed with six hundred soldiers on the impregnable island on 24

May. His landing had been fiercely opposed, but to no avail, and he had marched across the island to the settlement at New Westminster where he laid siege to the Governor's house and the church. Resistance soon collapsed, though several men got away to continue to annoy the Spaniards as corsairs. On 26 May High Mass was celebrated and a *Te Deum* sung in the town square of New Westminster in the presence of the Spanish troops and four hundred heretical English prisoners. The male prisoners were then shipped to Cartagena and so to Spain, while the women and children were treated very humanely and allowed to depart in English ships. The booty was immense, six hundred black slaves and over half a million ducats worth of treasure, the former property of Spaniards captured by the English and Dutch corsairs.[36] It was the greatest Spanish triumph in the West Indies for many years, and Pimienta had rightly become a famous and much-fêted man. Campos had no wish to share anything with a hero. His fleet would sail for Spain before Pimienta arrived in Havana, whatever condition the ships were in. Business demanded silver in Spain in 1641, not 1642, and Juan de Campos was a businessman, not a sailor.

In fact some delay was inevitable in Havana. There were stragglers to wait for, and it was not till 6 September that the whole fleet and its escort was once again assembled. It was also necessary to stock up once again with provisions. Much of what had been bought in Vera Cruz had turned out to be of very low quality. The area round Havana was famous for its food and drink, especially for its fruit and vegetables, and in the city itself there were 'all sorts of shops' where officers and passengers could purchase those delicacies which alone could make bearable the two-month voyage back to Spain. All this took time, and it was not till 13 September, seventeen days after their arrival in Havana, that the fleet set sail. Seventeen days was a long time, long enough to have carried out considerable repairs on the Almiranta, if the time had been spent working rather than arguing.

On the first night of the voyage, a peaceful calm night when the fleet was only twelve hours out of Havana, the Almiranta was found to be leaking. Juan de Villavicencio ordered the depth of water in the ship to be measured and found the leak was serious. He signalled to the Capitana to heave to, by lighting a lantern in the maintop, and lowered a boat to carry the pilot over to the flagship to tell Campos what had happened. Campos was surprised, but there was little he could do but order the fleet back to Havana where the damage to the Almiranta could be surveyed.

Three divers were lowered, who quickly discovered the cause of the leak, a breakage in one of the planks attached to the sternpost about a fathom below the waterline. The plank was replaced and the water pumped out.

Villavicencio reported the state of affairs to Campos and repeated his demand that the Almiranta be properly careened and the fleet await the arrival of Pimienta before leaving for Spain. Campos had already decided what he was going to do, but he went through the good old Spanish motions of convening a junta to discuss the problem. It was composed of the senior officials of the silver fleet and the Armada de Barlovento, and the Governor of Havana. All the old arguments were repeated, and it was quickly apparent that there were two directly opposed views represented. Villavicencio and Volumbozcar wanted to stay and wait for Pimienta. Volumbozcar felt that the cargo carried by the fleet was so valuable that two or three months' delay in reaching Spain was far better than taking the risk that the treasure never reach Spain at all. On the other side, Campos and Diego Centeno, the son of the former admiral whose opinions seemed to carry considerable weight, wanted to set sail at once. The argument was heated. Villavicencio accused Campos of wanting to leave for his 'own ends and interests' and without thought of the risks to which he was exposing His Majesty's treasure. Campos accused Villavicencio of exaggerating the danger and using the need of careening as an excuse 'to take the glory from him of entering with the fleet (without [Pimienta's] galleons) into Spain'. A sensible compromise was put forward by Antonio de la Plaza, the Almirante of the Armada de Barlovento, who suggested that some of the silver be transferred to the two biggest galleons of his squadron which, although 'less luxurious', were newer and safer ships. Campos ignored all such suggestions and, since he was Captain-General, it was he who had the final word. The silver would remain where it was and 'if it became necessary to remove the silver from either ship and transfer it to another vessel, it would be very easy and this was frequently done at sea'. The fleet would sail immediately. 'If he arrived he would take the thanks and if he was lost, he would have no one to account to as he would pay with his life.' So, of course, would many other people, but Campos made no mention of them. The junta was dismissed and the fleet set sail for the second time on 20 September, a full month after the almost mystical 20 August, the last safe date to leave for Spain. To quote Pierre Chaunu, the great French historian of the Carrera de Indias, 'In 1641, after a century and a half of dearly bought experience, the men, or at least the officers, who left Havana so late in the year and with ships in so poor a condition, could hardly be ignorant of the risks they were running. The sea which was waiting for them would not have come as a complete surprise.'[37]

CHAPTER FOUR

Shipwreck

There was no time for fireworks and fiestas to entertain the passengers and crews of the Spanish silver fleets bound for home. The long passage from Havana to Seville was fraught with potential danger for nearly every mile of the route, danger which was heightened by the fact that ships and men were nearly always in poor shape after their many months of inertia in American ports. The condition of the *Concepción* was by no means exceptional. Indeed, it comes as something of a surprise that any ships got home at all, so many were the obstacles to be encountered. The route lay due north from Havana for twenty or thirty miles until the fleet was shot into the Gulf Stream or Florida Current about halfway between Havana and Key West. The current took control of the lumbering ships, sweeping them along to the east at increasing speed, perilously close to the Florida Keys, or the Martyrs as they were known for good reason by the Spaniards, and then north into the Straits of Florida. Here the north-bound current reaches its maximum speed of four and a half knots and there was little the sailors could do but ride the conveyor belt, while masthead lookouts searched the seas each side for the reefs and shoals of Florida and the Bahamas. The wind was often opposed to the current, whipping up the sea and pushing the top-heavy ships to port or starboard at its whim. Distance travelled was difficult to judge, as was the drift of the ships, and the pilots tended to hug the Florida side of the Straits in an attempt to fix their position, but conditions often made it impossible to know exactly where they were. A moonless night, a change of wind, a sudden drop in the rate of flow of the current or an idle lookout and the ship could take the path of so many previous Spanish galleons and end up helpless on the poorly charted reefs. Spaniards praised the early navigators who had discovered the merits of the Gulf Stream which so speedily carried their fleets six hundred miles to the north on the way home, but there was a heavy price to pay.

New dangers faced the fleets as they turned east from the coast of Carolina hoping to pick up westerlies to carry them to within sight of

Bermuda, where they could set a course for the Azores. At first they were within easy range of corsairs based on the English North American colonies, who waited hopefully to pick up stragglers as the fleet sailed by. Then there was Bermuda itself, notorious for 'right Bermuda weather', a region of storms and low visibility, a dangerous speck in the middle of the ocean, whose barrier reefs had claimed many Spanish victims, the most recent only two years before, in 1639. There was little to hit and few enemies to fear in the long haul from Bermuda to the Azores, but it was an unpleasant passage, especially in winter when storms and black skies replaced the pleasant days and nights spent speeding along before the north-east trades, some fifteen hundred miles farther south, on the outward voyage. As the fleet approached the Azores a fresh danger of corsairs was added to that of the elements, a danger which increased as they neared the coast of Spain and saw at last the towering cliffs of Cape St Vincent, the long-sought landfall of the homebound fleet. It was not for nothing that the sailors' nickname for St Vincent was the Cape of Surprises, for its deeply indented coastline was a favourite haunt of corsairs. There was one last potential surprise for the long-suffering, weary Spanish sailors who had managed to get this far, a surprise which they knew only too well since it lay at the mouth of the Guadalquivir River, just sixty miles from Seville where an impatient government was waiting for its silver. The river was obstructed by a dangerous sand-bar, so close to the surface that only the most favourable conjunction of wind and tide enabled the great silver-carrying galleons to cross it, and this Barra de San Lucar had claimed innumerable ships which had survived every other obstacle only to sink within sight of home.

It might be thought that no one would be so crazy as to sail twice in the silver fleets, but nearly all the officers and most of the crew of the *Concepción* who set sail from Havana for the second time on 20 September 1641 had done the round trip several times and were well aware of the dangers. No doubt they hoped to do it several more. The first couple of days were frustrating as they waited for an off-shore wind to carry them north to pick up the Gulf Stream, but when the wind came it brought good weather and they were soon being happily propelled along by the current. On the fourth night out three shots rang out in the darkness, and the Almiranta sailed forward to investigate the trouble. The shots had been fired by a shallow draught frigate, *La Garca*, which had sailed ahead of the fleet on her captain's own initiative. This sensible action saved the fleet from the first and most obvious obstacle on the route, for *La Garca*'s leadsman had sounded and found only four or five fathoms of water, and the general opinion was that the fleet had narrowly missed running up on the Florida Keys. The Capitana changed course and there were no further problems met in the passage through the Straits of Florida, from which they emerged on 27 September, a lovely day only slightly marred by the fact that there was one sail too many in the fleet, 'which we determined to be the enemy'.[1] The corsair gave no trouble, however, and the current bore them on along the coast of Florida as they tacked into the north-east wind in preparation for the long beat towards Bermuda.

The first sign of a change in the weather came on the following morning when the lookout in the Almiranta, which had retaken her station at the rear of the fleet, saw a long swell coming up towards them from the south and a threatening bank of clouds on the horizon. At the noon sighting of the sun it was found that they were in the latitude of 30° north, the latitude of the Spanish settlement at St Augustine, Florida. In the afternoon the wind swung round from the north-east to the south-west and then the south, and the bad weather which they had seen on the southern horizon caught up with them. The sea got up and the freshening wind from the south swept them along before it. It was clear that they were in for a bad storm and normal precautions were taken. Most of the guns and other heavy gear on the upper decks were taken below, hatches were fastened and the upper and lower gunports were closed and fitted with washers. 'By nightfall the weather was becoming increasingly violent and by midnight it was an all out storm.'[2] Huge waves struck the great 'mountain of wood' in the darkness and already many of the older sailors were saying that they had never experienced such a savage storm. But there was much worse to come.

By now the Almiranta was running before the storm with her foresail alone, trying to keep the towering poop directly before the wind, but forced by the proximity of the eastward-trending American coastline to head as much as possible to the north-east. With the wind now blowing from the south this exposed the starboard quarter to the fury of the waves which threatened every moment to overwhelm the ship. At dawn, such as it was in the driving rain, a momentary error by the exhausted pilot laid the whole side of the ship open to a freak wave which broke right over the poop lantern, fifty feet above the water level, sweeping four men and one of the ship's boats into the sea and rolling the ship over so far that the decks on the port side were under water to the foot of the mainmast. Hen-coops, crates of provisions, casks of sugar, anchors, cables, guns, two more lifeboats, everything vanished into the sea from the decks which looked as if they had been stripped with axes. It was a quarter of an hour before the Almiranta righted herself, and during this time the sea poured through the rotten washers in the gunports and through the gaping holes in the gundecks, whose seams were so bereft of caulking that you could place a bolt between them, and so down into the bowels of the ship where the water sluicing down from the decks above was like a heavy rainstorm. Desperate attempts were made to repair the gunports, under conditions of great hardship and danger, but to no avail. The sea continued to pour through as each new wave struck the crippled ship. Soon the sea found a new place to enter. The thunderous waves smashing at the stern ripped to pieces the repairs which had been done in Havana, washing away the new oakum with great ease and flooding through the ship. The pumps had been manned since the storm began and now all those not needed to work the ship joined in bailing with jugs and bowls, anything that could hold water, but it was no good. The wind continued to gain strength, and the water level kept rising, as fresh waves broke over the sides of the ship and the weight of water in the hold dragged the lower gunports down below sea-level.

First light on that terrible 29 September, St Michael's Day, revealed that the Almiranta was not the only ship in trouble. The fleet had been scattered by the storm, and each ship sought to save herself. Three of the merchant ships had been swamped and sank in the night with the loss of all aboard. But at dawn there were still a few ships to be seen, dismasted and helpless or running before the wind with the minimum of sails. Early in the morning the Capitana, the *San Pedro y San Pablo*, was seen coming up fast on the starboard quarter, still apparently in good condition. She sailed past the waterlogged Almiranta and headed north, followed by the Almiranta for a couple of hours until she was lost to sight. At ten they had a brief glimpse of one of the galleons of the Armada de Barlovento. She had lost her mainmast and was as helpless as they were as she ran before the storm with her mizzen and foremast bare of sails. Then she was gone and the *Concepción* was alone, wallowing out of control as the weather got worse and worse, 'intensifying into a fully fledged hurricane, the strongest that had ever been experienced or seen at sea'.[3]

At one in the afternoon Don Juan de Villavicencio discovered that there were seven and a half feet of water in the hold and it was still rising. On the advice of the ship's officers he ordered the mainmast to be cut and several guns to be cast overboard to lighten the ship. Shortly afterwards the foresail, the only means of keeping the ship running before the storm and preventing her from being continually broached by the waves, was torn away in three pieces by the wind. Now the Almiranta lurched side on to the sea and 'the sea and wind tossed the ship so much and she took in so much water over the side that we decided we had no hope of salvation'.[4] Soon there were over ten feet of water in the hold and a couple of feet in the storerooms above. Barrels of gunpowder and foodstuffs were tossed about and smashed open and their contents were ruined by the water.

Now, alone and with no possibility of help, the passengers and crew began to despair. 'We thought that we were in such danger that now no one tried to do anything but that which was most important, to save their souls. Each person said goodbye to the others. Not even the bravest had any hope of life.'[5] People tried not to look at the sea and the gigantic waves, each one of which seemed determined to bury them for ever. The priests and friars on board worked hard as everyone made their confession, including some who had not confessed for fifteen years. Now was the time to regret the absence of the Viceroy's relics. All that they could hope for was that their own contrition and 'the total kindness and compassion of God' would save them. They waited for a sign but, when it came, it only deepened their despair. The image of Our Lady of the Conception, the patroness of the ship, fastened to the poop deck by two massive bolts, was swept away and vanished for ever into the deep. 'With this, everyone was sure that they would all lose their lives.'[6]

The destruction of the Virgin marked the worst moment of the storm. Between five and six in the afternoon the weather yielded a little and the mate, Francisco Granillo, led a party of the bravest sailors, 'who were very few at that point for most of them considered themselves already dead',[7] across the pitching, wave-swept decks to rig a jury foresail. The ship was once more brought under some control and the people recovered a little hope of life. All night they took shifts at the pumps or bailed with jugs, and the water level was lowered a little, only to rise again when the pressure forced the oakum from between the planks in the prow and let a fresh torrent of sea-water run into the ship. But now there was no more despair, and this new blow merely provoked a fighting spirit. They remembered that they were Christians and Spaniards, and love of life overcame their fear of death. All next day and the following night the pumps clanked, and passengers and crew struggled to keep the Almiranta afloat. That day, 30 September, the wind swung round to the north and north-west, and, at a meeting of the ship's officers, it was decided to make their way before the wind to one of the islands of the Bahamas where they could beach the ship and do the necessary repairs before continuing their voyage to Spain. By late afternoon the weather became more settled, although the sea was still very rough, and by midnight the exhausted men at the pumps had lowered the water level in the hold to just over two feet. The people rested, and God repaid their efforts, bringing dawn on Tuesday, the first day of October, an hour early – and what a dawn; a brilliant topaz sky and calm weather. The storm was over.

Advantage was taken of the fine weather to do some repairs. A raft was lowered with a diver, carpenters and caulkers who filled the gaping seams with barrel staves and then recaulked them. This work took three days and, when it was finished, the Almiranta was sound enough to pump out dry. 'God miraculously permitted this', wrote Don Juan de Villavicencio, 'it should not be attributed to human energy, for that alone would never have saved a ship from such a dangerous situation.'[8] When the ship was dry Villavicencio ordered the Vedor to go below with other officials to check the extent of the damage to the stores. His report was not encouraging. Nearly all the gunpowder was ruined; there was just enough to load eighteen of the guns once and many of the provisions were so saturated by sea-water as to be useless. This was serious. They might be weeks in the Bahamas, putting the ship in sufficiently good order to make the passage back across the Atlantic to Spain. Without powder they would be at the mercy of the pirates and privateers who had their bases on the north coast of Hispaniola and in the island of Tortuga. There was no Spanish garrison, indeed no inhabitants at all, in the Bahamas to help them. A fresh junta of senior officials was called, and it was unanimously agreed that, with so few provisions and virtually no gunpowder, there was no alternative but to sail the damaged ship to Puerto Rico, the nearest Spanish base and dockyard. It seemed likely that many other ships in the fleet would do the same. On the first day after the storm they had seen two ships in the distance, one to port and one to starboard, headed in that direction. Both were dismasted except for their mizzens. The Almiranta had signalled to them and had kept a lantern lit at the masthead during the night, but the following day they had disappeared, and the sea was once more completely bare of other ships. A few days later they got a further unhappy indication that they were travelling in the same direction as their friends when they saw some masts with rigging and sails in the sea. But there was no sign of the ships which had shed them. The *Concepcíon* would have to solve her own problems.

It is not quite clear exactly where the Almiranta was when the decision was made to head for Puerto Rico. She must have gone a long way to the north and north-east, as she ran before the storm for a day and a half and was probably approximately in the latitude of Bermuda, but a long way further west, when the wind changed direction and she started sailing towards the Bahamas. If this supposition is correct, she must have been about a thousand miles north-west of San Juan de Puerto Rico when Villavicencio gave the order to make for the Spanish port, a very long way in a ship with no mainmast and in serious danger of foundering in the next storm. There was no assurance that the hasty repairs just made by the diver would hold any better than those done in Havana, once the ship was subjected to heavy weather. Confidence was not increased when it was learned that neither Bartolomé Guillen, the senior pilot, nor his assistant, Mathias Destevan Arte, had ever done this particular voyage before and would have to rely on their rudimentary charts to find Puerto Rico. None of our witnesses make any comment on the next stage of their voyage, but it must have been a frustrating and worrying time with stores and powder so low and not a sight of land or another ship. Days and weeks passed by as the Almiranta struggled against contrary winds and currents or remained motionless in the notorious calms of the Sargasso Sea. But there was some progress, and slowly she made her way farther and farther towards the south-west.

On 23 October, three weeks after the repairs had been completed, they found themselves in the latitude of 22° north, the latitude of the Caicos Islands at the far end of the Bahamas but considerably further east.[9] The two pilots now declared that the ship was due north of Puerto Rico and they should turn south to search for land. Don Juan de Villavicencio protested. 'I, along with other practical persons, felt that it was not possible to have gone such a long way or to be as far to windward as the pilots made out and affirmed.'[10] They had wandered in their navigation and their attempts to measure the ship's way had been blighted by the many days of calm and contrary winds and currents. In his opinion they were three hundred miles farther to the west than the pilots claimed, an enormous margin of error. To turn south now would be foolhardy for, by his reckoning, they were due north of the Abrojos, a dangerous and well-known bank of shoals and reefs some fifty miles north of Hispaniola. 'It was essential to leave sufficient sea-room for the galleon to avoid the Abrojos. And in order to do this, we should steer another five or six days to the south-east.'[11] The pilots stuck to their opinion. It was not possible that they had made an error of such magnitude. 'How did he think that in three hundred leagues, they should be mistaken in half of them.'[12] Bartolomé Guillen reinforced his statement by pointing with his finger at the chart which lay on the Almirante's table. Villavicencio was still unconvinced. 'I continued to see the aforementioned risks.' The Gobernador, Don Bernardo de Tejada, who, although a commander of marines, was a dab hand at navigation, was also not convinced; nor was the mate, Francisco Granillo, both practical people who aired their opinion of the pilots' competence to the widest possible audience. But the pilots persevered in their belief and, in accordance with the regulations of the Carrera de Indias, Villavicencio had no choice but to accept the pilots' opinion on a matter of navigation. But he was going to make quite clear where he stood. Calling his steward, he asked for a silver bowl full of water to be brought to him on the poop deck and then, in full view of the assembled crew and passengers, he washed his hands. He then gave the order to turn south.

A week of calm weather postponed the day when it should be seen who was right. But on 30 October the wind got up a little from the north-east, and they began to make more rapid progress to the south.[13] At sunset the Almirante ordered the sails to be furled and the ship hove to till the next day dawned, lest they run aground in the night. Next morning, All Souls' Day, soundings were taken at intervals and no bottom was found, nor could the lookouts see any land from the masthead, so it was felt that the ship could proceed safely through the following night with just the foresail. The weather was good and the night was clear when, at half past eight, a shudder ran through the ship as she touched bottom. The senior pilot, Bartolomé Guillen, immediately ordered the anchor to be dropped, but this manoeuvre took half an hour in which time the ship's way ground her forward, tearing her bottom on the submerged coral reef.

Next morning the long-boat (*lancha*), the only boat remaining after the storm, was lowered, and an attempt was made to find a passage through the reefs. No exit could be found, nor was it possible to tow the ship back off the reef. Cables kept breaking as they ran over the sharp coral and there were not sufficient anchors to kedge the ship off. Indeed there was a serious shortage of the necessary equipment to cope with the emergency. Some had been lost in the storm; some had been carelessly left at Havana when the ship set sail. The Almiranta had only two anchors, far too few for this situation. 'The warps, capstan hawsers and other fittings which these ships are supposed to carry for this sort of occasion took away our little luck, for they were not aboard. The anchors and two cables had been taken overboard by the storm, as they were not taken below in time.' Having failed to tow the ship off, an attempt was made to sail her off backwards. 'The pilots decided to let out the sail to see if this would help the ship to exit the way it had come in. However, God did not find sufficient merit in us to grant a miracle and so we could not free the ship.'[14] The Almiranta was firmly stuck and remained at anchor all day.

On the second night on the reef the wind got up from the north and there was a serious danger that the ship would be forced farther on to the reef. A lantern watch was kept on the cables of the one anchor holding them against the wind. At two in the morning the worst happened. The cables parted and the ship began to grind forward. Cables were attached to guns and other heavy objects which were thrown overboard in a desperate attempt to check the ship's progress. These cables snapped as well, and the wind and sea jerked her farther and farther forward on to the reefs, which ripped open her bottom and sides. At daybreak on 2 November the ship was clearly sinking, her bows tipped down into the deeper water beyond the reef and her stern resting at a crazy angle between two sunken rocks. The *Nuestra Señora de la Concepción* had made her last voyage.

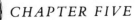

CHAPTER FIVE

Sauve Qui Peut

The documents which describe the last few days in the life of the *Concepción* are surprisingly silent on the reactions of the passengers and crew to the desperate situation in which they found themselves. Perhaps their authors had exhausted the vocabulary of despair in describing the horrors of the hurricane. Still, it takes little imagination to envisage the mood of people who had already endured so much and now found themselves stranded in a sinking ship on a coral reef in the middle of nowhere. No land could be seen from the tilting mizzen masthead, and the weather was becoming increasingly dirty as the wind continued to blow from the north bringing heavy rain. Nothing could have seemed more desolate than the crescent of sunken reefs stretching to the east and to the west, their position clearly marked by the line of waves breaking on them, breakers whose spray rose higher and higher as the north wind grew in intensity. Through the rain to the south and south-west more breakers marked the existence of further reefs, while close at hand there were a number of flat rocks which remained uncovered for a few hours each side of low water. The reefs were formed from coral heads, the peaks of crazily shaped formations of coral rising forty or fifty feet from the sea-bed. What struck many observers was the density of these coral heads. Sometimes the individual heads were only separated by a few yards of sea, sometimes by a hundred yards or more, but the general impression at low tide was of a whole forest of extremely dangerous looking tree-stumps; a 'pruned vineyard [*viña podada*]' was the vivid expression used by Gaspar Romero Maldonado, a young passenger who described the reefs many years later. 'The distinguishing mark is like a pruned vineyard. When the tide goes out, everything can be seen; when it comes in, several tops of the reefs can be seen.'[1] The Almiranta was held fast in the midst of this desolation, her stern jammed between two sunken coral heads, while her bows dipped farther and farther into the sea as water poured in through the gaping holes in the prow and hull. The sea was soon lapping the foot of the mainmast, but the afterdecks and poop remained clear of the water, providing a precarious footing for the ship's company who had retreated aft up the sloping deck.

Where were they? On the day after the ship hit the reef, a party made their way to one of the uncovered rocks to try to answer this critical question. A number of separate estimates of the ship's latitude were made, and their disparity provides a startling illustration of incompetence in navigation. A gunner, who was standing next to Bartolomé Guillen, the senior pilot, heard him calculate that they were in the latitude of 20° north. Guillen later corrected this and told Don Juan de Villavicencio that they were in $19\frac{30}{4}$° north, and that the reefs which they had struck were to the north of Anegada in the Virgin Islands. It will be remembered that it was Guillen who, a few days previously, had declared that the ship was due north of Puerto Rico. He was now saying that, after sailing due south with a north-east wind, they had struck a reef which was a hundred miles east of the most easterly part of Puerto Rico. It was a truly extraordinary piece of navigation. A second independent estimate of the ship's latitude showed that she lay in 22° north, over two full degrees north of Guillen and in a region where there were no reefs at all, a region which in fact is distinguished by some of the deepest seas in the world with depths of up to 20,000 feet. A final estimate was made by Don Bernardo de Tejada, the Gobernador, who first calculated that they were in $20\frac{1}{2}$° north and later in 21° north, thus neatly splitting the difference between the other two wild estimates. Don Bernardo had been one of the group of 'practical persons' who had supported Don Juan de Villavicencio in his assertion that they were in danger of running on to the Abrojos if they headed south as Guillen wished to do. Now he said that that was exactly what they had done. The Abrojos lay between $20\frac{1}{2}$° and 21°, and that was where they were. Needless to say he was quite correct. The wreck, in fact, lay in 20° 43' north, almost exactly halfway between Don Bernardo's two estimates. But once again Bartolomé Guillen refused to be corrected. When it was suggested that he might be wrong, he simply reiterated that they were on the shoals to the north of Anegada and 'that was the end of it'. There was no other reef on the chart. 'If it had been on the chart, we would have noted it.' Later he reinforced his calculation by saying that he had actually seen the island of Anegada from the masthead at dawn and that it was about twenty miles away from the ship. Was his error simply the result of incompetence or was it a bad case of wishful thinking? We cannot tell, but the error was colossal. Anegada is nearly four hundred miles away and a full degree further south from where the *Concepción* really sank. But so convinced was Guillen that he was right that, in the end, even Villavicencio believed him and made his plans for saving the people and the treasure on the ship in accordance with Guillen's estimate of their position.[2]

On the morning of the second day on the reef Villavicencio decided that he would have to abandon ship. The position was hopeless. Every possible effort had been made to save the ship, but shortage of the necessary equipment and the rising wind from the north had foiled them all. Even if by some miracle she could still be got off the rocks, the ship was so badly holed that she would sink anyway. Now 'there was no more important task than to save the silver, artillery and people'.[3] This would not be too easy, since only one boat had survived the storm. The only solution was to build rafts on which the passengers and crew could make their way to the island which Bartolomé Guillen had proclaimed was so conveniently near. When everybody had got ashore the long-boat would return to save the treasure and what remained of the guns, a manoeuvre which would presumably involve several trips to and from the wreck in view of the colossal weight of silver and artillery that would have to be moved. In the circumstances, and with the fallacious idea of his location which Guillen had given him, Villavicencio's plan was reasonable enough. There was, however, one problem. To move from the reef to Anegada might simply mean that the long-suffering ship's company of the *Concepción* exchanged one form of death for another, since the island was said to be inhabited only by cannibals.[4] But no doubt it was thought that the landing parties would be sufficiently well armed to defend themselves until help and ships could be brought from Puerto Rico.

Villavicencio gave the order for the rafts to be built, while the long-boat was left with an armed guard in case anyone should try to seize it before the final order was given to abandon ship. As the day wore on the ship settled a little farther into the water and the Almirante tried to hurry along the work. It was clear that there was not much time to lose. All the provisions that were still dry were brought up on deck, and there was a discussion as to whether to bring the silver up too. Don Juan was at first in favour of this as it would make the subsequent salvage easier. But it was pointed out to him that an abandoned ship with her decks piled high with silver would be an attractive proposition for any enemy ship that might hear of it. It was also thought that if the ship broke up completely, which now seemed very likely, silver left on deck would be scattered about the sea bottom, while if it were left where it was, in the hold and the padlocked storerooms, the weight would keep the wrecked ship in position and thus make salvage comparatively easy for the divers who would later be brought to the site. All this made good sense, and so the silver, save that which was already on the deck in casks and boxes or in the poop cabins, remained where it was. Much of it was already under water.

Meanwhile, the sailors continued to build rafts under the supervision of the ship's carpenters. With the ship listed at an increasing angle, it must have been a tricky task making rafts out of deck-planking, casks, hatches and what spars still remained, but the work went on steadily, and by nightfall one raft had been completed and fitted with a mast and sail and waterbutts, and other rafts were nearly ready. They were lowered into the sea, now not far from the deck, and provided with armed guards. Villavicencio decided to wait till daybreak to assign as many people as possible to the long-boat and the raft that had been finished, while those who remained would continue to build more rafts to take them off in their turn. He assured everybody that he, the Almirante, would be the last man to leave the ship.

There was little chance of sleep for anyone that night, the third which the ship's company had spent on the reef. The weather got worse and worse, and by midnight had developed into a full-scale thunderstorm. The wind howled, the rain lashed down, and flashes of lightning revealed huge waves breaking on the stern of the ship and on the reefs each side of them. It seemed that God had spared them from the storm at sea only to pound them to death on these desolate rocks. At four in the morning Juan Mexias Araias, the sergeant-major of the fleet who was commanding the guard on one of the rafts, saw the ship suddenly lurch forward and plunge much deeper into the water, which now rose to the level of the quarter-deck. Morale, which had been good up to this point, collapsed completely. People clambered up on to the poop or into the rigging, while many threw themselves into the sea and swam towards the long-boat and the rafts in a desperate attempt to assure themselves of a place of safety. The guards fought them off with pikes and lances and only a few managed to get aboard. Most of the rest were drowned. Fighting broke out on the poop deck as well, and many people were seriously wounded and a few, including a priest, were killed.

Don Juan de Villavicencio was faced by an appalling scene as he came out of his cabin with sword drawn to try to restore order. Men were fighting on the decks and in the water, and all the time more people were hurling themselves into the sea. The thunderstorm provided a suitable backdrop to the pandemonium. 'I commanded them to cease and wait for daybreak to divide themselves between the long-boat and the rafts,' wrote the Almirante when he described the scene much later. 'I assured them that I would be the last to leave as I had proclaimed the day before.'[5] But no one listened. His authority had collapsed. Making the best of a bad job, Villavicencio ordered a number of the senior officials to make their way to the long-boat while he stayed on deck and waited despondently for the dawn. As he stood there the mate, Francisco Granillo, came up and urged him to get off the ship while he still could. 'Now there is no time to wait any longer,' he was reported as saying by a passenger who was standing nearby.[6] But the Almirante made no move, and Granillo decided to make his mind up for him. He grabbed Villavicencio by the breeches and threw the Almirante into the sea and then jumped in himself. Villavicencio could not swim and, as he came up gasping for breath, he looked around desperately for a means of saving himself and grabbed the foot of Don Felix de Paz, a young passenger, who towed him to the long-boat where the guards hauled the now unconscious Almirante to safety. Or, at least, that was Don Juan's story, and there were many people who were later prepared to give evidence in support of it. Let us hope for his sake that it was true, for Don Juan de Villavicencio needed a very good reason indeed to explain why he abandoned his ship, leaving no one to command in his place and leaving several hundred people in a situation of the most terrible confusion and despair. It is hardly surprising that Granillo later denied the Almirante's version of the story, saying that 'he and Villavicencio threw themselves into the water', but it is only fair to the mate, who had played such a heroic part in saving the ship from the storm, to point out that many other people, including Don Felix de Paz, also said that Don Juan jumped and was not pushed or thrown into the water. Readers may decide for themselves what really happened.[7]

When Don Juan recovered consciousness he found that the wind and current were so strong that the long-boat had already been carried three miles away from the ship, and there was no chance of returning, as there were only four or five sailors to man the oars.[8] He did not, of course, think of asking the many distinguished people on board to do anything so servile as to row the boat themselves. There was nothing for it but to continue sailing south till they found the island of Anegada which, according to the pilots, was only twenty miles away and then return to help the rest of the people on the wreck when the weather improved or the wind changed. Needless to say they did not find Anegada, as it was in fact four hundred miles to the east of them, and Don Juan was forced to choose a fresh course. Common sense indicated that the pilots' estimate of their position was too far to the east which meant that they were probably somewhere north of either Puerto Rico or Hispaniola, and that if they sailed south or south-west they should hit land unless they were incredibly unlucky. What was more serious was that they had left in such a hurry that they had neither food nor water on board and the prayers of all thirty-three men in the long-boat were concentrated on getting ashore as soon as possible. Their prayers were answered. Don Juan sailed south, south-west and west-south-west all day and all night 'and at dawn we saw land which we prayed would be Puerto Rico'. At two in the afternoon they landed, still believing that they were in Puerto Rico, although in fact their landfall was near Puerto Plata on the north coast of Hispaniola. The mistake is understandable. Both islands are very mountainous, and few Spaniards ever sailed along the north coast of Hispaniola, a region which had been abandoned over thirty years previously and was now mainly the resort of corsairs, who knew it well.

They sailed west along the coast of the island, which they soon identified correctly, looking for somewhere where they would be able to find food and water. A few years later, George Gardyner, an English travel writer, was to describe this region in glowing terms. Referring to the north coast he wrote: 'This island is so full of harbours, as he that will coast it, cannot well misse of one where he pleaseth, most of which afford refreshing of fresh meat and good water.'[9] Don Juan de Villavicencio and his party were not to be so lucky. On the second day of coasting they turned in towards the port of Isabella but discovered an enemy ship anchored in the bay and hurriedly set sail to the west again. Two days later they sailed into a small bay, but found no food or water in the vicinity. 'It was now four days since we had eaten or drunk anything, as we had left the galleon so quickly and without thought', wrote Don Juan. 'I and thirty-two men who had been on the long-boat entered the densely forested but unfruitful mountains without a guide or path. Barefoot and wounded and on the point of breaking, we could not find anything among the trees and we were so overcome with thirst and hunger that we collapsed and were unable to lift ourselves from the ground for many hours.'[10]

They returned to the boat and continued to coast along the island. It was not until the eighth day after leaving the ship that they found a supply of fresh water. 'We undressed ourselves to our skins and wet our shirts in the water and wrung them across our mouths, taking away the thirst which had afflicted us for eight continuous days.'[11] They also found crabs with which they were able to assuage, if not satisfy, their hunger. Four days later they arrived at the foot of Monte Cristi, the prominent headland which had so impressed Christopher Columbus when he approached it from the west on his first voyage, 'a very high mountain which appears to be an island, but is not, for it has a very low-lying piece of land uniting it with the shore. It is shaped like a very lovely pavilion, and he called it Monte Cristi.'[12] Here there were more shellfish to eat and plenty of water to drink, and Villavicencio decided to rest most of his exhausted party, while the five men who had survived the experience best were sent inland to look 'for people or civilisation', with orders that if they did not meet anyone after six days they were to return. 'Three people went one way and two others another way. The two returned with no hope of finding anything but the three others met with a youth. We attributed this to a miracle.'[13] The boy was shocked by the appearance of the famished, ragged and weatherbeaten party from the longboat, but there was little he could do to help on the spot except try to preserve the Almirante's dignity by giving him his hat. He then went to get his brother and father and the three of them guided Don Juan up the valley of the Yaque del Norte river to the town of Santiago de los Caballeros and then over the mountains and down to Santo Domingo, a distance of 170 miles in all. People on the way gave them bananas, cheese, cassava, meat and other things to eat, but they were still in a terrible state when they arrived 'barefoot and naked' in the city of Santo Domingo on Monday, 25 November, twenty-two days after that terrible night when they had leaped into the sea to escape from the sinking ship.

It soon became clear to the remainder of the passengers and crew that the long-boat party was not going to return to the *Concepción* in the immediate future. Many people were none too happy about the Almirante's desertion of them, especially as the long-boat had been capable of carrying many more than thirty-three men. There was muttering about dishonourable behaviour, and dishonourable it certainly seems to the historian. For, even if we accept that Villavicencio's departure from the ship was unpremeditated, it still seems a pretty poor show that the long-boat party should have included so many senior people, such as both the mate and the second mate. No doubt the officials of the Casa de la Contratación, not to mention the King, would also like to know why the Vedor, the Provedor and the silver-master, the three men most responsible for the treasure, should have left their posts so soon and abandoned so much silver to a crew who, for all they knew, were quite capable of building a new ship from the wreckage and sailing somewhere safe to share out the treasure. It was indeed very much a case of officers and gentlemen first, though to be fair there were still many senior officers, such as the pilots, and many distinguished passengers left on board.

Grumbling and righteous indignation have never saved anybody's life, and it did not take long for those remaining on the wreck to think of themselves and forget about the long-boat. The situation was bad, but not quite so desperate as it had seemed at four in the morning during the thunderstorm. The weather improved after a few hours, and the ship does not seem to have sunk any farther during the next three or four days. No one seems to have taken command of the survivors, who must still have numbered nearly four hundred and fifty men, but it must have seemed obvious to everyone that the best thing to do would be to complete the rafts and then try to find land. It is hardly surprising that the different accounts of the various departures from the wreck are rather confused and it is often difficult to tell whether two witnesses are describing the same raft. There seem to have been between eight and ten rafts built altogether, the smallest carrying twenty-five men and the largest sixty or seventy. All were grossly overloaded, and there are some sad stories of men swimming out to rafts only to be thrust back into the water by those in possession, who felt that one more passenger would sink them all. On nearly all the rafts the weight of people on board meant that they were actually sitting in the sea, sometimes up to their waists, and these were shark-infested waters. Another problem faced on several rafts was a shortage of drinking water. None of the raft parties made the mistake of the men in the long-boat of travelling with no provisions or water at all, but it seems clear that several underestimated the time that they would be at sea and quickly exhausted the meagre supplies that they had brought, reducing some men to the fatal expedient of drinking sea-water. Most of the rafts which reached land took three or four days to get there. But three of the eight rafts never reached land at all.

The first to leave was the big raft which had already been completed before the thunderstorm. It set sail on the same day as the long-boat with seventy men on board and provisions for four days. For some extra-ordinary reason the pilots had suggested to the leaders of this party that they sail west and try to make a landfall on Cuba, a suggestion in the best tradition of these particular pilots since the nearest part of Cuba was three hundred and fifty miles from the wreck, while the nearest land to the south or south-west was only about eighty miles away. None of the seventy men on this raft was ever seen again and it was presumed that they all drowned. There is only one bizarre piece of evidence relating to their fate. Weeks later a ship arrived at Santo Domingo from Cuba and the crew reported that a unicorn horn had been washed up on the north coast of the island. It was well known that Don Francisco de Villagortia, one of the men who travelled on this raft, always carried a unicorn horn as a lucky charm.[14] There is no evidence at all as to what happened to the seventy men on the other two rafts which were complete losses.

There was also a heavy death toll on two other rafts from which there were survivors to tell the tale. In one raft twenty-eight died out of sixty-four. Some were lost to sharks who took men right off the raft. Others died from drinking sea-water. Others threw themselves into the sea after going crazy from lack of sleep and from sitting up to their waists in water on the overloaded planking.[15] A survivor from the other raft, Francisco Andres, later told the story of what happened to his party. They were just approaching land when a huge wave overwhelmed them, drowning nearly half the party, including the chaplain of the Almiranta. Some of the thirty-two survivors swam to shore; others managed to right the raft and came safely ashore on that. Three more men died as they wandered through the mountains of what they thought was Puerto Rico, and it was twenty days before they met someone who told them that they were in Hispaniola and showed them the way back to civilization.[16]

Much the best documented survival story involves one hundred and twenty men, over half of the eventual survivors, who set off in two rafts under the guidance of the pilots. This might not seem the best company in which to travel to safety but, in fact, all but one of this large party survived, though not without adventures on the way. Work was started on the two large rafts after the departure of the long-boat and they were completed after four or five days' continuous effort. They seem to have been particularly well made and indeed many witnesses described them as boats (*barcos*) to distinguish them from the other rafts (*jangadas*). What this distinction involved is not quite clear, but they seem to have been more buoyant and seaworthy than the rafts. No witness mentions anything so unpleasant as sharks swimming on board or men sitting for days in sea-water. Most of the more distinguished people who were left on the wreck seem to have travelled on these two boats, including the two pilots, the constable, several priests and friars and many wealthy passengers such as Don Diego Centeno, the son of the Captain-General who had died in Vera Cruz, and his friend Don Diego Sandiel. Fortunately for the historian, the party also included the anonymous author of what we have called the 'Jesuit letter' and his son.[17]

The two boats set sail on the morning of 8 November, eight days after the Almiranta struck the reef and five after Villavicencio departed in the long-boat. The pilots were still sure that they were to the north of Anegada, but had apparently regretted the advice which they gave to the men who had set out on the first raft to sail west, and they steered southwest hoping to find the coast of Puerto Rico. On the third day they saw land at dawn and wild guesses were made as to their whereabouts. One man said later that he thought they were approaching the island of Virgin Gorda, which is actually south of Anegada in the Virgin Islands.[18] That day they were hit by a storm 'which seemed to want to eat them and they were afraid the cliffs would tear them to pieces during the night. Fortunately, God miraculously saved them. . . .'[19] God was saving them for an ironic fate. The two boats separated in the night and at dawn on the fourth day one of the boats found itself under the guns of an English corsair ship, no doubt the same ship which the long-boat party had seen in Isabella Bay. The corsairs had no pity. They took all sixty men aboard and stripped them of everything they had, from their fine clothes and jewellery to 'their few damp provisions', giving them some cheap English and Dutch clothes in return to cover their nakedness. Then the English captain proceeded to question them. It was quite clear to him that there was only one sort of Spanish ship which could be carrying people so well dressed as some of these were, and he wanted to know where they had been wrecked. The pilots told him that their ship had struck the reefs to the north of Anegada and that they were now making their way to Puerto Rico. The English captain looked at them in amazement. How could anyone be so ignorant of these waters? 'Drunkards,' he retorted, 'that wasn't Anegada where you were lost. Those were the Abrojos.'[20] He also pointed out that the island which they were approaching was Hispaniola and not Puerto Rico.

Just then the lookout called out that he had seen a second boat full of

Sauve Qui Peut

survivors. This boat contained the author of the 'Jesuit letter', and we can leave it to him to tell us what happened next.

We came upon a sail which we felt belonged to the enemy. It had met the first boat at dawn and had taken all the people aboard and from what was said they had also recognized us. They put the people below deck and then came after us, letting off a cannon and we took in the sail. They took us on the ship and we painfully thought about what we had brought with us. We recognized the others from the Almiranta who were there. Before the hour of prayer, they put us on land, having taken our clothes and shirts and exchanged them for worn out ones from Holland and Brittany. We were left there near Puerto de Plata without shoes. We did not know where we were and in the morning we began our journey without knowing which path to take.[21]

They could at least congratulate themselves on being alive. There had been only one casualty from the party of one hundred and twenty men. This was Don Geronimo de la Rodo, who had died on the corsair ship from wounds which he had received when he tried to get into the long-boat during the panic on the night of the thunderstorm. The survivors now broke up into smaller parties. The strongest went off ahead to try to find a good route through the mountains to the south. Others wandered off along the coast. The majority followed in the wake of the 'most vigorous ones', through mountains 'so high that they competed with the sky' and across rivers so deep 'that the water went above our chests'. Here we can once again follow the marvellous narrative of the author of the 'Jesuit letter'.

We walked together for five days without having anything to eat except a few palmitos [the tops of the palm tree] and guavas which are not enough to give a human resistance. This was particularly true for me as I was the oldest. Our bodies were so wasted that they were hardly recognizable and, even after we had reached the city of Santiago, I could not believe myself when I looked in the mirror. On the fourth day I was so exhausted that I made my confession to Canon Don Juan de Roa, as I had decided to stay behind and die. This would have happened, if my son had obeyed me and had gone on with our companions leaving me behind. On the fifth day I took heart and, under incredible hardship, went with the others and they stopped a thousand times for my sake. That day, at four in the afternoon, God guided us to a small farm where wild pigs and cattle used to be rounded up and slaughtered.* I stayed there with a few friends

* Presumably the farm was deserted and was used during the periodic round-ups of the runaway animals which roamed the island of Hispaniola. See above pp. 38–9.

73

who were almost as tired as I was. The resolution was made that forty-four of us would remain while the others carried on, with the understanding that they would let us know as soon as they met anyone. This they did, fifteen days after leaving us. We remained there in the utmost misery. We had nothing to eat but the palmitos from the palms surrounding the farm. The others had left us an axe with which we were able to cut them down and we found a pot which was a help as we cooked the hard part of the palmitos in it. We were able to eat the soft part raw. The poor pot did not stop boiling all day long. Finally an angel came and showed us the path to someone who had been sent by our companions four days after they left us. But, as they got lost, it took them fifteen days to return for us. From there we walked to the city of Santiago, a city of this island thirty-six leagues from this city [i.e. Santo Domingo] where we stayed for a few days to recover our strength and bodies. We were treated with the greatest kindness and they provided us with supplies beyond the limits of charity, and I was one of those who received it. Others, they treated well for their money such as those who arrived in the long-boat.[22]

The departure of the two boats which were to be robbed by the corsair left just thirty men on the wreck, perhaps still hopeful of the return of the long-boat, perhaps too scared to leave the relative security of the flat rocks and the wreck itself for the terror of the unknown seas to which they had seen their friends commit themselves. There is nothing more terrifying then to leave the solidity and familiarity of even a wrecked ship which has been home for several months for the pitching insecurity of a raft or lifeboat, fragile craft which look so pitifully small when set against the immensity of the ocean. Shortly after the departure of the pilots' two boats the wreck sank a little farther into the water, and the thirty castaways shifted to the rocks, taking with them all the silver that had been in chests and casks on the upper decks so that it might serve as a guide to future salvors, if they were forced to abandon the site before help came. There seems to have been no shortage of provisions, which they were able to get from the wreck when they needed them, but this is the only comfort which they had. They must have presented a pitiful picture. The flat rocks were only dry for a few hours each side of low water and conditions must have been appalling for this last party of survivors, standing in the water much of the time and searching the southern horizon for the return of the long-boat or some other assistance which never came.

Three days they waited on their own on the rocks. But then on the third day, the eleventh that they had spent in the Abrojos, the same storm which had struck the pilots' two boats as they neared land struck the reef and ended the long vigil of these last few men over what remained of the Almiranta. The wreck fell apart; the bows broke up, as did part of the stern, thus releasing the ship from the two underwater rocks which held her, and the Almiranta finally sank beneath the sea. Those who were left made a raft from planks, chests and pieces of the side of the ship and set out for land. 'The men started to drink sea-water and then go crazy and throw themselves into the sea.' Later, the raft struck a rock and over-turned. Only two reached land – Andres de la Cruz, twenty-three years old, the Indian servant of a lawyer from Mexico City, and his friend Luis. 'After they reached land, Luis went back into the water because he thought he saw a little barrel floating which might contain fresh water. However, as he went into the sea, he was caught and eaten by a shark.' Now Andres was alone, the last man to leave the *Concepción* and live to tell the tale. 'Then this witness left by himself and went into the mountains. He walked until he met some people who took him to Santiago.'[23]

It is impossible to say exactly how many people died as a result of the various sad events of the last voyage of the *Concepción*. No one called the roll of the ship to determine precisely who survived. The authorities were mainly interested in the fate of officers and gentlemen, and most of these escaped to safety in the long-boat and the two boats which were captured by the corsairs. But even if the roll had been called, it would not give us the correct answer, as not everybody turned up in Santiago and Santo Domingo to be counted. Survivors were wandering around lost on Hispaniola for weeks after the wreck. One source said that eighteen people died of starvation in the mountains.[24] Some probably took the opportunity to desert, quite certain that they were never going to take the risk of being sent to sea again. There were survivors living near Puerto Plata more than forty years later.

However, there is no doubt that well over half the passengers and crew died in one way or another, swept overboard in the hurricane, trapped in the ship when the bows plunged under water, killed in the fighting on the night of the thunderstorm, drowned in mad attempts to swim ashore from the wreck, drowned in the fruitless effort to sail to Cuba, drowned when madness forced them to jump into the sea or when their rafts overturned, eaten by sharks, or dead of the long slow death of despair and starvation in the mountains and forests of Hispaniola. Don Juan de Villavicencio said that 190 escaped and 300 drowned. Antonio de Volumbozcar said that 'in all we are 200 men who were saved, poor, unclothed, asking for charity. More than 300 comrades and friends were drowned.' Another source gave the same figures and added that it 'has been very sad'. All three may slightly overestimate the dead, but it was certainly very sad.[25]

CHAPTER SIX

Santo Domingo

Don Juan de Villavicencio had plenty to occupy his mind as he followed his guides up the long valley of the Yaque del Norte river on his way to civilization. It was no small matter for an Almirante to lose his ship, and there was much to be done if his future reputation was to be secured. He must organize an expedition to return to the wreck to take off any people who might still remain on it and to salvage the treasure and artillery. And, even more important for his own security, he must make sure that blame for the disaster was correctly apportioned; in other words, he must make sure that he himself bore no blame at all. Don Juan had no doubt who was responsible for the wreck of the *Concepción*. The pilots were in charge of navigation, and, if a ship hit a reef in calm weather, that was clearly the fault of the pilots, a verdict which no one who has read the evidence would question. The pilots must therefore be arrested. There was also the matter of Villavicencio's precipitate desertion of his command. Don Juan had no doubt who was responsible for that as well. No one was going to accuse him, the Almirante, a Knight of Calatrava, of leaping off his ship in a moment of panic.

Don Juan was able to make a start on his programme when his bedraggled party reached the town of Santiago de los Cabelleros on 19 November. Here he discovered other survivors who had escaped from the wreck on the rafts and had taken a more direct route after their first landfall. And among them was Mathias Destevan Arte, the assistant pilot. Villavicencio ordered the mayor of the town to arrest him and place him in the public gaol. Further orders were given to the local constable to take a party to the north coast to help survivors and to search for the other pilot, Bartolomé Guillen. Meanwhile, Villavicencio sat down and wrote a description of the shipwreck to be sent ahead to the President of the Audiencia of Santo Domingo and governor of Hispaniola, Don Juan Vitrian de Viamonte y Navara.[1] His business done, the exhausted Almirante could now relax, eat a decent meal and sleep in a bed for the first time since he was so rudely tossed into the sea eighteen days previously.

The arrest of Mathias Arte in Santiago was just about the only successful piece of business which Villavicencio was to achieve during his long stay in the island of Hispaniola. What we have to record now is a story of frustration, accidents, arguments, incompetence, pettiness and sheer bloody-mindedness which may well be typical of the management of Spanish colonial affairs in the middle of the seventeenth century. It would be tedious to record every non-event and to itemize every piece of obstruction which Villavicencio had to endure, but it is important, and in fact quite amusing, to understand just how difficult it was to do what the Almirante conceived to be His Majesty's urgent business. The first thing to go wrong happened before Villavicencio had even left Santiago. Don Juan was just about to set out on the road to Santo Domingo when he heard that Arte had smashed the lock of his gaol and had put himself under the protection of the local convent. But this was not to help the pilot very much. The Almirante got permission from the church authorities to enter the convent and to place the pilot in chains in the ecclesiastical prison. A proclamation was published that 'no one of any status or quality as well as Blacks, mulattos, Indians or women are to help or provide the said Mathias Destevan Arte with provisions, tools, files, hammers, pliers or any other instrument that the delinquent might use to escape'.[2] Despite these precautions, Arte was to escape again, and four months later no one had any idea where either he or Guillen were. Most people presumed that they had fled the island. We do not know how Arte escaped the second time, but one thing is clear. There was very little enthusiasm on the island for the men in Santo Domingo who attempted to uphold the King's authority, and there were very few people who were prepared to give them any assistance, proclamation or no proclamation.

Such distressing truths of colonial life were not yet apparent to Villavicencio when he left Santiago on 22 November. With Arte in chains and a posse searching for Guillen, he could feel that the matter of the eventual punishment of the pilots for their negligence and incompetence had been satisfactorily set in motion. He could now get on with the business of the wreck itself. When he arrived in Santo Domingo, capital city of Hispaniola, three days later he can hardly have imagined that it would be more than a week before he was back on the Abrojos recovering His Majesty's treasure. His confidence was increased when he saw in the harbour three ships from the Armada de Barlovento – General Sosa's

Capitana, the galleon *Rosario* and the *petachio* – as well as one of the most richly laden merchant ships from his own fleet. All four ships had lost masts and bore other signs of damage from the storm, but this could soon be remedied, and then they would be available to provide Villavicencio with the naval protection which he would need while salvaging in the Abrojos.

General Sosa had arrived in Santo Domingo on 13 November after a peregrination even longer than Villavicencio's own. He, too, had been heading for San Juan de Puerto Rico after the storm, but his pilots did just the opposite from those on the Almiranta and underestimated the distance that they had sailed east, with the result that they had sailed right round the island of Puerto Rico and had arrived at Santo Domingo from the east. This had done nothing to improve the General's normally bad temper, already at a very low ebb as a result of the disastrous maiden voyage of his Armada. Now all he wanted to do was to repair his ships as quickly as possible and sail for Cuba where he had heard that three other galleons from the Armada had gone to refit after the storm. Nothing ever happens as quickly as seems possible to a bad-tempered general. Sosa stormed round Santo Domingo, shouting at the dockyard authorities who objected to him removing their carpenters without written permission from the President, insulting the butchers who supplied his men with meat and then demanded to be paid, and generally making a nuisance of himself. He was in no mood to want to provide assistance to Don Juan de Villavicencio, even though he knew it was his duty.[3]

On 27 November, two days after Villavicencio's arrival in Santo Domingo, senior officials from the local bureaucracy, from General Sosa's Armada and from the *Concepción* met to discuss what should be done about the wrecked Almiranta. Everyone knew that they would have to do something, and also that they would have to do it quickly, before the ship fell apart or floated away. But there were serious problems. What ships should Villavicencio use for the salvage? There were many ships in Santo Domingo harbour, including a fleet of merchant vessels waiting to take the produce of the island back to Spain. The best thing would be to hire some of these for the work. But who was going to pay? Neither Villavicencio nor Sosa had any money, and so it looked as though expenses would have to be borne by the Real Hazienda, the royal treasury on the island, which like most royal treasuries was short of cash and very reluctant to spend more than the bare minimum which good manners and the officials' interpretation of the

King's business demanded. They were prepared to pay the freight of one or possibly two merchant ships to be used for salvage for a short time, but really felt that it would be much better if the ships were provided from what remained of General Sosa's Armada. In any case it was obvious that Villavicencio was going to require considerable naval protection, and who else could supply that but General Sosa? The men in Santo Domingo had all heard by now of the English corsair ship based at Isabella which had robbed the men who had escaped on the two rafts with the pilots. There was no doubt in anyone's mind that this ship would now be waiting for a salvage expedition to lead them to the treasure. There were also reports of many other corsairs in the vicinity, most of them based on the island of Saona lying off the south-east corner of Hispaniola, directly on the route which any expedition would have to take to reach the wreck.

It was finally decided that these were risks which must be borne. Speed was essential if the treasure were to be recovered. Don Juan de Villavicencio must leave as soon as possible, 'accompanied by the most capable survivors from the wreck' and a number of musketeers from the local garrison. Just how many survivors were capable at this stage is not clear, but General Sosa provided a typical comment on the situation when he remarked that forty-three men stayed behind, 'as they were lazy'. Villavicencio was to sail in the *petachio* from the Armada de Barlovento, together with three smaller boats paid for by the Real Hazienda of Santo Domingo which were to do the actual salvage work on the reef. General Sosa was to follow with his two galleons as soon as they had been sufficiently repaired.[4]

In his letter describing the aftermath of the wreck, Villavicencio boldly wrote that, despite bad weather and reports of enemy ships, 'I decided to set out, offering my life in the face of the many dangers that I might encounter.'[5] All of which sounds very noble but, in fact, Villavicencio did not set out until 14 December, over a fortnight after the meeting. At the last moment it had been decided that a certain delay would be more sensible in view of the weather conditions, new reports of enemy concentration at the island of Saona and, perhaps most importantly, the fact that Villavicencio had no diving tubs or other equipment to use for salvage.[6] Even now, General Sosa's galleons were not ready, and Villavicencio sailed out of port on his own with the *petachio* and one of the merchant ships whose master had been forced to unload his cargo of fruit and join the expedition. The rest of the merchant fleet were ordered to remain in

Santo Domingo, lest they return to Spain to tell the story of the fate of the Almiranta before there had been any chance of salvage to counterbalance the news of the disaster.

Don Juan's expedition did not last very long. He sailed east along the south coast of the island, and on the second night encountered two enemy ships. For a couple of days his ships alternately chased and were chased by a varying number of corsairs and then sailed back to Santo Domingo to inform General Sosa of the situation and to ask for the assistance of his galleons. Villavicencio sent two officers to report to Sosa, who arrived at the General's house just as he had finished eating his evening meal. They got the most extraordinary reception. The officers made their report 'with the courtesy that is used between people of office', but all they received back from Sosa was a stream of abuse to the effect that they were exaggerating the danger from the enemy, that he knew it was his duty to protect shipping from corsairs and there was no need to tell him his job, and that he would come out in his own good time, even though his Capitana was leaking. All of which was said 'with great anger and violence and harshness to the sergeant without letting him talk'. The General was in one of his bad moods, probably caused by indigestion. The last remark in his tirade was that 'this has been the most vile meal possible'.[7]

The presence of General Sosa's two galleons did not add much to the effectiveness of Villavicencio's expedition. The galleons sailed out to sea while Villavicencio hugged the coast, with the result that they lost sight of each other on the first day. Then, oddly enough, Villavicencio ran into a completely different galleon from the Armada de Barlovento, the Almiranta, the only ship which had actually found Puerto Rico after the storm. She was now sailing to Santo Domingo after a refit. This was a strange coincidence, but it did not help Villavicencio to get anywhere near the wreck, for the next thing that happened was that he met up with Sosa once again, only to discover that both the General's galleons were damaged and that he was returning to Santo Domingo. Villavicencio himself, seeing that he no longer had an escort, 'followed him and entered port that same day'.[8] The whole affair seems extraordinarily futile. It was now near the end of December, seven weeks since Villavicencio had left the wreck in the long-boat, and no progress at all had been made in the business of salvaging the treasure. Meanwhile waves continued to break on the reefs of the Abrojos, slowly destroying what remained of the *Concepción* and making her harder and harder to find.

Preparations for salvage had to start all over again, but now all the old problems seemed magnified. The President and his treasurers were becoming seriously worried about the cost of what was increasingly seen to be a rather hopeless expedition. But it was too soon to dismiss the whole affair. The treasure was too big for that. It was agreed that the Real Hazienda would pay for the construction of two *barco-lenguos*, shallow-draught oared vessels which were much used in the Spanish West Indies and would be ideal for working close up to the reefs, as well as being well equipped to get away from corsairs. A special boat with reinforced decks capable of carrying a derrick to raise the guns of the sunken Almiranta was also to be built. Later the President complied with Villavicencio's request for the use of a 250-ton cargo ship which was to be hired for 1200 pesos a month. Slowly the costs built up, and there was nothing to show for it. The officials were very reluctant to pay out any more, unless they received special instructions from the King.[9]

General Sosa had promised to escort Villavicencio past Saona to the north coast of the island, once all his ships had been careened and fully repaired. But he was getting more and more fed up with the prospect of an extended stay in Hispaniola. On 7 January 1642 he called a meeting of the officials of his Armada to discuss a proposal put forward by the President that Villavicencio build his boats on the north coast of the island. This would greatly reduce the distance that they would have to go to reach the wreck. It would also relieve Santo Domingo of the expense of provisioning the salvage team and the men building the boats. In General Sosa's view it would also mean that Villavicencio would require no escort to get to the Abrojos, and so the Armada would be able to return to Vera Cruz, picking up the galleons which were refitting in Cuba on the way. This would be the best employment for the ships of the Armada. If they went with Villavicencio to search for the wreck, they would probably spend as much as 'the silver which will be salvaged'. Sosa also emphasized the physical problems of escorting Villavicencio to the Abrojos. The area was notorious for bad weather, and there was nowhere amongst the reefs where a ship could be safely anchored. Furthermore, if the weather forced them to seek shelter they would have to find it in the ports of the north coast of Hispaniola, ports which were difficult to find at night, 'as the coast is so difficult and unknown'. Most of what Sosa said was grossly exaggerated, as later chapters in this book will demonstrate, but he was determined to make as strong a case as he could and get away from the boredom of Santo

Domingo as soon as possible.

The record of this meeting of the senior officials of the Armada de Barlovento provides an interesting illustration of the 'democratic' way in
which Spaniards ran their affairs. For Sosa was to be overruled by
officials junior to him in rank. The General, as we have seen, was completely opposed to giving Villavicencio any more help, and he was supported by two other men, one of whom, Captain Gutierrez de Sosa, was
probably his brother or his son. Other captains and officials were well
aware of the dangers of sailing to the Abrojos so early in the year and
wanted to wait until March or later when the weather would be better.
But the meeting was swayed by the Almirante, Antonio de la Plaza, who
made the unanswerable point that 'as His Majesty's aim in forming the
Armada was to guard the Windward Islands and the treasure which is
sent from New Spain to Spain, it is the duty of the Armada to help Admiral Villavicencio'. He was strongly supported in this view by the
Vedor who said that 'as the aim of the Armada was to escort the fleet,
the Armada should be prepared to go immediately and save the silver
from the Almiranta before the enemy discovers it'. In his summing-up
General Sosa capitulated. He reported that, although the members of the
meeting were aware of the risks and inconveniences referred to in his
proposal, they felt that they should help Villavicencio.[10]

While Villavicencio supervised the building of his boats, Sosa argued
with his officers and the dockyard officials, and the treasurers of the Real
Hazienda watched with alarm the money trickling out, other officials on
the island were getting very worried about a completely different problem. From an early date there had been rumours that many of the survivors of the wreck had brought treasure with them and had then hidden it
on the island. No one was more certain of the truth of this rumour than
Don Francisco de Alarcon Coronado, the Fiscal of the Island, who felt
that people should be sent out immediately throughout the island to discover the whereabouts of this treasure. When pressed as to how he came
by his information he was a little vague. 'He said that it is the voice of the
public which has informed him. He has also heard news of it from some
religious people and even from the black men who walk in the street.'[11]

Great efforts were made to find this treasure. Every survivor from the
wreck who could be found was interrogated. So were officials and resi-
dents from Santiago and the other towns through which the survivors
had passed. Some people admitted to having heard the rumour, but there
was not a scrap of evidence to prove that it was true. No one had actually

seen any treasure, and all the islanders interviewed stressed the extreme destitution of the survivors who had arrived barefoot and dressed in rags and whose baggage consisted at the most of a bunch of bananas or some cassava which they had received from charity. The survivors, too, pleaded their innocence. When they left the ship they were not thinking about treasure, but about saving their lives. No, none of them had seen any treasure on the rafts, except a silver bowl which they had used for bailing.[12] It all sounds very convincing, and no one was to change his evidence, even though the President arranged for all those responsible for hiding treasure to be excommunicated. 'Let all persons know, whether they be men or women of whatever standing or quality . . . that the Bula de la Cena has a sanction of excommunication to all persons without exception or reservation who took and hid any gold, silver, pearls, merchandise, silk, chinchilla and other things which were on the lost ship.'[13] But somehow one gets the impression that the rather bored officials who made these enquiries were faced by a conspiratorial wall of silence which they had neither the energy nor the desire to destroy. It just does not seem very likely that no one took anything, whatever the conditions, and some evidence that the rumours heard by the Fiscal were true comes from a statement made by an 'intimate friend' of the first mate, Francisco Granillo, over thirty years later. Granillo had told him that 'a great quantity of silver' which had belonged to private individuals had been taken ashore by the survivors.[14] This was the silver which was mainly kept in chests on the deck and so would have been easily available. Most of the King's silver was in padlocked storerooms and was under water when the rafts left the ship.

Further efforts to find treasure were made by coastguards and other officials who had orders to patrol the north coast looking for survivors and searching the beaches for the harvest of the sea. The main harvest that winter was corpses, and the coastguards had orders to search the dead bodies for gold, silver, pearls and other valuables before they buried them. Once again the complete absence of any treasure, except '38 minute pearls in a little box half full of sand', seems too good to be true. The evidence given by the coastguards, fishermen and other beach-combers is bizarre in the extreme. Two examples out of many will suffice. On 17 January the Mayor of Santiago reported that three men working for him had brought 'a small wooden half-painted barrel, an empty box with a broken lid, an empty wine skin, two rotten hats, a hammock, five broken glass flasks, six rosaries, six or seven *chicaras* [for

84

drinking chocolate], several locks big and small, and half an iron bolt'. A couple of days later a fisherman brought him 'two wooden saucers, a *chicarita* to drink chocolate in, a hat, a worked cup made from a coconut and a cup with a silver whistle'.[15] At least the whistle was made of silver. It was not long before much bigger things than whistles, or even corpses, were being washed up on the beaches of Puerto Plata and farther to the east. Winter storms had smashed up the wreck still further, and great ship's timbers were being driven ashore. Soon there would be little indication of the site of the wreck at all.

During this long idle period in which his *barco-lenguos* were being built, Don Juan de Villavicencio ordered all the evidence against the pilots to be collected, 'in order to proceed against those who are guilty and give notice to His Majesty in the Council of the Indies'. A local lawyer, Don Christoval de Aragon, was commissioned to conduct the proceedings, which began on 8 January 1642. In the next two days he examined eight survivors of the wreck, including two lieutenants and the constable of the Almiranta, Diego de Castro. The witnesses described the reasons for the decision to head towards Puerto Rico, the controversy between Villavicencio and the pilots over their position and the decision to turn south. All blamed the pilots for the ship striking the reefs and completely exonerated Villavicencio from responsibility for the wreck. They also gave evidence that Granillo had thrown him overboard and that it had been his intention to return to the ship as soon as possible.[16] Many more witnesses were examined in the next few weeks, mainly in connection with the possible removal of treasure from the ship and the deaths that had occurred during the fighting on the night of the thunderstorm.[17]

Early in March attention was turned on Granillo, whose behaviour seems to have been condoned up to then. Perhaps the Almirante was not keen for too detailed an enquiry to be made into the circumstances of his departure. However, the Fiscal had seen the evidence and thought that it was clear that Granillo was 'very gravely guilty' for having 'violently taken hold of Admiral Villavicencio' and having thrown him into the sea, knowing that the Admiral did not know how to swim. On 18 March the President ordered his arrest, though Granillo did not stay around to be arrested. It was also discovered that the mate had been in trouble in a former shipwreck, that of the Almiranta of the 1631 New Spain fleet which had sunk off Campeche. Evidence was taken from five men regarding Granillo's behaviour on that occasion. It was hardly conclusive, being mainly hearsay, but the evidence suggested that Granillo had deserted his post and had gone off in the ship's boat with some gold, a silver chain and some money. Things looked black for Granillo at this point, but, despite his present guilt and this evidence of his past misbehaviour, no action seems to have been taken against him, and he was allowed to sail with Villavicencio when he eventually set off again to search for the wreck. Indeed his presence was considered essential if the expedition was to have any chance of success.[18]

This left just the two pilots to be dealt with. The whole island had been searched, but there was no sign of them. The search parties had visited a number of religious foundations where the pilots were said to have taken refuge, but each time the reports turned out to have no basis. It seemed probable that the two men had fled the island, or possibly had gone west to join the international community of corsairs and other ruffians who flourished on the west end of the island and in the island of Tortuga.[19] Or perhaps they were planning to sneak aboard one of the four ships of the Armada de Barlovento when it set sail to escort Villavicencio to the Abrojos. An officer was sent to deliver to General Sosa a proclamation that no officials were to 'hide, take or receive the pilots aboard any of the ships of the Armada'. Sosa refused to see him, but that was hardly evidence that the pilots were aboard.[20] It was simply what everyone had come to expect from General Sosa.

It will come as no surprise to the reader to learn that there were delays in the preparations for Villavicencio's second salvage expedition. General Sosa's four ships were careened and repaired and ready to sail by 22 February, but the construction of Villavicencio's boats took much longer and cost much more than had been expected, and the expedition did not in fact set sail until 7 April. In the meantime much more had been learned about the state of the wreck. On 14 February President Vitrian ordered a lawyer to interrogate Andres de la Cruz, the Indian servant, who claimed to have been the last man to leave the Almiranta, and who had only recently turned up in Santo Domingo.[21] His evidence made it clear that the wreck had completely broken up only eleven days after it struck the reef, and the truth of this was becoming increasingly manifest to the coastguards who reported large timbers being washed up. It was suggested that a boat be sent out to the wreck and 'that a few buoys could be placed in the water before the ship disintegrated, to mark the place for the later search'.[22] However, there is no real evidence that this very obvious precaution was taken, though one report does mention the despatch of two boats to search the reefs and look for the hull of the ship. No dates are given for this expedition, and it was in any case a failure, the boats being forced back to Hispaniola by bad weather.[23] When Villavicencio eventually did set out, he was going to have to rely on his memory to locate the wreck, an additional obstacle for which the Almirante can have only himself to blame. He had had five months in which to make a quick voyage to locate and mark the position of his lost ship. On 3 April he wrote a letter in which he claimed that 'until now, he has proceeded with great diligence in all that has been necessary regarding the loss of the galleon'.[24] This seems more like wishful thinking than the truth.

As the date of General Sosa's departure from Santo Domingo drew nearer, people living in the vicinity were able to learn the General's views on the correct method of manning and provisioning an Armada. It would not be said again, as it had been when he left Vera Cruz, that there was 'not one ship with four seafaring men'. Squads of soldiers were sent off in boats to press all the fishermen and sailors they could find into His Majesty's service. They quite often took the boat and the catch as well. Other groups did the rounds of the farms, removed everything that caught their eye – hens, cocks, bananas, maize, vegetables, firewood, clothing and crockery, as well as sons and brothers-in-law – and took them back to the ships of the Armada. The pressed men were given the option of buying their release for fifty pesos. Manuel Luis de Flores, for instance, was tricked into going aboard the Capitana by a party who told him he was required as a witness. When he came on board he was taken below and held for four days before he persuaded the sergeant to let him go for forty-one pesos, as he had not got the full fifty. A soldier went ashore to Manuel's house, got the money out of a locked box and then returned to the ship where the ransom was distributed – thirty pesos for the sergeant, four for the quartermaster, three for a corporal and two each for two soldiers. Manuel was then set free. When asked why he did not report all this immediately he said he was afraid that 'they wouldn't have paid any attention to him [*no le diessen alguna puñalada*]'. The four-man crew of a fishing-boat had a piece of luck, since one of them was a friend of Anna Garcia who had some influence in the Armada, since she had washed the clothes of one of the officers and had also lent him a mattress. Anna's intervention freed the fishermen, but there were many other men who had neither money nor friends and were forced to serve with General Sosa. It was quite clear that he had no intention of returning to Santo Domingo for a very long time.[25]

It was, then, a well-equipped Armada which set sail on 7 April 1642 to escort Villavicencio, whose own fleet consisted of a hired frigate called *La Santissima Trinidad* and the two *barco-lenguos*. It had been decided to build the special boat for lifting artillery at Puerto Plata, which was to be the base from which salvage operations would be carried out. Two days later the expedition reached the island of Saona. That was the last that anyone saw of the two *barco-lenguos* which had taken so long to build. Villavicencio went on to Puerto Plata, while the four ships of the Armada waited in turn at Cape Engaño, Cape Cabron and Cape Francés – three rendezvous which had previously been agreed between Villavicencio and Sosa. No boats turned up. Sosa even sent two ships to search for the missing boats in the Abrojos. But they were not there either. It was later learned that they had been wrecked.[26]

Perhaps one should grieve for Don Juan de Villavicencio. So many things seemed to go wrong. But the comedy was not ended. It was not until he arrived at Puerto Plata that he decided that the frigate was not really suitable for the salvage operations, as she drew too much water, and that the only way that it would be possible to sail her to the reef would be to make a very long detour through the Caicos Passage, between the Caicos Islands and Mayaguana, the most easterly of the Bahamas, and approach the wreck from the north. Needless to say, this was complete nonsense and simply indicated just how little the Spaniards knew about the waters in which the wreck lay. But this was Villavicencio's view, and so he settled down in Puerto Plata to build not only the special boat with the derrick, the materials for which he had brought with him in the frigate, but also another lighter-draught frigate which he hoped would be able to replace the missing *barco-lenguos* and work safely among the reefs.[27] There was a fair bit of ship's timber, masts and other fittings around from the remains of the rafts and the wreckage which had been washed up by the sea over the winter. It looked as though there would be enough materials for his carpenters to work with. All the same it seemed probable that Villavicencio might be in Puerto Plata for rather a long time.

This was also the opinion of the officials of the Armada de Barlovento, who dropped anchor alongside Villavicencio's frigate on 7 May, a month after leaving Santo Domingo. If they had felt fed up before, it can be imagined how they felt now. A week later the Almirante of the Armada, Antonio de la Plaza, examined the pilots and other technical experts of the squadron to hear their views on the situation. They were all very gloomy. There were not sufficient provisions or naval stores in the neighbourhood for the Armada to be able to remain much longer where they were. The salvage enterprise had already been going on for a very long time without any benefit to anyone, and such a situation was likely to continue into the indefinite future, now that Villavicencio was planning to build a new frigate as well as his boat with a derrick. Neither of these two vessels would really be suitable for the salvage work even if they were built, which was unlikely in view of the shortage of suitable materials for the new frigate in the vicinity. And even if everything else went right, they did not think that Villavicencio would be able to find the wreck. Captain Baez, the pilot of the *Almiranta*, made this point most clearly. 'According to the chart, the shoals of the Abrojos are such that he doubts that the ship will be found. They are thirty leagues across in each direction and are covered in water. There are only a few rocks which mark them.' Captain Alvarez made it sound even harder. 'He says that the reef on which the ship was lost is 8 or 9 fathoms deep and there are no markers along it except a few rocks which appear at low tide.' All the experts thought that the Armada would be much better employed elsewhere.[28]

This was all the evidence that General Sosa required. On 16 May he called a meeting of the senior officials of the Armada. There was to be no dissension on this occasion. Everyone agreed that there had been a time when they could have played a useful role. That time had long since passed. 'The best solution is for this part of the Armada to sail to Cuba where it can join the remainder of the fleet. Then the Armada should sail along the coast past the other ports of the Windward Islands, checking for the enemy, until Vera Cruz is reached. As it has been seven months since the *Almiranta* was lost, the search is futile.' General Sosa needed no convincing. He ordered the Armada to set sail on Sunday, 18 May.[29] Villavicencio made a desperate effort to stop the squadron sailing. He wrote a letter, pointing out that the search would be impossible without Sosa's help and that he would be at great risk with only the frigate for defence against corsairs. He ended by imploring General Sosa not to leave port. This letter was given to a public notary who set out in a sloop at six on the Sunday morning to try to deliver it. 'I followed in the said sloop for one and a half leagues out to sea, but the Capitana had set her sails . . . I made every possible effort to reach her . . . but it was not possible to over take her.'[30]

The Armada had one last kick in the teeth for Don Juan de Villavicencio. He had been worried that some of his men might take this oppor-tunity to desert his enterprise and had placed a guard on their quarters. However, in the middle of the night before the Armada sailed, his two master-carpenters escaped, taking some workmen with them. At dawn the Armada sailed, and, before the soldiers searching for the carpenters could stop them, the *petachio* from the fleet sent out its boat to take them aboard. Villavicencio had no other specialists capable of supervising the building of the boats, and now it would be impossible to finish them.[31] The Armada was also carrying another stowaway, our old friend the mate, Francesco Granillo, who had gone aboard the Almiranta the day before she sailed. He was obviously not prepared to take any chance that he might later be charged for throwing Villavicencio overboard. Don Juan sent word to Antonio de la Plaza, but was answered that Granillo was not aboard. He asked again and de la Plaza still answered: 'I know nothing of him.'[32] The Armada sailed towards the western horizon carrying Don Juan's two master-carpenters and the one man who was absolutely certain that he knew where the wreck lay, the very practical Francisco Granillo. But, even now, the long-suffering Villavicencio did not despair. The last letter written by the Almirante in the big bundle of papers which provides most of the evidence for this chapter was written on 5 June 1642, eighteen days after Sosa's departure. He said that in spite of the risks of the enemy, the lack of boats and naval protection he was once again going out in search of the wreck to begin the salvage of the silver, 'if the weather permits'.[33]

Here perhaps we may leave Don Juan de Villavicencio. Things were not to get any better for him. It was not long before the treasurers of the island gave up paying his bills, and there was no money forthcoming from a penniless Spain. In the summer the President finally let the cargo ships in Santo Domingo harbour and most of the survivors of the wreck go home. It seemed extremely unlikly that there would ever be good news from the Abrojos. Other survivors remained on the island, some settling near to Puerto Plata. Perhaps they were what remained of Villavicencio's salvage team. The Almirante himself did not give up for a long time. He made many more attempts to locate the lost ship from his base at Puerto Plata, but always something went wrong. The weather drove him off the shoals. Corsairs seized his boats. He was nearly wrecked on the coast of Hispaniola. There seemed to be a curse on the wreck of the Almiranta, and indeed on Don Juan himself. In the end, even he gave up, and the *Concepción* became just one more disaster in what was to be an extremely disastrous decade for Spain as a whole. But the wreck was not forgotten. Too many people knew that a fortune lay somewhere beneath the waters of the Abrojos. Many people thought that one day they would try to find it.

The sad story of Villavicencio's abortive attempts to get together an expedition to search for the wreck of the Almiranta provides a fitting end to the series of events which started with the appointment of Juan de Campos as Captain-General of the homebound Mexican fleet of 1641. Juan de Campos had a lot to answer for. It was he who decided to leave Havana with a fleet of leaking ships in the middle of the hurricane season. It was he who had appointed Bartolomé Guillen as pilot of the Almiranta. By the spring of 1642 the full measure of the disaster caused by these decisions had become apparent. Every single ship in the new Armada de Barlovento had been badly damaged, and the fleet was ruined for many months as an effective fighting unit by the wide dispersal of the individual ships. Three had gone to Santo Domingo after the storm, three to Cuba and one each to Florida and Puerto Rico. It is still not quite clear just how many of the twenty-one ships in the Mexican fleet itself were lost. Three sank with all hands on the day of the storm. Various estimates suggest that up to five were wrecked on the coast of Florida. One other ship sank only a few miles from safety, just outside Havana. All the rest of the fleet were badly damaged, and only one ship, the *Nuestra Señora de la Candelaria* from Honduras, arrived safely in Spain.[34] Then there were the two great ships which between them carried the whole of that year's consignment of silver. We know about the Almiranta. But what happened to the Capitana of Juan de Campos, last seen sailing strongly past the waterlogged Almiranta on the day of the storm? It was months before the news arrived in Santo Domingo. Juan de Campos got all the way back to Spain, only to sink on the notorious Barra de San Lucar at the mouth of the Guadalquivir river. It was Juan de Campos who had proclaimed in Havana that 'if he arrived he would take the thanks and if he was lost, he would have no one to account to as he would pay with his life'.[35] This proved to be untrue. Juan de Campos did not pay with his life, but he was to spend the next few years trying to account to government officials for the fact that much of the treasure brought up by divers did not appear on the register of his sunken flagship. These divers were quite successful. Salvage was rather a different proposition in the Guadalquivir river than it was in the Abrojos, and much of the Capitana's silver was later raised.[36] This may have brought the shadow of a smile to the King's face, but it was not enough to erase the general gloom with which the news of the disaster of the Mexican fleet of 1641 was met. It was a very bad year for Spain.

CHAPTER SEVEN

Sea Change

The lost treasure in the *Concepción* was not forgotten. The King had spent 30,000 ducats on the search for the wreck and was not prepared to spend any more, but this did not mean that no one else was prepared to finance expeditions to locate and raise the treasure. There was a long tradition of private entrepreneurs who tried to salvage wrecks after the Crown had given up and it was not long before such adventurers began to show an interest in the *Concepción*.

The first record that we have of a private expedition to search for the lost Almiranta was the petition of Juan Gomez Cavallero in 1650. He offered to pay all the costs of the venture himself and to give two-thirds of all treasure recovered to the Crown. He also asked for permission to recoup some of his expenses by trading free of tax between the West Indies and Spain. All the subsequent treasure-hunters also asked for this concession, and it is clear that the Spanish bureaucracy suspected that it was illegal trade and not salvage that was foremost in the petitioners' minds. On this occasion, Cavallero was refused permission to engage in any kind of commerce, but was granted a licence to search for the wreck. He seems to have fitted out two expeditions, one in 1650 and another in 1652, both of which were unsuccessful.[1]

There were no further official licences granted during the rest of the 1650s and the next application we have record of is that made in 1665 by Gaspar de los Reyes Palacios, a pilot from Cadiz. Palacios was already famous as a wreck-hunter and salvor for he had discovered the wreck of another Almiranta, the *Nuestra Señora de las Maravillas*, which had been swept off course in a storm in January 1656 and wrecked on Los Mimbres, a reef now identified as Matanilla Shoal on the Bahamas side of the Straits of Florida. He was said to have salvaged more than a million pesos of silver and forty guns in several expeditions to the wreck. Now, in 1665, he claimed to have information about the *Concepción* which made him think he could find the ship and the treasure.

He asked to be allowed to take two ships of 300 tons each, and, like

Cavallero, he requested permission to load a cargo in the West Indies free of taxes in America and Spain. He, too, would pay his own expenses and give two-thirds of the treasure to the Crown. Palacios also asked the Crown to free him from the payment of a 2,500 peso fine, which had been imposed for some offence connected with the salvaging of the *Nuestra Señora de las Maravillas*. The officials of the Case de la Contratación looked very favourably on Palacios's petition, considering him a man of great 'intelligence and experience', and they granted all his requests, except one. Only if he found the treasure would he be allowed to pay no taxes on his trading venture. Palacios sailed out to the West Indies with the Tierra Firme fleet of 1667. However, he failed to find the wreck of the *Concepción*, due to the bad weather and 'because of other accidents which overcame them'.[2]

The next application came in 1672 from Antonio Petri y Arce, also of Cadiz, a man who had spent forty years sailing in the Indies. He was a friend of Francisco Granillo, the mate of the *Concepción*, who had recently died. Arce claimed that Granillo had left him 'very particular information and descriptions of the place where the silver is located'. No one else who had searched for the wreck had had such good information. 'Today, he is the only man possessing such particular information regarding the location of the ship and, when he dies, the treasure will remain lost and it will be impossible ever to recover it.' This was strong stuff, and Arce was granted a licence on similar conditions to the previous applicants. He was just completing the preparations for his voyage when he died.[3] Palacios applied to take Arce's place. The Casa de la Contratación thought he should be given permission as he was the only man available with the experience and necessary information. He was granted a fresh licence and set out once again for the Abrojos, but he had no better luck than on his first voyage.[4]

Palacios's second voyage in 1673 seems to have been the last licensed expedition of search for the wreck of the *Concepción*. Manuel García de Villegas was granted a licence in 1675, but never set out. Captain Don Juan Baptista García was licensed in 1678, but died in Santo Domingo before he had begun his search. There still seemed to be a curse on those who sought to find the wreck of the *Concepción*.[5]

The longer the wreck remained unfound the more difficult it would be to find.[6] Wrecks in shallow tropical seas do not remain conveniently preserved intact for searchers to locate and divers to salvage at their leisure. Much of the more easily visible features of the Almiranta had disappeared long before Villavicencio set out on his very first expedition to locate his lost ship. Men and the sea had hacked away most of the masts and spars during the storm. What remained, together with much of the deck planking, had been converted into rafts by the survivors. The vast poop and the hull of the ship would last for some time beneath the sea, but they coud not resist for ever the remorseless battering of the waves. Sailors who know these shoals have described the seas piling up across the deep water to the north and east and then striking the reefs with a wall of water up to forty feet high. The effects of such storms had been seen on the north coast of Hispaniola where great pieces of the side of the ship had been washed up during the very first winter after the wreck. By the time that Gaspar de los Reyes Palacios started searching for the *Concepción* in 1667, twenty-six years after she had been wrecked, there can hardly have been any timber left at all.

Rough weather was not the only enemy of the salvor. Cousins of the shipworms which had such fun picking their way through the holes in the ship's sheathing in Vera Cruz could have a field day, now that the bottom had been broken wide open. As their small pincer beaks slowly nibbled their way through the submerged wood of the hull, the high sides of the ship, which had done so much to protect it in its prime, would collapse and fall away to be eaten at leisure as the years went by. If the shipworms had had no competition they would have eaten the whole ship in a matter of time.

But the teredo was not the only living thing rapidly disguising the wreck from the human eye. The Abrojos are the most extensive open-water concentration of coral in the Caribbean, and it was on a living coral reef that the *Concepción* was wrecked. Looking down through the transparent, blue-green water in a bid to locate the lost ship the searcher would see patches of sand 'as white as snow' interspersed with fantastic outcroppings of every kind of coral, rising from the sea bed in weirdly shaped towers and spires and pinnacles of beautiful colours, sometimes thirty or forty feet high, each one looking like the weed-covered masts and spars of a sunken ship. Coral loves wrecks and slowly it covered what the shipworm had not already digested. The *Admiralty Pilot* tells us that the maximum growth of live coral in these parts is a little over three inches a year, but even at a fraction of that rate it would not take long for a ship to disappear completely, to become indeed an integral part of the coral reef on which it had been wrecked. Some things would remain untarnished, uneaten and uncovered, a few bronze cannon lying on the sea bed, perhaps a heap of ballast stones and an anchor or two, but it would take a lucky man to find them in a region of shoals and reefs which modern charts show to be about forty miles long from north to south and thirty-four miles wide.

While the Almiranta broke up and became a prisoner of the coral the whole world of the Spanish empire in the Indies was crumbling in its turn.[7] The disintegration was slower than that of the wreck, but it was just as remorseless. The year 1640 had been an *annus terribilis* for Spain, the beginning of the end of a long period of glorious history for the great Iberian power. We have already seen the serious inroads that had been made into the supposedly Spanish monopoly of the Caribbean in the 1620s and 1630s. The next four decades were to see the process accelerate while Spain looked on helplessly, too short of men and money to stop the rot. More of the Lesser Antilles were settled by foreigners, and those which were already settled became more populous, as black slaves were shipped in to work the sugar plantations which were gradually becoming the sole source of income in many of the islands. Black slaves made the poorer whites redundant in the smaller islands, but there was work for them too. They could fight each other during the numerous European wars of the period. They were also available to fight and rob the Spaniards, an activity which many found sufficiently congenial to make their main profession. Some remained in the small islands of the eastern Caribbean, but many more moved nearer to their prey into the empty lands of Hispaniola and Cuba where they could join the ranks of those enemies of cows and Spaniards, the buccaneers. Here they could learn to accustom themselves to hardship and discomfort, extreme even by the standards of seventeenth-century Europe. Here they could learn the necessity of making sure that every scarce bullet hit its mark, be it cow or pig or Spanish lancer. Here they could also learn the joys of dissipating sudden wealth by joining the crews of the corsair ships which sailed from the island of Tortuga, now the busy home of desperadoes of all nations, somewhat uneasily controlled by a French governor.

Soon the corsairs and the buccaneers were to be provided with an alternative base, bigger, more fertile and just as attractive as Tortuga. The English were not to be outdone by the French. That curious mixture of the puritan, the pirate and the planter which represented the ideal of empire as seen by members of the Providence Island Company in the 1630s was to get a new lease of life in the 1650s under Cromwell, a man who shared the Elizabethan instincts of so many of his countrymen in believing that anything that belonged to Spain was fair game. The actual implementation of Cromwell's 'Western Design' to extend English power in the West Indies does no credit to Cromwell himself or to the English army and navy, whose reputation had never stood higher than it did late in 1654 when the expedition set sail from England under the command of Admiral Penn and General Venables. There have been few military enterprises so poorly organized, so poorly equipped and led, but, even so, an army of nearly seven thousand men was enormous by contemporary West Indian standards, even if it was recruited from the rejects of English infantry regiments, the scourings of the London slums and the poorest and most miserable of poor whites from Barbados and other islands in the Lesser Antilles, and should have been sufficient to seize any target in the thinly manned and unconfident Spanish Indies. Corsair captains with a few hundred men had held great cities to ransom in the past and were to do so on innumerable occasions in the future. But the Penn–Venables expedition seemed doomed to fiasco from the start. The army was landed near Santo Domingo in April 1655. Twenty days later what was left of it was back on the ships, defeated by disease, a handful of Spaniards and their own cowardice and incompetence. Terrified at the thought of what Cromwell would say if they returned empty-handed, the leaders decided to attack Jamaica, an island practically deserted by the Spaniards, which even their miserable army could hardly fail to conquer. But Jamaica, once conquered, was fortified and held, and slowly the Spanish settlers who had retreated to the mountains to fight a long, guerrilla war were rounded up or driven from the island. Meanwhile, the great harbour at what was later to be called Port Royal became the base for a privateering war against the Spaniards, in which many of the same men who appeared so incredibly unmartial outside Santo Domingo were to amaze the world by the daring, the bravery and the sheer impudence of their exploits. This was the first of the large islands to fall completely to the foreign intruders, and the loss of Jamaica was a terrible blow to Spain, however little was thought of the island before the English set foot on it.

While the English, French and Dutch consolidated and expanded their settlements in the Caribbean, the links between Spain and her American empire became progressively weaker as Spain herself became absorbed in protecting her territories in Europe, and Mexico and Peru became more autonomous, economically if not politically. Spanish officials continued to rule the islands and the mainland territories.

Decisions continued to rest on the consent of Spain. The flow of bureaucratic paper back and forth across the Atlantic continued to keep clerks
busy. But the paper took longer and longer to reach its destination. The
system of regular fleets connecting Spain and America, which had often
been interrupted in the 1630s, now completely broke down. There were
sometimes intervals of three years between the arrival of fleets in Vera
Cruz and, in the meantime, colonists had no alternative but to look to
foreign interlopers for their supply of European goods, a supply which
was readily forthcoming. The system of maritime defence also broke
down. The Armada de Barlovento which had been launched so optimistically in 1641 to sweep the coasts of corsairs and smugglers was soon
withdrawn to be employed in other roles, first to escort the silver fleets
and then in 1648 to be incorporated in the home fleet of Spain operating
on the Atlantic seaboard of Europe. For nearly twenty years after this
there was to be no permanent squadron in the West Indies and, with so
few silver fleets sailing out, the coasts and islands of the Caribbean were
left practically defenceless against the raids of foreigners. Only in the
great fortified harbour towns of the islands, such as Havana, Santo Domingo and San Juan de Puerto Rico, and in a few mainland ports, such as
Cartagena, could the colonists feel safe from attack, and much of the
Spanish population of the islands clustered close to these strongpoints,
ready to take refuge behind their walls in time of danger. Elsewhere the
only refuge was in the mountains and forests behind the coastal fringe of
settlement.

Spanish policy in the Indies ignored the lack of naval power with
which to implement it. Foreigners who settled in the area were still
intruders to be punished severely if caught, even if their settlements were
now several decades old. Trade between foreigners and Spanish colonists
remained illegal and those who were attracted by its profits took the risk
of being captured and imprisoned for many years by the governors of the
towns with which they traded. The fact that there was often no alternative source of supply of European goods or African slaves and that
practically everyone who lived in a Spanish colony wanted to buy cheap
foreign goods was totally irrelevant. Illicit trade continued to flourish
but at the same time illicit traders continued to be captured. The knowledge that their countrymen were languishing in chains in Spanish prisons and that their ships and goods had been seized and sold at auction in
Spanish cities provided an excuse, if one was needed, for continued
attacks on Spanish property in reprisal, attacks which when reciprocated

by Spanish corsairs carrying commissions from colonial governors provided further excuses for further reprisals. There continued to be no peace beyond the line.

It was in this strange world of Spanish inflexibility and weakness that the buccaneers were to thrive, to amaze the historian just as they did their contemporaries, who could read a somewhat exaggerated account of their exploits in a book written by the buccaneer turned author, the Dutchman John Esquemeling (Oexmelin).[8] Such exploits place the fiasco of the English expedition against Santo Domingo in perspective. On literally hundreds of occasions between 1640 and 1680 the 'Brethren of the Coast' set sail from Tortuga or Port Royal, rarely with as many as a thousand men aboard a flotilla of often minute ships, to appear suddenly several hundreds of miles away outside some largely unsuspecting Spanish city whose garrison and forts would be overwhelmed by the dash and courage inspired by the buccaneers' lust for loot, or, as they called it, 'purchase'. Purchase made brothers of Englishman and Frenchman, Dutch and Portuguese, Indian and Negro. Purchase kept them together, but not for long. They would follow a successful leader just as long as he remained successful and just as long as was necessary to achieve a new success. But then what discipline they had was likely to disappear. The loot from the most incredible of all their exploits, the sack of Panama in 1671, was disappointingly small, mainly because a detachment of the buccaneers were so drunk on plundered wine that they could not be bothered to capture a ship carrying most of the treasure of the Spaniards who had fled the city. The buccaneers rarely missed such an easy prize as this, but, once the expedition was over and the booty had been scrupulously shared out and spent in a glorious spree in the bars and brothels that flourished in their home ports, the brethren quickly broke up. Those individuals who avoided the debtors' prisons which were so often their homes merged once again in the crowds that thronged the ports or returned to chase cows in the forests of Hispaniola, until the word went round that Morgan or de Grammont was preparing a new expedition and the contract 'No purchase, no pay' promised fresh excitement and the possibility of an even bigger spree.

The fact that the most notorious of the 'English' buccaneers, the Welshman Henry Morgan, was able successfully to sue the London publishers of Esquemeling's book for libel merely highlights the strangeness of the buccaneering episode in history.[9] For Morgan never did anything that was illegal under English law, even if the Spaniards quite naturally regarded him as a pirate, as they had regarded Drake a century or so before him. Some of the rovers were pirates by anybody's law, but few of the more famous buccaneers took the risk of being hanged by their own countrymen. Morgan never sailed without a commission signed by the English Governor of Jamaica, and, whether the King and his ministers at home approved or disapproved of Morgan's exploits, it was the Governor and not Morgan who was ultimately responsible.

Whether the governors thought that robbing Spaniards was a good thing or a bad thing, and most did not think it too bad, they were almost forced to employ the buccaneers to protect the new colony. For the English government soon withdrew the royal ships which had provided the naval backing for the original conquest, and it was rare for there to be a single frigate in West Indian waters. Without the manpower and the threat of the buccaneers, Jamaica would have been wide open to Spanish reconquest and reprisals. The buccaneers did not have a mon-opoly of violence and greed, and there were many Spaniards who would have gladly sailed with a commission from such men as the Governor of Havana, if they had been able to do so safely. In any case, if the English did not commission the buccaneers, the French or Portuguese would, if they did not simply turn to piracy, and then English shipping would be in danger not only from the Spaniards but from the buccaneers them-selves. So it made good sense to grant commissions to men who, although not prepared to engage in mundane naval tasks like the protec-tion of merchant shipping, were quite prepared to wreck any hope that the Spaniards might be able to protect themselves. In 1669, for instance, Morgan was to destroy the new Armada de Barlovento before it had a chance to do any police work in the Caribbean, merely as a by-product of his raid on Maracaibo in modern Venezuela.

Most people in Jamaica supported the governors' decison to use the buccaneers. Planters were glad of protection from the danger of Spanish raids. Ship-chandlers were happy to give credit to such good customers. Shopkeepers and publicans in Port Royal had no objection to receiving the plundered pieces of eight when the buccaneers returned, drums beat-ing and flags flying, after a successful voyage. The only group who really objected to the buccaneers were the great merchants of the island, who thought that the best way to make money out of the Spaniards was to trade with them, not to rob them, and were therefore keen for peace in the Caribbean, the recognition by Spain that Jamaica was an English possession and, just possibly, permission for Englishmen to trade with

Sea Change

Spanish colonies. Even if Spain never allowed this, peace would provide
a better background for illegal trade than war.

Such an attitude was shared by many in England. Popular opinion
might make a hero of Morgan but the populace did not rule England.
Shopkeepers and ship-chandlers in London did not make any money out
of his raids. They were more likely to be making money out of the legitimate trade with metropolitan Spain which was growing fast, but which
would cease just as rapidly if the exploits of the buccaneers led to war this
side of the line as well as beyond it in the West Indies. Great merchants,
like their colleagues in Jamaica, were interested in developing trade with
the Spanish Indies. The Royal African Company, the Company which
had a monopoly of the supply of African slaves to the English colonies in
the West Indies and America, was keen to break into the potentially
profitable business of supplying slaves to the Spanish colonies as well.
Spain was worth wooing; a valuable trading partner and a valuable ally
in a Europe in which the power of France was becoming uncomfortably
great. Arguments presented by Jamaican governors seemed less convincing in London than in Port Royal. There was no danger of a Spanish
raid on England; no citizen of London need fear that he might suddenly
be transported from his comfortable home to a Spanish gaol. On the
other hand, King Charles II was not prepared to spend money on naval
protection in the West Indies, and no one wanted to lose Jamaica. So letters from London to Jamaica were sometimes hot and sometimes cold on
the subject of the buccaneers, sometimes encouraging them and sometimes calling for the cancellation of their commissions, while diplomats in
Madrid worked slowly towards more favourable relations with Spain.
An attack by the buccaneers might make the Spaniards very angry and
unlikely to be friendly to the diplomatic representatives of the country
which commissioned them. But the same attack was added proof of
Spain's weakness and her need of friends. At last, in July 1670, the Treaty
of Madrid was signed, incorporating the basic requirements of the
English negotiators. 'All offences, losses, damages and injuries which the
English and Spanish nations have, for whatsoever cause or pretext, suffered from each other at any time past, in America, shall be buried in ob-
livion and completely effaced from memory, as if they had never
occurred.' After more than half a century of English settlement across the
Atlantic the Spaniards recognized English sovereignty over 'all the
lands, regions, islands, colonies and dominions, situated in the West
Indies or in any part of America, that the said King of Great Britain and

his subjects at present hold and possess'. It was an enormous admission. In their turn the English promised to 'revoke all commissions and letters containing powers either of reprisal or marque, or of making prizes in the West Indies'.[10] There was still no mention of reciprocal trading agreements, but the era of the buccaneers was coming to an end.

Naturally it was far easier to sign a treaty in Madrid than to implement it in the West Indies. While the treaty was being signed Morgan was preparing to set sail towards Panama on his last and most famous raid. The news of Morgan's astonishing march across the isthmus of Panama, his destruction in open battle of the Spanish garrison and the capture and sack of one of the richest cities in Spanish America might bring pride to Englishmen who heard it, but was hardly likely to cement the new relations between the two countries. First Sir Thomas Modyford, the current Governor of Jamaica, and later Morgan himself were to be brought back to England in an attempt to appease the Spaniards. They were forced to remain in England for some years cooling their heels, but they were never charged with any offence. It was not their fault that correspondence took so long to cross the Atlantic. Modyford was replaced in Jamaica by Sir Thomas Lynch, the most consistent advocate of friendship with Spain amongst the Jamaican merchants and planters. Lynch was the factor in Jamaica for the Royal African Company and hoped to make a fortune by selling slaves and other goods to the Spaniards, legally if that should prove possible. Much of Jamaican politics in this period can be seen as a struggle between Lynch and Morgan, a struggle which was reflected in London where both men had their advocates.

Morgan indeed found himself very popular in a London society that liked hearing a good story, and he was to make some useful friends. The most important was Christopher Monck, second Duke of Albemarle, who had just succeeded to his title and riches on the death of his famous father, George, the architect of the Restoration of King Charles II. Albemarle was close to the King, and Morgan was to return to Jamaica a Knight and Lieutenant-Governor, a poacher turned gamekeeper whose job was to suppress the buccaneers who had made him a rich and influential man and one of the most important planters on the island. He certainly made a better job of this task than Lynch, who had no credit with the buccaneers and virtually no royal ships to enforce his policy. Lynch was forced to watch helplessly as the buccaneers turned pirate or accepted French commissions, while Spanish corsairs took the opportunity to attack English shipping and plantations.

Morgan was reluctant to hang men who had been his friends, and who might well prove to be the only defence of the island in the next European war. But he did hang some. He also got the Jamaican Assembly to pass a law making it a capital offence for Englishmen to take commissions from foreign princes to attack the nationals of countries who were not at war with England. This closed the main loophole, since many of the former English buccaneering captains had left Jamaica to receive commissions to attack the Dutch and Spanish from Bertrand d'Ogeron, the French Governor of Tortuga. Morgan also made it easy for buccaneers turned pirates to make their peace with the Jamaican government by offering a free pardon to any who came in before September 1681. Many took the opportunity, and, although Morgan was to lose his office to the Lynch faction in the same year, the mechanism for the suppression of piracy and buccaneering was now becoming properly established. The other European powers followed the English lead. The Dutch made a similar agreement with Spain in 1673, the French in 1683; and, although all three nations and the Spaniards themselves were prepared to cheat a bit, it would be fair to say that it now became generally accepted that it was possible, if still difficult, to have peace beyond the line. The last really spectacular exploit of the old-time buccaneers in the West Indies was the capture and sack of Vera Cruz in the summer of 1683. The incoming fleet from Cadiz arrived while the buccaneers were still ashore but so feeble had Spanish resistance become that the Spanish fleet were content to wait out at sea until the buccaneers had finished their business and sailed out to divide the booty at a nearby cay. The world had changed a lot since 1641. Now, in the early 1680s, the Spanish government were forced to leave the defence of shipping in the Caribbean to the English, who at last began to back the new policy with naval power.[11] From 1681 there were nearly always at least two royal ships on the Jamaica station. Soon there were to be more. A fifth-rate, like the 28-gun *Guernsey* which sailed for Jamaica late in 1682, was more than a match for any buccaneer. Indeed, her long-boat alone could deal with most of them, if they could be found and caught. Many buccaneers began to move out of the area, first to the west coast of South America and later to the Indian Ocean, where Madagascar was to be the centre of international piracy in the early eighteenth century. Only a few big pirate ships remained in West Indian waters. Small-scale piracy was to survive for many, many years, but Jamaica now became moderately respectable, a place where planters and merchants could make money and moan about the price of sugar; a good market for English industrial goods, for slaves from Africa and wine from Madeira; a regular port of call for ships from Ireland and New England carrying provisions; a centre of the contraband trade with the Spanish Indies. Jamaica was still the home of many former buccaneers. They sailed to the Cayman Islands and the South Cays of Cuba to catch the turtles, whose meat provided a staple of Jamaican diet. They sailed to their old haunts in the coastal swamps of central America, to the no-man's-land between the widely scattered Spanish settlements, to cut the valuable logwood, a dye-stuff much in demand from the textile industries of faraway Europe. Such innocent activities were often combined with the old, old game of trading illegally with the Spanish colonists. Sir Thomas Lynch, back as Governor of Jamaica after ousting Morgan and eager for more trade, legal or not, has left us a good description of the business of these half-reformed men.

We have about twenty trading sloops from fifteen to forty-five tons; built here, admirable sailers, well armed and treble manned, some carryng twenty or thirty hands, who receive forty shillings a month. They carry from here some few negroes and dry goods of all sorts, and sell them in the islands, and all along the coast of the Main in bays, creeks, and remote places, and sometimes even where there are Governors, as St. Jago [Cuba], St. Domingo, etc. for they are bold where they are poor. But at Carthagena, Portobello, Havana, etc., the Spaniards admit no one. This trade were admirable were we not undersold by great Dutch ships that haunt the coast of the Main and islands, and were we not fearful of pirates, which is the reason why the ships are so strongly manned. . . . This trade employs all the privateers that are come in, and would bring in the rest had I your Lordship's order to connive at it.[12]

Such voyages often ended in violence or with illegal traders in Spanish gaols, an instant challenge to a former buccaneer, but they would have to wait for the next European war before privateering became respectable again.

CHAPTER EIGHT

The Wreckers*

Men might do well or badly as privateers or planters, as merchants or illicit traders, in this brave new English world beyond the seas, but there
was another way of making a living, 'a lazie course of life', which may
well have been more attractive to many restless spirits than even buccaneering. Indeed, even today, the occupations of beachcombing and
wreck-hunting have not lost their charms. The most famous wreckers in
American waters were the settlers in Bermuda, an English colony whose
initial settlement was the result of a shipwreck in 1609. 'We found ourselves on the dreaded islands of Bermuda . . . called commonly the
Devils Islands', writes William Strachey in his superb description of the
shipwreck of the *Sea Venture* on its way to Virginia. They 'are feared and
avoyded of all sea travellers alive, above any other place in the world. . . .
Well may the Spaniards and the Biscani [Biscayan] pilots with all their
traders into the Indies, passe them by.'[1] The Spaniards beseeched God to
save them from the dreaded rocks of Bermuda, but they often prayed in
vain. The route of the returning plate fleets went either just north or just
south of Bermuda, according to season, and too often storms and poor
visibility left the ships wrecked and the survivors faced with a none too
Christian welcome from the Bermudans who took to their boats to seize
what they could. The most famous Bermudan wreck of the seventeenth
century was the *San Antonio* which was driven on to the rocks of Long
Bar during a hurricane in September 1621.† Later the Spanish ambassador in London was to complain that 'gold, silver and merchandise, to the
value of more than 6000 crowns, was seized by the English there, who
also took possession of the cock boat, and even of the clothes belonging

---

* Throughout this book I will use the word 'wrecker' in its contemporary sense, i.e. one who
searches for and salvages wrecks, rather than in the later meaning of one who induces shipwrecks by
showing false lights on land, etc.

† This wreck was located and salvaged in 1960 by the famous Bermudan treasure-hunter, Teddy
Tucker. There were still plenty of artifacts and valuables which had been overlooked by his predecessors.

to the passengers'.[2] There were to be many more wrecks. Two in 1639 provided an easy prey for the Bermudan wreckers, as their hulls lay in shallow water. In 1648 a Bermudan correspondent of John Winthrop Jr. wrote an enthusiastic account of 'a Spanish shipp of three hundred and fifty tonnes cast away uppon our rockes' which was thought to 'bee the richest shipp that hath bin cast away there since the iland was inhabited'.[3] And so it was to go on. The main business of Bermudans was planting and trading, but they would have been foolish to spurn the bounty of the ocean. The fact that the highest point of Bermuda is only 240 feet above sea-level and often covered in cloud; that Spanish navigators liked to be able to see the islands so as to know where they were; that the area is notorious for storms – all meant that Spanish ships (and those of other nations) continued to pile up on Bermuda's rocks, and, even when they did not, the sea often washed up goods from previous wrecks to keep the wreckers busy. Houses were built of wreck timber, the forts were provided with salvaged Spanish guns, and most men on the island had a few pieces of eight hidden away.

The wreckers of Bermuda were not to go long without competition. Most Spanish ships were wrecked in places too close to Spanish settlements to be easily salvaged by foreigners. Others were wrecked in waters too deep or too remote. But there was one area, empty of Spaniards and surrounded by shallow, transparent, 'gin-clear' seas, which had claimed large numbers of wrecks in the past and was to claim many more in the future. This was the Bahamas, the extraordinary, sprawling, low-lying archipelago of some three thousand islands, small cays and rocks, which stretches from the eastern side of the Straits of Florida to the north of Hispaniola, a maritime labyrinth of small slivers of dry land and shallow banks, separated by incredibly deep trenches, such as the aptly named Tongue of the Ocean, an inlet several hundred fathoms deep extending a hundred miles into the very centre of the Great Bahama Bank. Most of the Spanish ships which had been wrecked in this area had suffered a similar fate to the fleet of 1641, leaving Havana too late in the season and being hit by a hurricane as they passed through the Straits of Florida. But the navigation of the Straits was so difficult for the lumbering plate ships that many struck the myriad cays in fine weather as well. Spanish ships tended to keep to the Florida side of the channel, preferring to be able to check their navigation by sight of the land rather than to try to steer up the centre of the Straits, and it was on the Florida Keys and the coastline farther north that the majority were sunk. Here they were fairly safe from foreign wreckers who would think twice before risking their lives at the hands of the Indians or the Spanish garrison of St Augustine. Here, too, the Spaniards were able to use their own shore facilities as a base for the salvage of a fairly high proportion of the treasure from the wrecks, though they left plenty to occupy the modern treasure hunters who flock the Florida coast. But the Bahamas took a large toll as well.

It was in the Bahamas that Columbus made his first landfall in 1492, and he found considerable numbers of peaceful, friendly Arawak Indians living in the islands.[4] But the Lucayans, as they were called, were not to be left in peace for long. The discovery that they were superb divers meant that many of them ended up in the great pearl fishery based on Margarita Island off the coast of Venezuela. The rest were enslaved to replace the rapidly dwindling Indian population of Hispaniola and Puerto Rico. Within a very few years there were no Lucayans left in the Bahamas. Indeed there were none left anywhere; they died just as fast as the Indians farther south and soon became extinct. Nor were there any Spaniards who saw good reason to inhabit these barren islands so far from the gold and silver of the Caribbean and the mainland of America. The Bahamas became a backwater, completely uninhabited for well over a century and almost forgotten; occasionally visited by English and French corsairs who found good uses for islands with plentiful wood and water far from the centres of Spanish populations; and sometimes visited by Spanish ships who loaded up the timber and other marketable products that could be found growing wild in the islands or searched the coasts for wreck goods or the incredibly valuable ambergris.* But, despite their strategic position, despite the fact that they threatened the homeward passage of the silver fleets, the Spaniards made no attempt to settle the islands.

In 1647 there appeared in London an intriguing publication entitled *A Broadside advertising Eleutheria and the Bahama Islands*, a colonizing puff which was to lead to the formation of the Company of Eleutherian Adventurers. This body was devoted to the establishment of an idealized republican community in the Bahamas whose members would be able to worship God in a spirit of complete religious freedom, hence the choice of the name from the Greek, *eleutheros*, free. Londoners at this time were

* A secretion of the sperm-whale, used in perfumery and cookery. Ambergris was often found washed up on the Atlantic islands. The early colonists in Bermuda were lucky enough to find about 180 lbs which sold in London for between £3 and £3 2s. an ounce, a revelation to the Spaniards who had never realized the island could be so valuable and began to think seriously about re-taking it.

bombarded by pamphlets and broadsides advertising various kinds of
utopia, and probably few people took much notice of this latest piece of
wishful thinking. But its promoter, William Sayle, a former Governor
of Bermuda, an independent in religion who had been at odds with the
island's conformist majority, went ahead with his plans. In the following
year he returned to Bermuda and then set sail for the Bahamas with a
party of seventy prospective settlers. The settlement did not turn out to
be quite the utopia that its promoters had planned. Shipwreck, near starvation and feuds among the settlers made for a harsh and lonely life.
Many settlers returned to Bermuda or later made their way to Jamaica or
the colonies of North America. But a few remained, to be joined on occasion by people whom the government of Bermuda saw fit to exile,
such as seven Negroes, who had been involved in an abortive slave
rising, or Neptuna Downham, who had conceived a child in her husband's absence. In the 1660s there was to be a fresh exodus of willing settlers from overpopulated Bermuda who 'bred apace', so that by 1671,
when a census was taken, there were over a thousand people living in the
islands, of whom nearly half were slaves. Most of the colonists lived in
what had formerly been known as Sayle's Island but which changed its
name to New Providence some time in the 1660s.* The rest lived in the
island still known as Eleutheria, the isle of freedom. Although the islands
were now quite clearly English, by right of possession, no one was quite
sure who was responsible for their defence, a fact of some interest in the
early 1670s as war with Holland loomed closer. Charles II quite naturally
ignored the republican origins of the colony and had re-granted the
islands in 1663 to the Lords Proprietor of Carolina, the group of great
men led by the Duke of Albemarle and Lord Ashley (later Earl of Shaftes-
bury) who were busy trying to set up another idealist colony on the
mainland in modern South Carolina. The Lords Proprietor, especially
Ashley, often wrote to the settlers, usually to admonish them for not
working hard to improve their plantations, but they were very reluctant
to meet the islanders' demands for arms and money to build up defences
against possible attack. On the other hand, the newer settlers from Bermuda tended to look for assistance to the Governor of Jamaica, 'the rock
whence their first Government and order was hewn'.[5] Jamaica, in fact,
did provide help for the Bahamas, and the Governor of Jamaica
remained the most effective higher authority, but this did not mean that

* Providence Island in the Caribbean now became Old Providence. It was taken, lost again and
re-taken during the raids of the buccaneers.

the Lords Proprietor of Carolina withdrew their claim.

Those who described the settlers in the Bahamas during these years were agreed that they left much to be desired and were a long way from being an idealistic republic of hard-working, sober and religious men and women. The plantations, which were supposed to supply their backers in England with an income, were neglected, and most of the population spent their time in beachcombing or in complete idleness. An excellent description has been left by John Dorell, a planter who had been responsible for bringing many of the new settlers from Bermuda in the 1660s. In March 1670 he sent an account of the islands to Lord Ashley. New Providence 'produceth provisions of all sorts that other islands in America doeth and goods, cotton and tobacco, suggar cains, indico weed or anything they plant it is accomodated, with harbouring for ordinary shipps'. All of which sounded very promising. The trouble was that the people would drink themselves stupid given the slightest chance. The other problem was that the ablest young people 'runn a coasting in shallops which is a lazie course of life', looking for amber, turtleshell, spermaceti and wreck goods, 'and leaving non but old men, women, and children to plant, which will be the ruine of that plantation'. Mr Dorell might not approve of the young men of the islands, who seemed to live an almost amphibious life, half in and half out of the water that surrounded them, but there is no doubt that 'coasting in shallops' had made them superb small-boat seamen. Every year they abandoned beachcombing for a while to set forth on a much more demanding occupation, the hunt for the sperm-whale. 'Ther is not more abler men in the Englis Nation for killings of whales than our natives', wrote Dorell, glad to give praise where it was due.[6] The Proprietors were worried about the mischief which such 'a stragling unsettled course of life will bring'. They were also worried about the income that they had hoped to get from the islands and gave rather optimistic orders that no one was to go coasting in search of ambergris, whales or wrecks without a licence from the Governor and an agreement to pay one-fifth of their take to the Proprietors.[7]

Wreck-hunting had been a major occupation since the very first settlement of the islands, and few writers omit to mention it. The business had been given a great boost in 1658 when a lucky shallop crew found £2,600 in coin in a Spanish wreck. One could get drunk for ever on that. It was therefore not surprising that 'many of the inhabitants range amongst the banks and Kayos in pursuit of wrecks or other profitable drift, which sometimes usher in a small benefit'.[8] By the early 1680s the Bahamas were attracting 'all kinds of dissolute fellows', including several former buccaneers, who combined wrecking with drinking and the occasional bit of piracy. This free-spending crowd attracted in their turn many merchant ships, mainly from New England and Jamaica, eager to sell provisions and drink at high prices, eager sometimes to do a little wrecking themselves. New Providence became quite a busy port of call.

Much of the salvage work was concentrated on the wreck of a Spanish plate ship which was probably the *Nuestra Señora de las Maravillas* mentioned above. Not everyone was allowed to join in. A Spanish barque which came along to share the spoils of the deep was rudely chased away; no wonder, since the wreckers often got 'ten or twelve pound weight a man', worth between £40 and £50, a fair sum in a period when a slave in Jamaica was valued at £25. This was a situation which did not appeal at all to the hispanophile Governor of Jamaica, Sir Thomas Lynch, who in August 1682 wrote to 'Captain-General' Robert Clarke, an old Cromwellian officer who was the Governor of New Providence, complaining of the activities of the men under his jurisdiction. 'It is known that your islands are peopled by men who are intent rather on pillaging Spanish wrecks than planting, that they carry on their work by Indians kidnapped or entrapped on the coast of Florida, and that all the violence you complain of arises only from disputes about these wrecks, from which the English and French have driven the Spaniards contrary to natural right. For the sea ought to be free and the wrecks are the Spaniards.'[9] Worse still, it was known that Clarke had had the temerity to issue commissions for reprisals against Spaniards who had attacked English ships, in direct contravention of the Treaty of Madrid. The proper action was to make a formal complaint to the relevant Spanish governor, however useless this might turn out to be.

Clarke was dismissed, but the damage had been done. That process of attack and counter-attack, commission and counter-commission which makes up so much of the history of the West Indies in the seventeenth century had begun. It was to end on 19 January 1684 with a raid on New Providence by 250 Spaniards from Cuba under the command of Juan de Larco, a corsair carrying the commission of the Governor of Havana. Three Englishmen were killed, several were taken prisoner and the rest of the population made a hasty retreat to the woods. The Spaniards held the town from daybreak till four in the afternoon, 'in which time they took away all the wrought and unwrought plate that they could find, a quantity of English dry-goods, and such provisions as they wanted, and loaded their booty, valued by the English at £14,000, in a pink that they took in the harbour'.[10] The Spaniards still had some life in them. Some of the English prisoners later escaped and reported that the Spaniards had said that 'it was a return for Vera Cruz'. If it was, it was a poor return, since the raid on Vera Cruz eight months previously was the most profitable raid ever made by the buccaneers in the West Indies. The division of money, gold, silver and jewels was sufficient to give a thousand shares of 800 pieces of eight each which, at five shillings to the piece of eight, was over fourteen times the purchase at New Providence. And this does not include the 1,500 slaves who were seized at Vera Cruz. The Spaniards were just not in the same league. Nonetheless the Spanish raid convinced the weaker hearts that New Providence was a dangerous place to live, and many left the Bahamas to go to Jamaica. But some stayed to carry on wrecking or to look for new wrecks.

The wrecking communities in Bermuda and the Bahamas drew on a very simple technology to pursue their vocation. The professional wreck-hunter who scours these waters for Spanish treasure today has the whole gamut of modern technology to aid his search, a technology which owes much to the spin-off from the growing complexity of submarine warfare.[11] Low-flying light aircraft or glass-bottomed power-driven boats carry the treasure-hunter across the shallow waters in his quest for the tell-tale signs he seeks, heaps of rounded ballast stones or unnaturally straight lines on the sea-bottom, old cannon or an anchor shaft. Techniques exist to enable the diver to spend long periods under water. Echo-sounders, metal detectors and magnetometers can help him not only to find a wreck, but are so sophisticated that they can locate metal objects under several feet of sand or coral. The wreck discovered, the modern treasure-hunter can remove the accumulated débris of centuries with air-lifts, suction pumps or 'blasters'. Several hundred years of coral growth can be dislodged in a moment with explosives. All of which does not mean that modern wreck-hunting is either easy or cheap, but it is incredibly sophisticated compared to the methods available to the wrecker of the 1680s. All the same, the men of the seventeenth century did have one advantage over the modern adventurer: The wrecks that they were seeking were three hundred years younger. What is now completely covered in sand or coral or has been completely eaten away by salt and shipworm was then often still visible to the patient human eye.

The naked eye is not adapted to seeing underwater, and it had little to aid it in its search. Goggles were used in the Mediterranean and may also have been used in American waters, although no description of divers in the Western Hemisphere mentions such solutions to the problem of seeing underwater.[12] It is probable that both the wreck-hunter above water and the diver below depended mainly on their own unaided sight, though one does see occasional references to the use of a 'glass' by those searching for wrecks. This was never described in detail, but was almost certainly the same as the glass used even now by octopus fishermen in the Mediterranean, a glass-bottomed wooden bucket which is held just below the surface of the water to enable the fisherman to get a clear view of the sea-bed.

There was nothing very sophisticated about diving itself. Most divers worked naked and simply took a deep breath and jumped overboard, clutching a large stone to carry them quickly to the bottom. The capacity of the human lung dictated that work had to be done quickly, although extraordinary stories have been told about the endurance of the divers of the past. Those former inhabitants of the Bahamas, the Lucayan pearl-divers, who were considered the finest divers in the New World, were said to be able to dive to a hundred feet and stay under water for up to fifteen minutes. Strange to say, they attributed their endurance to tobacco smoking.[13] Similar descriptions can be found of the pearl-divers of the Indian Ocean or of the sponge-divers of the Greek islands. Such seventeenth-century tales should obviously always be taken with a pinch of salt, but there is no doubt that what might seem to be remarkable feats were regularly achieved by men and women who were forced by circumstances or inclination to dive for their livelihood. Even today there are free divers who can descend to over a hundred feet and stay under water for five minutes.

It was generally assumed in the seventeenth century that Europeans did not make very good divers. Nearly all the divers employed by the Spaniards for running repairs on their ships, for salvage, or in the pearl fishery at Margarita were either Negro slaves or Indians. Judging by the stories one reads about them, they were indeed better divers than Europeans, but, of course, the main point was that such expendable labour could be worked to the limit of their capacity or even to death. The common contemporary use of the expression 'fishing for wrecks' perhaps symbolizes this division of labour, with the European on his ship pulling in the line which has been made fast to cannon or chest of silver coins by the Indian diver working far below him. Nonetheless, it is clear that the wreckers of the Bahamas often did their own diving, even though, as we have seen above, they were quite willing to force the Indians of Florida to do it for them if they got the chance.

European divers were given a great boost by the only important technological development in underwater salvage of this period. This was the diving bell, an artifact known to the ancient Greeks, which was re-discovered in the sixteenth century. In the New World the diving bell normally took the form of the 'Bermuda Tub', reputedly invented by the former pirate Richard Norwood in 1612.[14] This ingenious and very cheap device was simply a large open-ended wine cask, heavily weighted at its open end, which was inverted and lowered into the water. Divers were able to re-charge their lungs, as occasion demanded, from the air that was trapped inside. A bigger form of the same thing, which was used in 1642 to salvage the wreck of a ship which had blown up in Boston harbour, was described by John Winthrop in his *Journal*.

He [Edward Bendall of Boston] made two great tubs, bigger than a butt, very tight, and open at one end, upon which were hanged so many weights as would sink it to the ground . . . It was let down, the diver sitting in it, a cord in his hand to give notice when they should draw him up, and another cord to show when they should remove it from place to place, so he could continue in his tub near half an hour, and fasten ropes to the ordnance, and put the lead etc., into a net or tub.[15]

The use of the tub seems to have become standard practice, and we find that the Bahama wreckers in the early 1680s were doing well, 'mostly by the ingenuity of a Bermudian, who has a tub that he puts perpendicularly into the sea so that it does not fill, but he can put his head into it when he wants breath, by which means he stays three-quarters of an hour under water'.[16] The Bermuda tub was an immensely valuable aid to salvage, particularly welcomed by the Spaniards who were able to recover much more than previously from their many wrecked ships, but it was not always practicable to use it. The tub could not be used in very deep water, since the farther down it was taken the more the air was com-pressed by the pressure of the water. Eleven fathoms was considered the maximum effective depth. At this depth the tub would be three-quarters full of water, leaving only just enough room for the diver to get his gulp of air. The tub also needed a fairly solid ship, both to take it to the wreck site and to lower and raise it in use. This meant that it was generally impractical to use it in reef waters, where safety dictated that a canoe or small oared vessel rather than a decked ship should be employed. In any case it was dangerous to use the tub in rough waters, since it was impossible to prevent it overturning.

The general knowledge that the 'fishing' activities of the New Providence men were quite successful seems to have aroused a much wider interest in wrecking in the early 1680s. Beachcombers in Bermuda and the Bahamas had, of course, been acquiring the odd windfall for decades, and wishful thinkers everywhere had always dreamed of buried treasure and sunken gold. But never before had there been quite such continuous activity, nor indeed had there been such wide knowledge of the possibilities of acquiring Spanish treasure in such an apparently easy way. The sailors on the cargo boats from Jamaica and New England which supplied the New Providence community told stories in the bars of Boston and Port Royal on their return home, stories which no doubt grew in the telling and sometimes ended up in letters written back to England by merchants or colonial governors. Stories led to speculation. Everyone knew that many ships from the Spanish silver fleets never got home to Spain. Most people could be reasonably sure that many of the wrecks had never been completely salvaged. Some people had very clear ideas where these wrecks were, or at least they seemed very clear until close questioning revealed that many stories were quite obviously apocryphal, and that all directions were incredibly vague.

Among these stories there was one that was repeated over and over again. The details of the story were as usual fuzzy in the extreme, but what substance there was seemed to be confirmed by repetition. This substance sounded very promising. The story that was going around was that about forty years before the Almiranta of New Spain had been wrecked somewhere on the shoals to the north of Hispaniola. She had been carrying an immense treasure and had never been properly salvaged. The details of the story naturally varied with the teller. Some thought the wreck had been in 1643, some in 1645. Some thought it was on this reef, some on that. Some thought there was just one wreck, some thought there were several. The most interesting and most circumstantial story was later written down by the English mathematician John Taylor, who lived in Jamaica from 1683 to 1688. He described how the *Golden Lion of Arragon* struck the reefs in 1644 and fired a gun for help. The six other galleons in the fleet, thinking the admiral had come up with an enemy, sailed towards the flagship 'and so they all struck on the rocks one after another and were all lost'.[17] Over three thousand men were drowned.

This story is interesting as it shows what the collective memory of many men can do. Some of the details of the story definitely relate to the wreck of the *Concepción* which we have described above. There is no problem in explaining why many such facts should be known in Jamaica forty years later. As we have seen, Hispaniola was swarming with English corsair ships in 1641 and 1642 and there were many English merchant vessels in the harbour of Santo Domingo. One can hardly be surprised that the sailors on these ships should remember at least something of what they had seen and heard and one would certainly expect them to pass on the knowledge to their friends and children. It was a sufficiently dramatic story. But only part of Taylor's story bears any reference to what happened in 1641 on the Abrojos. Many incidents and names which he mentions clearly relate to other famous Spanish wrecks of the seventeenth century, including that of the *Nuestra Señora de las Maravillas* in 1656. Even more remarkable is the fact that the main framework of this story of multiple shipwreck is almost certainly drawn from the terrible fate of a French fleet, under the command of the Count d'Estrées, which was wrecked on the island of Aves in the central Caribbean in 1678, only five years before Taylor arrived in Jamaica. A quotation from a modern description of this well-known disaster should make the point.

On the night of 4 May d'Estrées' flagship, the 70-gun *Terrible*, was leading the long column of ships when suddenly breakers were seen ahead, but before she could alter course the flagship ran up on one of the reefs of Aves. The Count immediately ordered warning guns to be fired but before the first gun could be prepared the ship of the line immediately astern had also smashed up on the reef in the darkness. The moment the flagship's guns began firing other ships mistook the warning for the standard signal for a council of war and promptly steered for the flash of the muzzles. By daylight seven ships of the line . . . were stranded on the reef.[18]

It is probable that most contemporary stories about wrecks and treasure have similar confused and multifarious origins. It would certainly have been extremely difficult to find an actual wreck from the sort of details contained in them, and most wrecks were found by chance and by keeping a careful eye on the locations where Spanish divers were working. Once again one sees the problems faced by the seventeenth-century treasure-hunter. Today, detailed information about Spanish wrecks is easy to obtain from the voluminous files of the Archivo General de Indias in Seville, but one can imagine what sort of reception a Bahaman wrecker would have had if he had turned up in Seville with such a motive in 1680.

The repetition of stories about the wreck of an Almiranta to the north of Hispaniola had its effect. However accurate the particular story which one heard, the general point was easily taken. There was no doubt in many minds that there was a fabulous treasure to be found. What made the story of the *Concepción* particularly attractive to the wreck-hunter was that it was known that her treasure was still intact. Most wrecks were discovered by watching the activities of Spanish salvage teams, which of course meant that by the time that foreign wreckers re-discovered the site, much of the silver had already been removed. But the wreck of the *Concepción* had never been discovered by the Spaniards, a fact which led many foreigners to try and find her for themselves. When Antonio Petri y Arce had submitted his petition to search for the *Concepción* in 1672, he had given as one of the reasons that he hoped for success, 'the removal of any motive for other nations to continue to look for it'.[19]

The fact that the Spaniards themselves had failed to find the Almiranta might well have been discouraging to foreign wreckers. After all, one would have expected surviving senior officials to know where they had sunk and contemporaries had not had the benefit of reading the evidence that we have discussed in previous chapters. But, in fact, Spanish failures did not dishearten the English. For many people said that the treasure could only be found by an Englishman. James Farmer of Bermuda had befriended an Englishman who had been for many years a captive in Hispaniola and who told him a strange and interesting story about 'a Spannish ship of burthen, being for ye most laden with plate and bound for old Spaine [which] proved so leaky that ye marriners could scarce keep her free'. The ship was eventually beached on an unidentified island and the sailors 'built a shallup in which they sailed for Hispaniola where they were furnished with a small vessell at times to bring off the said loading; to which intent they mad severall attempts but were alwais beat back by ill weather. . . . He also added that others were about to have gon in serch of it but were diswaded by a kind of Demonical prophites who said it should never be brout away but by sum of ye English nation.[20]

Many of 'ye English nation' believed stories like this. Some became obsessed with them, quite sure that it was they who were destined to fulfil the demoniacal prophecy. One such man was so confident of his destiny that he was able to convince no less a man than the King of England to aid him in his search for the wreck. He was going to have to compete with two other men, an Irishman and a Dutchman, who thought that they already knew where the treasure was and were not too worried that they were not Englishmen. The waters of the Abrojos were once again to be disturbed.

CHAPTER NINE

The Captains and the King

It would be difficult to imagine a king more likely to be interested in treasure-hunting than Charles II of England,* a man who was perpetually short of money, who loved gambling, and who had a great liking for plausible rogues with a good story to tell. So it is perhaps not all that surprising that in the year 1683 no fewer than three ships of the Royal Navy should have been fitted out to search for wrecks in the Bahamas 'or in any other place or places thereabouts', a suitably vague phrase which could serve to cover parts of the sea-bed which others might think belonged to Spain. Three ships were no great burden for a king who had plenty of other ships and was not at the moment at war. And if they found no treasure there were plenty of other jobs they could do in the West Indies.

King Charles certainly did not agree with his Governor of Jamaica that 'the sea ought to be free and the wrecks are the Spaniards'.[1] The seas round English possessions were clearly English, even if international maritime law was not yet sufficiently developed to define just how far out to sea such sovereignty extended. It was equally clear that the Bahamas were English possessions, a fact which even the King of Spain had accepted by the Treaty of Madrid. Finally it was clear that things taken up from the bottom of English seas (usually called 'lagan') were English things whose finder was bound in English law to pay part of his findings to the King of England. No one doubted the King's right to such a share, though few wreckers bothered to inform the King of his rights, and there was some dispute over the size of the royalty. Some thought it should be a tenth, others a half, a difference which was to be of some significance in the next few years until it was settled in the royal interest by a legal opinion of July 1687 which stated that the Crown's right to lagan was 'a moiety', unless a special deal had been made.[2] So even an unromantic king was likely to have some interest in wrecks.

The actual process by which King Charles II became involved in the

* By one of those awkward historical coincidences the kings of both England and Spain were called Charles II. Charles II of England ruled from 1660 to 1685 and Charles II of Spain from 1665 to 1700. In order to avoid confusion, I shall always refer to Charles II of Spain as the 'King of Spain', the 'Spanish King' etc. and to Charles II of England as 'Charles II', 'King Charles' etc.

treasure-hunting business is somewhat obscure. The first we actually know is that on 10 October 1682 the Secretary of the Admiralty wrote to the officers of the Navy Board instructing them to look out for a ketch of about forty tons which would be suitable for a voyage to the West Indies.[3] The Navy Board found such a ship, but there was a serious problem. The ship would cost £500 and the owner wanted to be paid cash down, something which all King Charles's servants found it extremely difficult to do. This time there was an easy solution.

Wee thinke it fitting also to acquaint you that his Majesty's sloop the *Bonetta* now at Deptford (which is about the burthen of this vessell) may with a small charge and in a little time be fitted for the sea. Her dimensions are as followeth vizt. length by the keel 61 feet, breadth 18 feet, depth in hold five feet, draught of water 4 feet 6 inches, burthen 57 tons. And in case she shall be judged a proper vessell for this designed voyage to the West Indies it will save his Majesty the charge of buying another for that use.[4]

The Admiralty quickly saw the sense of this suggestion. The *Bonetta* sloop was ideal for wreck-hunting, easy to manoeuvre in restricted waters, with a very shallow draught which would enable her to work up close to the reefs and, above all, cheap. Her normal complement of ten men was increased to fifteen and she was got ready for a voyage to the West Indies.[5] These fifteen men were to get to know the waters of the Abrojos in the next three years as no one had ever known them before.

What lay behind these orders? There is no direct evidence, but it is possible to piece together the story from a variety of later comment. Some time in the summer or autumn of 1682 two men had arrived in London and had approached Sir John Narborough and Sir Richard Haddock, two admirals who were at that time Commissioners of the Navy, with a rather convincing story and an extremely interesting document. The admirals were sufficiently impressed to introduce their visitors to the King and the result was, as we have seen, a royal commitment to treasure-hunting.

The vital link-man was without doubt Sir John Narborough, a man who had been fascinated by the story of the wreck of the *Concepción* for a quarter of a century, and who was now to play an important part in almost every stage of the long process that would eventually lead to its discovery. Sir John had made his reputation in two successful campaigns against the Barbary corsairs during the 1670s. He was also famous as the leader of an exploring and fact-finding expedition to the Straits of Magellan in 1669–71. But his early days as a seaman had been spent as the protégé of Sir Christopher Myngs, the man who had first established Jamaica as a privateering station. Narborough had first gone to the West Indies in 1657, when he was seventeen, and had heard tales of the loss of the *Concepción* from the motley crowd of soldiers and sailors who had conquered Jamaica two years previously. The wreck seems to have become an immediate obsession with the young naval officer. He made several attempts to find it during the four years that he spent in the West Indies with Myngs and again when he returned to the Caribbean during the Second Dutch War.[6]

It was therefore with close attention that Sir John listened to his two informants in 1682 when he discovered that they, too, were interested in the wreck of the *Concepción*. What made his informants especially interesting was the fact that they had in their possession a document which became known as 'the Spanish directions'. This document no longer survives, but there were to be sufficient comments on its contents during the next few years for us to be able to reconstruct it. The directions were reputed to have been written by the pilot of the sunken galleon. They gave the exact latitude of the wreck and a general description of its location. The directions also gave the course which 'ye galloone's boate steerd and fell in with Port Plate [i.e. Puerto Plata]'.[7] No treasure-hunter could really hope for more than this, and it is hardly surprising that the admirals and the King were excited.

But were the directions genuine? It must have seemed a little odd to an intelligent man like Sir John Narborough that the Spaniards themselves had never found the ship, if the pilot had survived and had been able to remember such details as this. Sir John, of course, did not have such an insight into the competence of the pilots of the *Concepción* as we do, since he had not been able to read the evidence given at the enquiry in Santo Domingo. But it is quite possible that the enquiry itself gave a false picture of the pilots. It is sometimes difficult to believe that they could have got their position quite as wrong as they appear to have done. Could they have deliberately lied to Villavicencio and the other officers of the *Concepción*? If they had done, it would not have been the first or the last time that the position of a shipwreck had been concealed by a survivor eager to benefit later from his special knowledge. This may well have been the approach that Sir John's two informants used to convince him of the value of 'the Spanish directions', but of course we have no evidence to prove it.

Who were these two men who approached the Commissioners of the Navy with such intriguing information? Their names were Sir Richard White and Captain Isaac Harmon (or Hermans), but, as with everything else in this particular stage of the story, it is difficult to find out very much about them. Nevertheless, what we can find out is instructive. Sir Richard White was a rather shadowy figure who crops up in a number of strange places in the records of the 1680s and the 1690s, and there will be several more brief glimpses of him as this story goes on. He was an Irish Catholic and had been born in Limerick in the early 1620s, the eldest of the four sons of Sir Dominick White. The four brothers had followed a pattern quite typical of well-born Irish Catholics in the seventeenth century and had all sought their careers outside Ireland. Sir Ignatius White, the second son, was created Marquis d'Albeville by the Emperor Leopold in 1677. He was a diplomat, 'who conducted the business of the English monarchy for several years at Brussels and Madrid' during the reign of Charles II and was later to be James II's envoy at The Hague. Andrew was naturalized in France and was created Comte d'Albi by Louis XIV, while Francis, the youngest son, spent most of his life in Flanders.

Sir Richard was more interested in money than in titles. His main business seems to have been dealing in men. He acted as a go-between in negotiations which resulted in the Royal African Company getting a contract to supply slaves to the Spanish colonies in America. He was also one of the main contractors involved in the shipping of convicted rebels from the West Country to the West Indies after the defeat of Monmouth's Rebellion in 1685. But more important for the purposes of this story was the fact that White had strong links with Spain. He claimed in a Chancery case of 1694 to have been 'educated or bred upp in or att the Courte of Spaine' and he certainly seemed to have considerable interest with the Spanish court and, indeed, with the Hapsburgs generally. He had been responsible for shipping 7,000 Irishmen for service in Spain following the Cromwellian conquest of Ireland in 1650, and it was from the King of Spain that he had received his knighthood. After the Restoration in 1660 he was once again in favour in England and was able to exploit his links with both Spain and England to make money, particularly in the West Indies. It is therefore not all that surprising that in 1682 he should turn up at Whitehall with some information about the wreck of the *Concepción*.[8]

It was, however, the man whom he had brought with him who had provided the information, for Sir Richard White seems always to have played the middleman. We know only one thing about the background of White's partner, the Dutchman Captain Isaac Harmon, but that one thing is the only real link that can be discovered between the English attempts to find the *Concepción* and the wreck itself. For Captain Harmon claimed 'that he had been a prisoner in Cadiz with the pilot who knew where the ship had sunk' and it was from this pilot that he had obtained 'the Spanish directions'.[9] We do not know whether the pilot was Guillen or Arte. We do not know why the pilot should give or sell such information to Harmon. Perhaps he was about to be executed, the normal punishment for a pilot responsible for the loss of an important ship. Whatever happened in the Spanish prison, Harmon thought that he had information that could lead him to the wreck and, from one or two hints which appear later in the story, it seems certain that he had already tried to use it. He must have realized quite soon that he had no chance of finding the wreck by himself. He needed backing and a well-equipped expedition, and this is where Sir Richard White and his wide-ranging contacts came in. Whether he picked Harmon up in Spain or in the West Indies is not clear but, once he had picked him up, he was sure that he knew where he could get a backer who would pay most of the costs of a fresh expedition and demand a much lower share of the treasure than the King of Spain. Sir Richard was quite right. No contract between King Charles and the adventurers has survived, but it was later stated by the captain of the *Bonetta* that White and Harmon were to have half the profits. The King was to get the other half and be responsible for the costs of the expedition.[10] This seems very generous compared with the Spanish contracts which gave the adventurers who paid their own costs only one-third of the treasure salvaged, but then it was not his own silver which King Charles was hoping to recover.

Arrangements were made for the *Bonetta* to sail out to the West Indies with the frigate H.M.S. *Falcon*, which was being sent to reinforce the Jamaica station. The captain of the *Falcon* was George Churchill, younger brother of the famous John, later Duke of Marlborough, and he was to be in overall command of the expedition. The *Falcon*, with 42 guns and 150 men, would be the most powerful ship in the West Indies when she arrived[11] and would be able to provide protection for the *Bonetta*, as well as having plenty of room to carry Sir Richard White 'and such men as he shall bring with him not exceeding fourteen' and 'ye

Dutch discoverer with others of ye same nation'.[12] But she drew three times as much water as the sloop, and so could hardly be expected to do much detailed searching among the reefs. This would have to be left to the *Bonetta*, and it was important to find a good man to command her. The first choice was an interesting one. Captain Bartholomew Sharpe was a famous buccaneer who had commanded the first major buccaneering expedition off the west coast of South America in 1680–1. He had only recently returned to England when he was offered the command of the *Bonetta*, and his name must have been extremely well known as the result of a book which came out in 1682 publicizing his exploits.[13] But on the eve of his departure, on 6 April 1683, he was replaced by Captain Edward Stanley. No reason was given, but it seems likely that Sharpe's presence was required in England to answer charges of piracy which had been brought by the Spanish ambassador.

Nothing much is known about Captain Edward Stanley. He was a member of a well-known English naval family who had first been commissioned as Lieutenant of the *Kingfisher* in 1681, so he was presumably quite a young man. There is no record that he had ever been in the West Indies.[14] But this was to pose no problem, for he carried with him, as his sailing master and pilot, his brother Peter, a former buccaneer who knew the area north of Hispaniola as well as any man alive. As we shall see in the next chapter, both the Stanleys were superb seamen. Edward was also a very conscientious and intelligent captain who was to go to enormous lengths to try to carry out his instructions. He had, in fact, all the qualities of the successful treasure-hunter except the most important: luck.

The *Falcon* and the *Bonetta* set sail from England on 30 April 1683.[15] There is no evidence that either captain had any idea of what the Admiralty had planned for them, except that they were bound for the West Indies. Two days later Captain Churchill sent for his officers 'to take note that ye orders which I had received was not broke up and opened them'. He discovered that he was to search for a 'rack' in the 'Abroxes', as the English called the Abrojos.[16]

While Captain Churchill was opening his sealed orders another would-be adventurer and treasure-hunter was making his way to Whitehall to knock on Sir John Narborough's door. This was a man who was truly larger than life, a man who was 'tall, beyond the common set of men, and thick as well as tall, and strong as well as thick', a man who could quell a mutiny with his bare hands and the force of his personality, a sunburned giant of a Boston sea-captain called William Phips. Phips was a man of destiny, who knew that he was bound to achieve great things and who was prepared to endure great hardship and disappointment on his way to achieving them, a man who 'would prudently contrive a weighty undertaking and then patiently pursue it unto the end'.[17]

He was born in 1650 'at a despicable plantation on the river of Kennebeck' in Maine, the son of an immigrant gunsmith from Bristol. His father died when he was a small boy, and Phips was brought up by his mother, who struggled to keep her enormous family alive in an impoverished farming and fishing community. At the age of eighteen Phips left home and made his way to the great port of Boston, where he bound himself apprentice to a ship's carpenter. Here he did so well that he was able to get married, well above his station, to the widow of a 'well-bred merchant', the first important step in his social progress from shepherd-boy to colonial governor. His wife was a good-natured lady, who listened patiently 'and with a sufficient incredulity' to the boasts of her overpowering husband, who said that 'he should come to have the command of better men than he was now accounted himself; and that he should be the owner of a fair brick-house' in the most fashionable and expensive part of Boston. Good wives have always known how to handle attractive boasters.

There seems no doubt that Phips had suffered some humiliation at the hands of wealthy Boston society in his youth and that much of his future behaviour can be explained by an overriding desire to raise himself to so eminent a position that he would be able to repay his humiliation with interest. He needed to earn both money and honour to be able to do that, and much of the fascination of Phips's career is that he should choose such an exotic way of achieving his ambition. Many men have wanted to be rich. Many men have searched for treasure in order to become rich. But surely no one can have searched for treasure with the conscious motive of acquiring honour by doing so? Phips's career is stranger still when one remembers that he was superbly equipped to achieve both fortune and honour by a completely different route. There was an obvious path to fame for a man who knew the ways of the sea and was immensely strong, who had the gift of the gab and could persuade men of all ranks from kings and dukes downwards to do his will. But Phips never aspired to follow in the path of men such as Henry Morgan, and there is no evidence that he ever did anything quite so obvious as to seek for purchase on a buccaneering voyage.

Phips did not become a buccaneer, but he did start trading to the West Indies and the Bahamas, first as the employee of others and then on his own account. It was here that he began to hear stories of sunken Spanish galleons and the immense treasures that lay on the sea-bed. This was the way to achieve his destiny. Phips quickly acquired a reputation for 'continually finding sunken ships' and was also said to have developed the techniques of underwater salvage.[18] But he clearly did not make much money during his apprenticeship as a wreck-hunter. In the early 1680s Phips was one of the many who worked the Spanish wreck near New Providence and managed to get a little profit from the exercise. He was also one of the many who heard the stories about another Spanish wreck lying somewhere on the shoals off the north coast of Hispaniola. Unlike the others, Phips decided to make a really positive attempt to find it. Success would require determination and luck, qualities which he was to prove that he had in abundance. More pragmatically, success would require money, equipment and a much better ship than he could at the moment afford. He tried to find backers in Boston, but the rich men of Phips's home port were not in the habit of backing wild-goose chases, nor were they particularly impressed by the upstart Phips himself. They knew him too well. So Phips got the rest of his money together, kissed his wife goodbye and sailed for England to make 'representations of his design at White-Hall'. He would share his profits with the King, the fountain of honour.

When one thinks just how humiliating Phips's visit to Whitehall might have been one has to admire his nerve and his incredible confidence in himself. Charles II and his courtiers were regularly besieged by impecunious suitors with stories to tell. The King had developed a particularly long stride so as to keep them at a distance. Why should he or any of his officers bother to listen to a Boston sea-captain? But Phips had no trouble. Sir John Narborough and the King seem to have been completely swept away by the sheer force of Phips's personality. He had no 'Spanish directions'; he had no idea where the wreck was; he just had 'a strong impression upon his mind that he must be the discoverer' of it and this impression was sufficiently strong to convince at least some sceptics that there must be something in his story.

In fact Phips was slightly more practical than this description suggests, for his design included a prior visit to the well-known wreck off New Providence. Here he was sure he could raise enough silver to pay the costs of an expedition to search for the wreck in the Abrojos. This must have appeared quite a reasonable proposition to the King, who had already heard from the Governor of Jamaica of the profits made by those who fished on the New Providence wreck. Phips asked for no money, just for the loan of a well-equipped ship. The crew and himself would be self-supporting. The King decided to rise to the bait. It could do no harm to have two men searching for the wreck, and Phips would probably make enough money to pay for the wear and tear of a ship. On 19 June 1683, less than two months after the departure of Stanley and Churchill, orders were received by the Navy Board to get the prize ship, *Rose of Algier*, ready for sea. And on 18 August they were instructed to furnish her with nine months' sea stores and hand her over to William Phips, 'unto whom His Majesty was pleased to lend her taking his indent for the same'.[19]

The ship which was indifferently called the *Rose of Algier*, the *Rose of Algeree* or the *Golden Rose* had been captured from the Algerian corsairs during the recent successful campaign to force them to respect the rights of English shipping. She was quite a big ship, equivalent to a sixth-rate, with eighteen guns and a complement of up to a hundred men. She was therefore quite capable of looking after herself in the event of any trouble. Captain Phips was very proud of her, and even prouder that he was her captain, the captain of a King's ship, 'an actual mann of warr', a second important step in his social progress. He gave orders to his crew to behave in a way befitting such a ship, 'to fire a gun evening and morning to set and discharge the watch' and to make all other ships strike their colours and topsails in honour of his flag.[20] Phips had been carried away by his pride. He was completely wrong in thinking that he had such powers and these breaches of naval etiquette, trivial though they may seem, were to cause a lot of trouble. But at the moment such trouble lay in the future, and there were no problems as Captain Phips reported to the Navy Board on 3 September 1683 and signed a detailed indent for the ship, a complete inventory of all the ship's equipment from the sprit-top-mast lanyards to four scrubbing brushes and forty tree-nails in the carpenter's sea-stores.[21]

On the following day he rode down from London to the Downs where the ship was lying ready to sail. Here he met two men, John Knepp and Charles Salmon, who had been commissioned by the Admiralty to look after the King's interest during the forthcoming voyage. The moment that Phips stepped aboard he was to find out that the presence of

Knepp spelled trouble. He had already had a row with the chief mate, Michael Coan, who objected to Knepp's insistence that the *Rose* was not 'an actual mann of warr', being only on the King's private business, and so was not entitled to fly her colours except on Sundays. Coan also objected to the very fact of Knepp's presence, arguing in forceful terms that 'as the King had interested Captain Phips with the ship he should have intrusted him with all that should be gotten in the voyage'.[22] It looked as though it might be an interesting voyage.

Knepp had also had considerable trouble in persuading the crew to sign the Articles of Agreement between themselves and the King. The crew insisted that they had made an agreement with Phips and not with the King; they were free men who had come on the voyage at their own expense and for their own profit, and they refused to be tricked into anything against their will. But finally, on 5 September, Phips and Knepp persuaded them to sign the agreement for a voyage to New England and so to the Bahamas, 'for the obtaining or gaining of all such plate, silver, bullion, gold and other riches as they or any of them can, in, by, from or out of any wreck or wrecks, lying or being amongst the said Bahama Islands or in any other place or places thereabouts in any of his said Majesty's, the King of England's, dominions'. It is an interesting document, modelled on the 'no pay, no purchase' contracts of the buccaneers, with which many of the crew were obviously only too familiar. The King was to lend the *Rose* fully fitted out for the voyage and was to receive a quarter of the profits together with his royalty, which was presumably reckoned at a tenth in this case. Each member of the crew was to pay out an equal sum to purchase provisions and to pay the wages of the cook, who was the only man on board who was to have no share in the booty. Each man was also to pay for his own small arms and ammunition. In return they were to receive equal shares of the remainder of the booty. It is clear that Phips was in the business for honour rather than money, since forty members of the crew signed this document, and so the captain only stood to gain less than five per cent of the booty.* But it was at least a cheap way of getting a crew and provisioning the ship. Where Phips acquired this crew we do not know, but they were a pretty rum lot and seemed unlikely from the beginning to honour the article of their agreement by which they were bound 'to be in all subjection and yield

---

* In fact considerably less, since one of Phips's three shares was to compensate him for providing the diving equipment at his own expense and several more men were brought in on shares in Boston. See below p. 148.

obedience to all the lawful commands of the said commander'.

Once the agreement had been signed there was no further reason to delay departure, and the *Rose of Algier* set sail the same night, just over four months behind Captain Stanley in the *Bonetta* in the race to find the wreck. The ghost of Admiral Juan de Villavicencio must have smiled.

1. A SPANISH GALLEON. Detail from an engraving commemorating the capture of two Spanish galleons by a Dutch squadron in 1628. The *Concepción*, which was built in 1620, must have looked very much like this.

2. THE NORTHERN WEST INDIES. This detail from *The West-India Pilot* of 1687 has little information, apart from changes of names, that was not available to the pilot of the *Concepción* in 1641. Note the enormous distance between the Abrojos, here called the Ambroches, and Puerto Rico.

La çiudad, y Castillo dela vera cruz

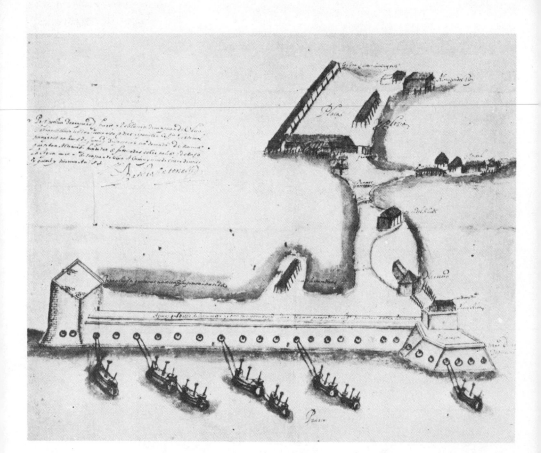

3. VERA CRUZ (*above left*). The arrival of the annual fleet, drawn by
Nicolás Cardona. The city is in the background and the island fort of
San Juan de Ulloa in the foreground.
(*left*) The silver fleet at anchor, drawn by the Dutch engineer Adrian
Boot. The man on horseback is looking down from the road to
Mexico City, towards which the mules are staggering with goods
unloaded from the ships.
(*above*) Detail of the fort and island of San Juan de Ulloa, drawn for
the Italian engineer Antonelli in 1590. Note the row of bronze rings to
which the ships were moored.

S.ᵗ FRANCISCO DE CAMPECHE

6. A STORM AT SEA. From a set of sea storms by Wenceslaus Hollar (1665). Although these four warships are not Spanish, the illustration gives a very good impression of the vulnerability of the small, clumsy ships of the 17th century.

4. HAVANA. The safest port and the main shipbuilding centre of the Spanish West Indies, where the Mexican and Spanish Main silver fleets usually combined to begin the journey home. Note the wide range of small island craft illustrated in this engraving.

5. SAN FRANCISCO DE CAMPECHE. Note the small ship being careened and having her bottom cleaned in the right foreground.
Plates 4. and 5. are from John Ogilby, *America* (1670).

7. THE CAPTURE OF THE MEXICAN SILVER FLEET. This engraving celebrates the unique feat of the Dutch Admiral Piet Heyn, who captured the entire homecoming silver fleet at Matanzas Bay in northern Cuba in September 1628. Not even Drake or Blake managed to do that. The illustration gives a good idea of the difference in structure between the Dutch ships, flying the tricolour, and the lumbering Spanish galleons.

8. SPANISH TREASURE. These examples of a silver bar and pieces of eight are taken from recently discovered shipwreck sites off the coast of Florida. The crude pieces of eight were chiselled from silver bars and then stamped with the Spanish royal coat of arms and the cross.

9. SIR WILLIAM PHIPS. This rather lifeless engraving hardly does justice to the incredibly vital Captain Phips, but it does give a good idea of the sheer bulk and power of the man.

10. SIR JOHN NARBOROUGH. 'That great commander and able seaman' who dreamed of the treasure of the *Concepción* for thirty years and lies buried on the site of her wreck.

11. CHRISTOPHER MONCK, DUKE OF ALBEMARLE. This not very flattering portrait of the man who provided a quarter of the finance for Phips's successful expedition may well be true to life. Albemarle was described by his physician as 'of a sanguine complexion, his face reddish and eyes yellow as also his skin, accustomed by being at Court to sitting up late and often being merry with his friends'. Artist unknown.

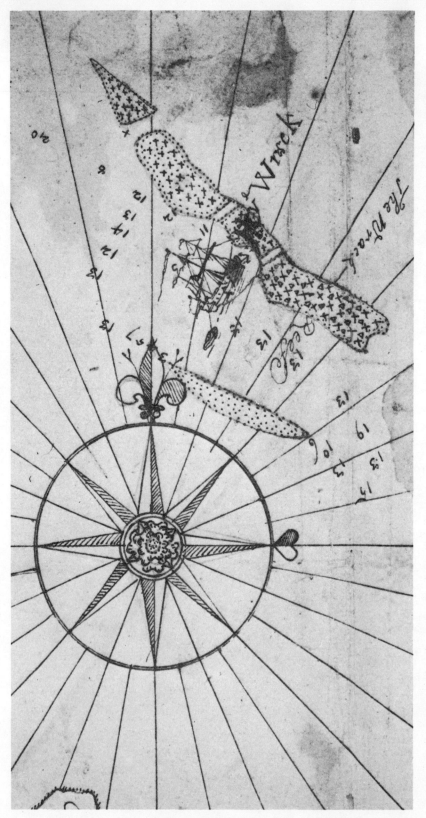

12. A CHART OF THE AMBROSIAN BANK. This detail is from one of three known contemporary charts of the reef. They were all probably drawn during Sir John Narborough's treasure-hunting expedition of 1688. Cape Cabron in Hispaniola can just be seen to the south (i.e. to the left) of this detail. (The other two charts are in the Institute of Jamaica and the National Maritime Museum, Greenwich.)

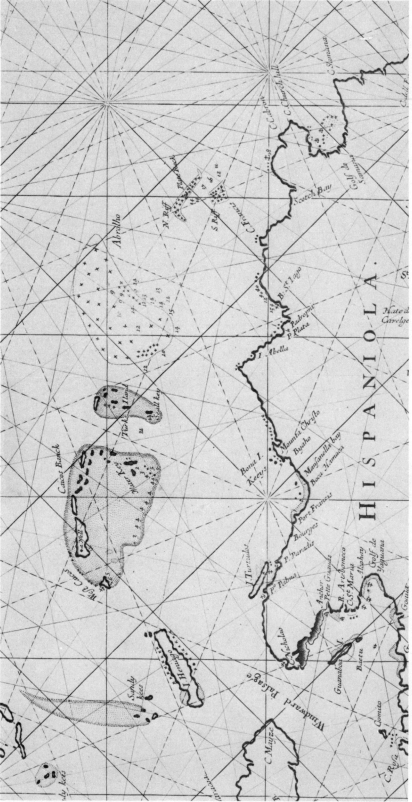

13. *(and endpapers)* HISPANIOLA. This chart should be compared with that of the northern West Indies (Plate 2). Both are from the same 1687 edition of *The West-India Pilot*, but here the cartographer has included the information brought back by Phips in June of that year. The North and South Riffs and the Plate Rack (i.e. the silver wreck) are all clearly marked, while the Abrojos (Handkerchief Bank) are here called Abrolho.

15. A DIVING BELL. This 18th-century engraving illustrates the major improvements in the diving bell which resulted from the boom in invention which followed Phips's successful voyage. Most famous of the inventors was the astronomer Edmund Halley, who introduced in 1690 this method of restocking the bell with air from a succession of casks weighted with lead. Fresh air was siphoned from the casks into the bell through a leather hose, while the stale air was released through a cock at the top of the bell. The attachment of another hose to a working diver's helmet came later.

14. CORAL DIVERS. This 16th-century engraving of coral divers in the Mediterranean may be somewhat fanciful but it shows that the divers wore goggles. No reference to the use of goggles in the Western Hemisphere has been found, but work underwater would have been very difficult without them and it is possible that their use was so commonplace that observers did not bother to mention it. Jean Stradanus, from the Frédéric Dumas collection.

16. and 17. A MEDAL COMMEMORATING PHIPS'S SUCCESS. The obverse shows the heads of James II and Mary of Modena and the reverse two boat crews fishing for treasure with the *James and Mary* in the background. Since the ship was lying in the Thames when the medal was struck this representation is probably accurate. The motto is from Ovid: 'Always let thy hook hang down.' 'Keep fishing' might be a better modern translation. 'Naufraga reperta' means 'Shipwreck refound,' which 300 years later could be said of PLATE 18, where two divers from 'Operation Phips' are at the base of the coral heads beneath the North Riff.

CHAPTER TEN

The Stanley Brothers at Sea

Captain Edward Stanley braced himself on the deck of the *Bonetta* sloop and looked back across the calm blue sea at the mountainous and densely forested coastline of Hispaniola. It was easy to distinguish his mark, the high mountain rising behind Puerto Plata whose flat summit with a large white patch could be seen up to seventy miles out to sea. He judged the mountain to lie twenty-five miles to the south-west and wrote the fact down in his log-book. It was noon on 3 July 1683, just under three months from the day when Stanley had taken possession of the ship at Portsmouth, 'being ordered to joyne Captain George Churchill in his Majesty's shipp Faulcon bound for ye West Indies'.[1] It was scorching hot summer weather, and Stanley must have been in high spirits as he veered a bit to the north and made his way towards 'ye Abroxes' to look for a wreck. He might have been slightly less cheerful had he known just how often he was to take a compass bearing on 'Port Platt hill' in the next two and a half years.

Stanley and Churchill had had an uneventful voyage from England, and, after calling at Madeira and Barbados, had arrived off the north coast of Hispaniola at the end of June. They located Puerto Plata, the port from which Admiral Villavicencio had tried to conduct his salvage operations thirty-nine years previously, and then set sail for 'ye Broxes' which were said to lie about sixty miles to the north. As they drew nearer to the shoals, Churchill ordered Stanley in the shallow-draught sloop to keep some three miles ahead of the frigate H.M.S. *Falcon* and to sound continuously until he struck the bank. At eight on the morning of 5 July the *Bonetta*'s leadsman found bottom at seven fathoms, and Stanley 'saw the ground very plaine and at the same time saw breakers a head'. They had arrived at the Abrojos. Stanley fired two guns to give notice of his discovery and Churchill sent the Dutchman Captain Harmon over in one of the frigate's boats 'to give instructions to find ye wreck'. No doubt everyone on both ships thought it would really be as easy as that, and they would soon be making their way in triumph to Jamaica laden with silver.

The Treasure of the Concepción

The Abrojos were the only area of shoals shown on contemporary charts in the wide expanse of sea between Turks Islands and Puerto Rico. They were usually located more or less accurately, some sixty miles north of Puerto Plata and some twenty miles south-east of the Turks Islands, and were normally drawn in a square or diamond shape. Because of their shape these shoals, which were quite well known to sailors, were often called the Handkercher Bank (or Mouchoir Carré) as well as by variants of their Spanish name, and today the area is called Mouchoir Bank. The shoals are potentially very dangerous, because they are very steep-to, rising suddenly from the immensely deep sea-bed with little or no warning to the navigator, who could only do what Stanley did, keep a good man sounding in the bows and a very sharp-eyed lookout at the masthead. Most of the area presented little danger to a ship like the *Bonetta*, which drew only four feet six inches, as most of the bottom, which could be clearly seen in good weather, was covered by ten to twelve fathoms of water. But in several places, and particularly on the more exposed north and north-eastern sides of the shoals, rocks and coral reefs rose much higher or actually broke the surface in a line of spray-tossed breakers. It was such breakers crashing down on the coral reefs in the north-west corner of the shoals that Stanley had seen.

Harmon told Stanley to keep sounding along the edge of the bank which ran south-east to north-west about half a mile from the breakers. Stanley patiently did what he was told. The weather was calm and there was nothing very alarming about the exercise as there were still ten fathoms of water quite close to where the breaking white seas indicated the presence of sunken rocks. And if such a rock should suddenly loom up dangerously close to his hull he could pull away quickly as he was on the leeward side of the bank. Captain Harmon tried to look knowledgeable and listened carefully to the call of the leadsman. But it was soon clear that he had no idea where he was, despite his confident judgement at one point that 'wee were five leagues to windward of the wrack'. After a day and a half plying up and down the bank he said he could not find his marks unless he came on the bank due north from Puerto Plata.

The two ships sailed back south until they got a fresh bearing on the mountain above Puerto Plata and then turned back to sail due north towards the bank which they found again on the morning of 8 July. But now the weather was not so good. Squalls whipped up the water, and it was not possible to see the bottom as easily as it had been on the first trip.

Next morning the weather improved a bit, and Harmon and Stanley's brother Peter went in two of the ships' boats to search round 'three great spotts which appear'd to have but little water'. Harmon felt sure that the wreck lay among these rocks, but he and Peter Stanley found nothing, despite searching all day. By the evening Harmon had changed his mind. Now he thought that the wreck lay four miles to the west of the rocks. But there was no chance to test his new theory, as the weather worsened that night and Churchill decided it was too risky to do any more work close up to the reefs. Next day the two ships sailed away from the Abrojos back to Hispaniola and so to Jamaica where they anchored in Port Royal harbour on 12 August. It had not been too promising an expedition. Nothing of interest had been discovered, and there was already some doubt about the extent of Harmon's detailed knowledge of the location of the wreck. He seemed to change his mind rather often. The only real benefit was that the Stanley brothers had learned quite a bit about the submarine geography of the Abrojos.

This first brief and abortive search for the wreck set the pattern for two further expeditions which Stanley made to the Abrojos. The first time the *Bonetta* sailed alone, a rather foolhardy decision in view of the navigational dangers of the region, once again with Captain Harmon as a passenger to guide the search. On this occasion, in October 1683, they spent only two days on the banks before being forced off by bad weather and nearly wrecked themselves when one of their cables broke and they were in danger of running on to the reefs. Captain Harmon decided that it was not a proper time of year to search for the wreck, a sensible decision since October and November, apart from being the tail end of the hurricane season, are the two wettest months of the year in those parts. The very experienced Spanish treasure-hunter, Gaspar de los Reyes Palacios, considered that the spring was 'the only time of year that it is possible to search in the Abrojos' and, judging from the evidence of contemporary log-books, he was quite correct.[2]

In April 1684 the *Bonetta* was back on the Abrojos, this time in company with another sloop, the *William and Martha*, which carried Harmon and several other Dutchmen, together with Mr Newell, 'a very good artice', whose drawings of the area have unfortunately not survived. The two sloops were under the general orders of Captain Tennett of the frigate *Guernsey*, which was based on the north coast of Hispaniola. Between the end of April and the end of June Stanley made five separate trips to the Abrojos and spent no less than thirty days actually on the banks searching for the wreck. The weather was by no means always good, and it is a tribute to his seamanship that, in all this time working close up to dangerous reefs, Stanley had only one major piece of damage to his ship, a broken main top-mast which was replaced by one of the *Guernsey*'s spars. Stanley, of course, knew the six hundred square miles' area of shoals quite well by now, and there are frequent references in his log-book to places he had already visited, such as 'the three rocks which I was formerly at an anchor by' or 'the reef which we saw in Captain Churchill's time'. But such familiarity, though cheering to the navigator, can hardly have been encouraging to the wreck-hunter, who had already made a thorough search of such places.

It must have been extremely frustrating work, rowing or sailing close up to the rocks in the ships' boats and moving from area to area at Harmon's whim. The actual details of the methods of search are a little vague in the log-book. There no mention of any divers on the expedition, and it seems clear that Harmon expected to see the wreck either proud of the water or easily visible to the naked eye or through a 'glass' beneath it. On one occasion the sloop and two boats sailed parallel to each other along the edge of the bank, Harmon having said that 'the wreck lay about a cable's length from ye edge of the banke'. It seems probable that they carried weighted cables between them to run foul of any interesting obstructions. But on this occasion, as on all others, they found nothing. Only once does Captain Stanley give the impression in his log-book that he had any real hope of finding anything. This was on 25 May, a lovely calm day, when he found himself at a section of the reefs which agreed 'with the Spanish directions in every thing except a rock which it says appears like a boate keele up'. Stanley sent his boat to search, but once again with no result.

Meanwhile Stanley, patient as he was, was getting more and more fed up with the expedition and especially with Captain Harmon, who had already had a row with William Abney, the master of the other sloop. Harmon's instructions were confusing and contradictory. What he seemed to be looking for was a certain pattern of soundings together with a single rock standing proud above the water. But he was probably not too sure himself. On 18 June Captain Stanley wrote in his journal what he had clearly been thinking for some time. 'I have noe hopes of finding ye wrack, Captain Harmon vareing in his oppinion'. He sailed back to Puerto Plata and begged Captain Tennett to relieve him of his command, 'for I saw noe hopes of Captain Harmons finding the wreck and that I did not think him a good man by reason that what hee ordered when hee was upon the bank hee denyed when hee was in harbour'.

Despite everything, Harmon had not yet given up, and he managed to prevail on Captain Tennett to agree to a rather strange compromise. Since Stanley refused to take any further orders from the Dutchman, another man, Alexander Watts, was installed as master of the *Bonetta* to follow Harmon's instructions. Stanley was to go as a passenger. 'I should not order nor contradict any course except I saw his Majesty's vessell in danger. This I agreed to.' This last visit to the Abrojos, Stanley's eighth trip to the shoals, had no better luck than any of the rest, and convinced Captain Tennett that there was 'noe encouragement of sending any more to looke for ye wrack'. It was a thoroughly frustrated group of men who were quickly borne along the north coast of Hispaniola by the current and the trade wind and who anchored once again in Port Royal harbour on 5 July 1684.

In the intervals of searching for wrecks Captain Stanley and the *Bonetta* were to prove a useful addition to the naval forces of Jamaica, despite the complaints of Sir Thomas Lynch, the habitual moaner who was governor of the island, that none of the naval captains on the station paid any more attention to his instructions, once they were out of port, 'than they would [to] a chapter in the Alcoran'.[3] There was plenty for Stanley to do in this uneasy, but comparatively peaceful, period which saw the gradual suppression of buccaneering and piracy and continued attempts by Lynch and his successor, Colonel Hender Molesworth, to bring about more satisfactory trading relations between the English and Spanish colonies. Stanley was often sent to the ports of Hispaniola and Cuba to request the return of English prisoners who had been seized by the Spaniards for illegal trading or other alleged offences. Colonel Molesworth was prepared to accept that what these men had done was illegal, but he did not think that the Spaniards played fair, as he pointed out in a letter which Stanley carried to the Governor of Trinidad in Cuba. 'We have the same law as you against trading with foreigners, but we do not treat your ships as you treat our sloops. If we suffer your ships to trade we protect them afterwards, and if not we give them notice to be gone. You permit the sloops to trade for a little to be the more sure of seizing them.'[4] This was all a very delicate matter, as Molesworth was actively encouraging Spanish ships to contravene the English Navigation Acts by calling at Jamaica to trade, especially for slaves, an activity which was condoned by the English government in London.[5] But the Spanish governors were neither merchants nor slave-dealers, as Molesworth was, and, although they usually agreed to deliver up their English captives, they were not prepared to go any farther in countenancing contraband trade.

Stanley was also able to assist in the long-drawn-out business of suppressing buccaneering and piracy, though the *Bonetta* was too small to go into action against the really big pirate ships which might carry 30 or 40 guns and well over a hundred men. *La Nouvelle Trompeuse*, for instance, a pirate ship which was on the rampage in West African and West Indian waters in 1682 and 1683, carried 36 guns and a crew of 198 men. The captain was a Frenchman, but his crew represented all nations and races – French, English, Dutch, Spanish, Portuguese, Scots, Irish, Swedes, Channel Islanders, New Englanders, Negroes, Indians and Mulattos.[6] Stanley's main function in connection with such ships was to try to stop them from robbing Jamaica's own turtling sloops of men, equipment and provisions and to prevent them from recruiting from the remoter parts of the island. Since neither pirate nor privateer had any wish to antagonize the English government any more than necessary, such activities were often quite successful, while the actual capture of pirates was left to bigger ships. Most pirates were prepared to respect the English flag, as Sir Thomas Lynch pointed out in a letter written when he feared that naval protection might be withdrawn. 'The privateers are civil to the traders only for fear of the men-of-war, and, if the men-of-war were taken away, they would enter every port and harbour, carry away our men, and intercept the very boats that carry goods about. So that in two years we should be all negroes, the increase of whom and lessening of the whites gives me great apprehensions'.[7] One notices here the usual exaggeration that makes Lynch's letters so entertaining to read, but the general point was fairly sound. Far less worried about the good wishes of the English navy were the almost unarmed galleys carrying up to 120 men which operated from the coast of Cuba. 'These galleys and periagos [large canoes carrying 50 to 70 men] are mostly manned by Greeks', wrote Hender Molesworth, 'but they are of all nations, rogues culled out for the villainies they commit. . . . They lurk in the bushes by the shore, so that they see every passing vessel without being seen. When our sloops are at anchor they get them by their compasses in the daytime, and steal on them by night with so little noise that they are aboard before they are discovered'.[8] The *Bonetta* was to fight these men off on one occasion, but it was obvious that a sloop with a normal crew of only fifteen

men was likely to be vulnerable, and the Governor used the depre-
dations of these galleys as an excuse to press for another frigate on the
station.

All this took up much of Stanley's time, but he was also able to spend
several weeks in Port Royal, careening and maintaining his ship, and we
must hope having a good time ashore. Port Royal was not quite the bonanza town that it had been in the heyday of the buccaneers, but it was
still quite a lively place, the largest city in English America which could
offer a sailor every amusement that he could wish for. Here in taverns
with names to remind him of home, such as the Windmill in Cannon
Street, he could drink his fill of rum, brandy, beer, several different sorts
of wine of which Madeira seems to have been commonest or the West
Indian speciality, mobby, which was made from potatoes. Here, too, in
low-class punch-houses he could sample the 'crew of vile strumpets and
common prostratures [*sic*]' which gave the town such a bad name, or if
he could afford it, patronize the establishment run by John Starr which
was exposed in the 1680 census as containing twenty-one white and two
black women.[9] All of which made Port Royal much like any other big
English sea-port, except for its exotic site on a long curving sand-spit
with the mountains of Jamaica in the background. But it is difficult for
the historian to be dispassionate about Port Royal, knowing as he does
that this pirate port, this city of shame and sin, this tropical red-brick
trading centre with its Thames Street, Queen Street and Lime Street, was
to vanish into the sea just a few years later following the terrible earth-
quake of 1692. Not even Gomorrah did that.

While Stanley was chasing pirates round the Cayman Islands or delivering letters to the governors of Cuban cities his mind continued to
work on the problem of the wreck. The official attitude was now that
there was 'noe encouragement of sending any more to looke for ye
wrack', but this did not prevent Stanley from thinking about it. He was
certain that there really was a wreck. There must be something in all
those stories. The Spanish directions could not be a complete fabrication.
But, after several several weeks of searching, Stanley was as certain as he
could be that there was no wreck of a Spanish galleon in the Abrojos; in
which case it must be somewhere else.

There was one piece of information in the Spanish directions which
seemed to confirm his doubts. After the shipwreck the galleon's boat was
said to have steered south-south-west and made its landfall at Puerto
Plata. But Puerto Plata was due south of the Abrojos, and there was no

possibility that the boat could have drifted east unknown to the survivors, since both the prevailing wind and the current would have borne them farther west, not east. Such doubts had been confirmed during Stanley's third voyage to search for the wreck. During one of the breaks between visits to the shoals, when Stanley had been weather-bound in Puerto Plata, he had met a man who claimed to be a survivor from the wrecked galleon. This man, who had been a boy of fifteen in 1641, told Stanley 'that several of them landed upon rafts at Porto-Plat, and some to the eastward of it'.[10] But a raft would have been even more at the mercy of wind and current than a ship's boat, and it was quite obvious to a man who knew the area as well as Stanley that it was impossible for rafts to have landed at Puerto Plata, let alone to the east of it, 'from any part of the Hankercher Reef [Abrojos]'. In other words the reef where the galleon had been wrecked must be much farther east than the survivors thought, 'at least twenty leagues to windward' in Stanley's opinion, and everyone who had since looked for it, including the Spaniards, had been looking in the wrong place.

But were there other reefs to the east of the Abrojos? There were none marked on most charts, but Stanley felt sure that he had once seen another reef shown on a printed map. He discussed the matter with his brother, Peter, who reinforced his suspicions. Yes, there was another reef to the east. He himself had been there and could find it again, a piece of information which was confirmed by the pilot of the frigate, H.M.S. *Ruby*. The two pilots were quite right. There are in fact two large areas of shoals and reefs to the east of the Abrojos. The first, now called Silver Bank, covers an area of nearly 1200 square miles and lies about thirty-five miles south-east of the Abrojos and between forty-five and eighty-five miles north-east of Puerto Plata. Farther to the south-east lies the smaller Navidad Bank, more than a hundred miles almost due east of Puerto Plata. The *Admiralty Pilot* says that both banks should be treated with the greatest caution.

Such general suspicions and calculations might have been enough to convince Captain Stanley that it was worthwhile setting up another expedition to search farther east for the wreck, but they were hardly sufficient to persuade the Governor to risk once again a sloop which was proving such a valuable part of Jamaica's meagre naval strength. But, in the early weeks of 1685, Stanley was to have a remarkable piece of luck, or at least it certainly looked like a piece of luck at the time. While the *Bonetta* was lying in Port Royal harbour, a sailor called Thomas Smith

made the acquaintance of Captain Stanley and told him a most extraordinary story which seemed to confirm every piece of information
which the increasingly wreck-crazy captain had acquired. In April 1684
Smith had been a seaman on a small ship bound from the island of La
Tortuga off the coast of Venezuela for New England. They sailed
through the Mona Passage between Hispaniola and Puerto Rico and

within three dayes after they parted from Cape Caberoon [Cabron] being the
northernmost part of ye eastermost end of Hispaniola, ye wind being southerly,
and they steering away east-north-east by east and by north they fell in accidentally (on ye 15th or 18th of said month of Aprill) with a reefe of rocks, one of
which was about fifty foot high, the rest being but low, and most even with the
water, upon one of which being flatt, they saw severall sowes and piggs of silver
heaped up upon one another, and allsoe one barre of gold; and within forty foot
from that rocke whereon the silver lay they saw ye hull of a ship, which lay upright wedged in between two rocks.

The ship's company had naturally wanted to get to the rocks to help
themselves to the treasure, but a gale blew up and forced them to leeward of the wreck 'and they haveing but one cable aboard and that not
good they were affraide to come to an anchor'. The three co-owners of
the ship were not prepared to risk their investment and their only livelihood in such bad weather and decided to return home, determined to
come back to the wreck when they had a chance. Smith himself was sure
'in his conscience' that he could easily find the wreck again, 'but being
noe artist he kept noe account of the ships way'.[11]

Stanley was not too worried whether Smith was an artist or not. The
story was totally convincing. The general description fitted the description in the Spanish directions. The location, even if rather vague, fitted
Stanley's current preconceptions. A course east-north-east from Cape
Cabron would have put Smith's ship well to the east of the Abrojos. By
combining Smith's course with the latitude which was recorded in the
Spanish directions he should be able to pinpoint the wreck quite easily,
with or without Smith's presence on board. Stanley carried Smith off to
Colonel Molesworth, who had replaced Lynch as Governor following
the latter's death in August 1684, and bade him repeat his story.

Molesworth was soon just as excited as Stanley about this new information. Smith stood up well to a long cross-examination from the new
Governor and continued 'stedfast to his first information, tho' he cannot

sufficiently satisfy me in some other circumstances, so as to take away all manner of doubting'.[12] Molesworth's main worry was that he 'could not find such a ledge of rocks (as this is described to be) set down in any of ye mapps'. But these doubts soon vanished under the joint pressure of Smith and Stanley. Stanley repeated the information he had received from the survivor of the wreck still living at Puerto Plata and told Molesworth what the two pilots had said about the existence of reefs farther east than the Abrojos. And Smith clinched the matter when he told Molesworth that he was prepared to enter 'into articles to be hanged if he did not show them the wreck, provided they brought him to the ledge of rocks beforementioned'. The man was either crazy or totally convinced that he was telling the truth. Molesworth decided to order a fresh expedition to search for the wreck.

Colonel Molesworth wrote to William Blathwayt, the secretary to the Lords of Trade and Plantations in London, explaining his decision to revive the wreck project. He warned him not to promise too much to the King. He himself was very cautious not to 'raise mountainous expectations for fear of ye ridicule that may follow it'. But it is clear from the general tone of his letter that he was really quite confident, despite his fears that 'the thing is too great for me to succeed in, and that I am not born to perform so considerable and acceptable a piece of service to His Majesty as this would be in case it takes effect'. In the end Molesworth did not accept Smith's own macabre contract, but the contract which he did make with him was bizarre enough, even by the bizarre standards of treasure-hunting. Smith was to get one-fifth of the treasure if the venture was successful. But if the wreck was not found on the reef which Smith had described, he was 'to serve ye King seven years in his ships of warr without pay, and to submit his body to such corporal punishment as I shall think fit, which I have threatened him to be very terrible and severe, if he did not answer expectation'. Smith did not flinch from signing these articles. He was clearly going to play the game to the end. Stanley's crew were to get £100 a man if the venture was successful in order to discourage them from mutiny and to provide them with some recompense for their 'extraordinary service'.[13] This was the first time any extra money had been promised to the crew of the *Bonetta*, none of whom seem to have caused Stanley any trouble, except the boatswain Thomas Challons who had been discharged for being drunk on duty while the ship was careening. Stanley had signed on and discharged several men in the West Indies but the nucleus of his crew, six men including his brother, had been with him ever since the *Bonetta* sailed from England.[14]

There remained only one more duty for Molesworth, to provide Captain Stanley with his sailing instructions. He was to sail as soon as possible 'and make ye best of your way towards ye ledg of rocks to ye eastward of handkercher reefe, and there use your best endeavour for ye finding of a Spanish wrack, and ye several bars of silver and gold sayd to be landed out of ye said wrack upon a flat rock neer unto it'. He was then to load the sloop with as much treasure as she could carry, 'of ye best and richest of ye said gold and silver', and make his way back to Jamaica, 'avoyding as much as convenyently you can your coming neer any cape land or place frequented by pyrats or pryvateers'.[15] It all sounds delightfully easy. Molesworth also ordered Stanley to try to give Smith the slip, 'in case he had thus long persisted in a wrong story'. Stanley was quite willing. He had no wish to share his triumph and quickly got off to sea, but there was no losing Smith now 'who immediately followed him in a wherry with all ye hast he could, as if he were affrayd to have been left behind'. So together they set sail, 'intending to look for a wrack', on the last day of January 1685.[16]

Stanley sailed along the south coast of Hispaniola, picking up some shipwrecked Spanish sailors and delivering them to Santo Domingo on the way. He then made his way north through the Mona Passage and steered north-west by west, 'my pilott saying that it would carry me upon ye banck'. The weather was appalling, and Stanley was twice beaten back by northers, but the pilot was right. On 17 March he struck ground on shoals, which appear from his bearings to have been the Navidad Bank. He sailed round in this region for several days, keeping his eyes open for the reef with a rock fifty feet high that Smith had described in his deposition, and taking bearings when he could on the white perpendicular cliffs of Cape Cabron and on the cliffs on the northwestern corner of Puerto Rico. But on the 22nd he was again forced to seek shelter by the weather. On 1 May he had refitted and provisioned and was back on the banks, this time on the eastern side of Silver Bank. This day he was to have his closest shave yet, when he got in among several sunken rocks, so close together that it was impossible 'to steere cleare of them all'. He managed to anchor and sent the sloop's boat to sound on the rocks. Luckily, they found one rock which was covered by nine feet of water, and Stanley was able to sail clear of the reef and anchor in its lee.

Nothing daunted, he determined to explore these new reefs the following day in conjunction with his boat which he fitted out with provisions, compáss, lead and everything else necessary, 'for feare of looseing company'. But he was unable to get very far with this exercise. The wind was blowing so hard from the east that he was unable to make any progress to windward. Worse still, he was unable to check his latitude accurately, as the sun was so near to the zenith, and could not really tell if he was searching in approximately the right place. On 5 May he decided to sail back to Jamaica, 'for there is noe possibility of finding the wrack except you can bee shure of your lattitudes'. On the way home he learned of the death of King Charles II, the man who had originally agreed to send him out on this strange and increasingly obsessive venture.

Stanley was now completely hooked on the idea of the wreck. He was convinced that only the bad weather, the time of year and the fact that he had not had an astrolabe aboard had prevented his mission from being crowned with success. He was totally confident of finding the wreck at the next attempt, so confident indeed that he told Molesworth that he was prepared to forfeit all his wages, 'which he said was about £300', if he should fail. Molesworth was convinced. Stanley would make one more trip when weather conditions improved, together with an astrolabe and a second sloop commanded by his brother. There was no time to waste as he had received 'a certaine account of two others, ye one from New England, and one from this porte, that are set out upon ye same designe (upon ye instigation of some that were in ye same vessell with Smith . . .) with a Spaniard aboard one of them who was cast away in ye wrack'. But Stanley had one major advantage over the competition. None of them 'have soe certaine account of ye lattitude as we have'. Molesworth was also worried that unnecessary delay would persuade Smith or members of Stanley's crew to desert 'and applye themselves to such others as will set them out in case they finde we doe not proceed upon it'. In order to conceal his activities, Stanley was given orders to cruise round all the creeks and bays of the island hunting pirates for six weeks or so until the weather enabled him to prosecute 'ye voyage for ye wrack on ye banck to ye eastward of ye Abrojos'.[17]

In the end it was not till late August that the Stanley brothers set sail once again along the south coast of Hispaniola, and they struck the bank for the first time on 3 October, at just the time of year that Captain Harmon had thought too dangerous for wreck-hunting in 1683. Once again they were in considerable trouble when they got in among the reefs. There was none of that leisurely searching in boats in calm weather which had been characteristic of the expeditions to the Abrojos. The afternoon of 10 October was a bad moment when Stanley came up under a reef with breakers breaking very high on the windward side. 'I louft [luffed] up under it and runn against sunken rocks. I fierd a gunn for ye sloop who was following mee as soone as I was gott cleare of yt. I gott among seaverall, louffing for one and beareing up for another, so that I had like to have lost her. My men being all amazed soe that they could not trimme sailes.' Well they might have been amazed, if not downright terrified, but by now they must have had enormous confidence in their captain's seamanship and uncanny ability to avoid the rocks.

The following day Stanley decided to test whether he was on the right reef by steering 'south-south-west being ye course ye galloones boate steerd and fell with Port Plate and if I fall with it I shall conclude shee was lost at ye ʒeef'. At ten in the morning on the following day he anchored in the harbour of Puerto Plata and all his calculations seemed to have been confirmed. This was all he needed to persuade him to return to the reefs, bad weather or not. Once again the two ships were soon in trouble, but nothing serious happened till 24 October, when Peter Stanley's sloop struck a rock. He sent canoes with cables over to his brother in the *Bonetta* in an attempt to warp her off. But, before the canoes could return and the sloop's men get aboard again, the stricken sloop had been washed straight over the rock by the waves and crashed into another one. 'She beate over seaverall and att last lett goe an anchor and it lookeing like bad weather they left her and came aboard me. Wee was almost in as bad a condition as she. It began to blow very hard at north-north-east with thunder and lightning and raine. I rid all night upon ye reefe, and at every flash of lightning saw ye rocks break all round me, soe that if it had not been for my chaine wee had perrished.' This passage is unusually descriptive for Edward Stanley, and perhaps gives some indication of just how scared he was that night. The next day the weather was better, and with superhuman efforts they managed to warp the sloop clear of the rocks and patch her up. Stanley had still not given up. 'I made the best of my way for Port Rico designing to gett anchors and not to give the designe over.' But this was really just bravado. The Stanleys had had enough, and, on 23 November, after some time spent refitting, they anchored once again in Port Royal harbour. Molesworth reported their arrival. 'He hath been several times in a great deal of danger beating upon the rocks without meeting with the markt rock which they lookt for, and with such hazard of their lives as wholly discourages him from prosecuting it further.'[18] The wreck of the *Concepción* remained unfound. In April 1686 the *Bonetta* got orders to sail home to England, and on 19 July the Stanley brothers were back at Deptford.

The reader of Stanley's log-book can only record admiration for his determination and incredible seamanship, which was never displayed to greater advantage than during the manoeuvres to save his brother's sloop on the last voyage. It is also necessary to commiserate with Stanley for his appalling luck. If the weather had been as reasonable on his last two voyages to the eastern shoals as on his third voyage to the Abrojos he must surely have had a good chance of finding the wreck. He certainly had the right general idea. But the weather was so bad that he was not even able to use his precious astrolabe.

One wonders also what happened to Thomas Smith. He completely vanishes from the records after Stanley's final voyage, the last comment being in a letter from Molesworth to Blathwayt. 'Yet Smith continues positive in his first affirmation. And Stanley is still of opinion that either Smith had really seen the wrack, or else the Spanish directions, otherwise it would bee impossible that his relation should soe exactly correspond therewith.'[19] He was not punished, since Stanley had never found the reef that Smith described, and, in any case, no one could justly be punished for failing to find a wreck under the conditions of Stanley's last voyage. What seems obvious to the historian, however, is that Smith was an extremely courageous confidence trickster. By the end of 1684 most of the information in his deposition could have been picked up in virtually any bar in Port Royal. Stanley and Harmon could hardly have kept the details of the Spanish directions concealed from their small crew during their many weeks on the Abrojos, and many members of this crew had since been discharged in Port Royal. The story of the treasure lying on a rock was a very old one. Everybody must have known of Stanley's failure to find anything in the Abrojos, and many people were dimly aware of reefs to the east of the Abrojos, as we have seen. Smith was able to put all this together in a convincing way and dress it up with the description of 'ye hull of a ship, which lay upright wedged in between two rocks'. There are two obvious problems in Smith's story. It seems extremely unlikely that anyone could have identified a single bar of gold at the distance which Smith's account suggests he was from the flat rock. Even more to the point, we know from the evidence given by survivors at the inquiry in Santo Domingo that the hull had already sunk below water forty-two years before Smith claimed to have seen it lying upright, 'wedged between two rocks'. So if Smith had seen a wreck it was not that of the *Concepción*. Smith was playing for high stakes, one-fifth of the treasure of the most fabulous sunken galleon known to contemporaries, and it is perhaps not too surprising that he should be prepared to take some risks. But now it is time to see how that other gambler, Captain Phips, was faring in the *Rose of Algeree*.

CHAPTER ELEVEN

The Cruise of the *Rose of Algeree*

Our knowledge of what happened on board the *Rose of Algeree* on her voyage from England to Boston, where she was to pick up diving tubs and other stores, depends entirely on the journal of John Knepp, the man from the Admiralty who had been placed aboard to represent the King's interest. Knepp clearly had a background in the navy. His journal was beautifully kept, illustrated with elevations of the various landfalls on the voyage, and provides plentiful evidence that its author was an excellent pilot who knew his way around the North Atlantic. But the tidy pages with their record of weather conditions, wind directions and bearings are punctuated with a sad story of disgraceful behaviour by the crew and dissension between the crew and Knepp. Indeed there can be few records of indiscipline on board ship to match this detailed account of Captain Phips's first command of 'an actual mann of war'. We have already seen that Knepp had a row with Michael Coan, the first mate, the moment he stepped on board, and this argument was to set the pattern for the rest of the voyage. Knepp was never able to win the confidence of the crew; indeed he never tried to. The crew, for their part, distrusted Knepp as a spy from the start. Phips himself seems to have been reasonably polite to Knepp, but he never made the slightest effort to follow his instructions or listen to his advice. Phips's attitude is perhaps summed up nicely by an exchange recorded by Knepp on the first day of the voyage. 'This day I spoke to Captain Phips and desired him that he would be pleased to appoint Mr Salmon and my self some place to lye in. He told me that wee must be contented to lye upon a chest till wee came for New England for all ye cabens and cradles were taken up already.'[1] It is true that the *Rose* was carrying passengers for Boston, including Edward Randolph who was on an important political mission to New England,*[2] but it is hardly likely that the ship was as full as Phips indicated, since she was

* He was delivering a writ of *quo warranto*, an order for an enquiry into the legality of the charter of Massachusetts which was to result in the colony losing its charter and coming under the direct rule of the Crown.

144

only carrying about half her potential complement of men at this point. The truth is surely that Phips was completely indifferent to Knepp's comfort.

Knepp was to get a good indication of the sort of men that Phips had enlisted when the *Rose* anchored in the mouth of the Shannon and Phips went up river to Limerick to buy provisions. It seemed rather bad management that he should need to buy provisions in Ireland. Why had he not provisioned the ship fully in England? And why did he want to go to Limerick? Cork would have been a more obvious port of call for a ship bound for Boston. Could Phips be deliberately wasting time for some reason? Knepp also had some doubts about the crew's method of supplementing the provisions which Phips was buying. They smacked more of a buccaneer than a man-of-war. Men on the King's ships did not normally go around shooting sheep and poultry in a friendly country in order to stock their larder. The local Collector of Customs also objected to the men of the *Rose* selling hats ashore. It seemed that such behaviour was illegal in Ireland. They must not do it any more or else he would have to place a tide-waiter on board to keep an eye on them. 'Mr. Coan told him if he put any man on board them he would throw him over board and bid him make hast and begone himself or else he would fling him over board for said hee you have noe business on board us.' When Phips returned from Limerick the Collector reported the mate's words. Phips said he was sorry. 'He could not help it but it should bee soe noe more.'

By 20 September the *Rose* had been fully watered and provisioned and her seams re-caulked, and she set sail again. The weather was appalling, and she made very slow progress. Four days after leaving the Shannon a serious leak was discovered in the powder-room, and there was so much filth in the bilges that the pumps would not work properly. The water-level rose, spoiling much of the gunpowder. What had Captain Phips been doing before he left England? Knepp noted down this further evidence of what appeared to have been manifest negligence and incompetence on the captain's part. Soon he was to have personal problems to add to his professional concern for the management of the ship.

'This day [4 October] I found that I had lost above forty gallonses of brandy out of several casks that I had in the hold and twenty-one bottles of canary eighteen bottles of clarret out of severall hampiers, severall cheeses and one piece of frease. Then I went and made my complaint to Captain Phips and he told me that he would have the ship searcht to see where the theif could bee found out.' Two days later, at the height of a storm, a drunken party indicated where the booze had got to. 'This evening our ship was in great disorder, most part of our company being drunk and for swearing and cursing I bless God I never heard the like before in all the ships as ever I have sailed in.' Knepp remonstrated with them but, by now, he must have expected the answer he got. 'They said God damn them they would swear and be drunk as often as they pleased.' At midnight Knepp discovered the boatswain and several others smoking and drinking brandy in the sailroom where what was left of the gunpowder had been stored after the leak. He complained to the captain who 'bid them doe soe noe more, that being their punishment'. A few days later one of the sailors, Richard Pickton, confessed that he had helped himself to Knepp's brandy and wine and named six other members of the crew who had done the same. Now surely Captain Phips would take some disciplinary action? But all he did was to promise Knepp that the men would pay him for what they had taken at the end of the voyage. 'For, said hee, they are some of the best men in the ship and, if I should punish them, I am afraid that their consorts will mutiny.' Knepp complained that if the men were not punished he would lose everything he had brought on the ship. Phips sympathized, but pointed out that he had really not got full authority over his crew of unpaid volunteers. 'He could not help me at this time, for men that paid for their owne victualls and received noe wages will not be corrected for every small fault.'

By now the crew were thoroughly fed up with Knepp's habit of snooping around and writing down everything that they did wrong. One of the sailors was overheard persuading his colleagues to maroon the government agent on the first island they came to in the Bahamas. The conversation was reported to the captain but, needless to say, he did nothing about it, simply telling the sailor not to say things like that again, 'that being his punishment'. Knepp must have been quite relieved on 22 October, when he saw 'abundance of gulls and gannets and some rock weeds and a small land bird', though it was not in fact until a week later that they anchored off Boston Castle.

Phips was supposed to stay at Boston for two or three weeks, 'to take in necessaryes for their undertaking'.[3] He in fact stayed for fifteen weeks, a period which saw the men of the *Rose* causing almost continuous trouble. Much of this arose from the determination of Phips and his crew to be treated as a King's ship. This was after all his home port, and he wanted people to appreciate his rapid elevation to his present dignity. But, as Knepp had pointed out, the *Rose* was on the King's private business and was not an 'actual mann of war'. Phips and his first mate, Coan, ignored this interpretation of their status and insisted on all ships striking their pennants and topsails in honour of his colours. Those who did not, either from ignorance of naval etiquette or because they thought rightly that they did not have to, had a shot fired across their bows, which was speedily followed by a boat's crew from the *Rose* demanding six shillings and eightpence for the cost of the shot. One old man, the skipper of a local boat carrying firewood, said that he 'had not soe much money in the world to buy his children bread'. He was brought on board where he pleaded that he was ignorant of the custom of striking and, in any case, it was too dark to see the *Rose*'s colours. In the end the old man was kept on board until he could arrange to borrow the money from his owners. Following this incident, most ships coming in and out of Boston harbour found that life was simpler if they humoured Phips, which only made him more furious at those who refused to strike. Matters were brought to a climax by one Captain Jenner, master of the *Samuel and Thomas* of London, who still refused to strike his pennant after the *Rose*'s gunners had fired five times at him. He claimed to have seen Phips's orders in London and said that they contained no powers to make other ships strike. He took Phips to court where Governor Bradstreet, who had seen Phips's papers on several previous occasions, upheld Jenner's complaint and sentenced Phips to pay five pounds to the country and five pounds to Jenner with costs. Phips said he had no money. The Governor said that he would wait for his fine until Phips returned from the wreck, as he did not wish to harm the King's interest.

The crew of the *Rose* also caused much trouble ashore, fighting, drinking, and generally abusing the good people of Boston. The worst occasion arose when the constables were clearing the taverns and ordered some men from the *Rose* who refused to stop drinking to go aboard or to their lodgings. The men started to swear at the constables and said that they would go aboard in their own time. The argument soon degenerated into a fight, in which two of the sailors got badly beaten up, and the rest ran off towards their boats. By now Phips had arrived, and he ordered them to go aboard, which they did. Phips was then reported as saying that 'he did not care a turd for the Governor' and inviting the constables to kiss his arse. Once again Phips and his men found themselves in court, where they claimed that the constables had started the fight and denied that they had insulted the government. The Governor, in his summing-up, said that it was clear that Phips and his crew had abused the government but, as they were on the King's private business, he would say no more about it as long as they behaved respectfully in the future. He did, however, allow himself one last dig at Phips when he remarked 'that every body in Boston knew very well what he was and from whence he came and therefore desired him not to carry it soe loftily among his country men'.

Meanwhile there was little indication that Phips was getting on very fast with the King's private business. Much of his first fortnight in Boston was spent trying to persuade the Governor to stop a local ship, the *Good Intent* commanded by William Warren, from going to the wreck off New Providence. The Governor was not sure if he had such powers, and asked to see Phips's orders, but after looking at them carefully he said that in no part of the orders was he empowered 'positively to stop all ships and vessells that are bound to the Bahama shoalds . . . but simply not to molest W. Phips mariner in his proceedings at the Bahama shoalds'. He could do nothing unless Warren had hindered or molested him since he had been in Boston. Phips repeated his attempts to prevent the *Good Intent* from sailing, claiming on many occasions that he had some further secret orders which gave him such powers, but, since he never produced them, the Governor was unable to help him. In the end Phips solved the problem of Warren's potential competition by taking him into partnership, agreeing to share their profits man for man. Now Knepp was worried, since there was every indication that the *Good Intent*'s men had no intention of splitting their share with the King. Phips also took into partnership a sloop from Bermuda, commanded by William Davis. The arrangement was that Phips was to take about 80 men (he actually took 103 according to Knepp), Warren was to take 60 or 70, and Davis in the sloop 18. So, if Knepp's fears were realized, the King stood to lose nearly half his profits. There was little Knepp could do about this, and, on 28 November, Warren set sail for Providence 'to stay and get what divers he can against Capt Phips coming there to him'. He was flying the King's jack and pennant as he sailed out of Boston harbour, and claimed that he, too, had the power to make all ships strike to him. Governor Bradstreet warned Phips that 'if Warren should doe any mischief to the Spaniards under his Majesty's colours you must answer for it'. God knows how Phips thought he had the right to issue a commission to another ship, but Knepp noted down this new misdeed in his already fat dossier.

It looked indeed as though Knepp's journal might be the death of him. Neither Phips nor his crew had come to love the King's spy any more during their stay in Boston than they had in the voyage across the Atlantic. Knepp soon learned to feel the extent of their dislike. On Christmas Day 1683 he heard from a man with the good Boston name of Adams that one of the crew had told him in a local tavern that 'Knepp was a suttle dog and did keep an account of all their actions'. He would never come alive from the wreck to tell tales to the Commissioners of the Admiralty in London. Knepp reported this to Phips who admitted that the crew had taken a dislike to him, but said that 'it could not be expected that he could hold his mens tongues'. Gossip became reality on New Year's Eve, when Knepp was attacked and wounded in the dark streets by two men with rapiers. He successfully fought them off and once again complained to Phips, who shrugged the matter off. 'It could not be expected that he could carry a strict command where every man found his owne provisions and receives noe wages.' However, he promised Knepp that he should have satisfaction once the *Rose* was again at sea, a promise that was treated with the scorn it deserved.

A few days later Knepp heard from the other King's agent, Charles Salmon, that Phips's wife had persuaded the captain to make sure that Knepp went on the voyage so that he could not go home and persuade the Commissioners to stop Phips from carrying on with the wreck-hunt. This was the last straw. Knepp now decided that nothing on earth would get him back aboard the *Rose*, a decision which was later reinforced when he heard of a plot to kidnap him at the King's Head Tavern. He continued to keep a close watch on all the doings of the crew and reported them in his journal. He also took heed of the many warnings he received to 'have a care how I walked abroad in the evening or at any time except I were certaine of not meeting with any of Phips men'. He did not have long to wait now. On 14 January 1684 Phips sailed without Knepp, much to the delight of the crew, and the King's agent spent the evening covering several pages of his journal in an attempt to explain just why he had deserted the King's business at this crucial moment. In view of the fact that the other agent, Charles Salmon, was still on board and was to come to no harm, it was to take quite a bit of explaining.

How much of Knepp's journal should we believe? He does seem to have been somewhat paranoiac, and he almost certainly exaggerated to justify his own misbehaviour in deserting his post. It is interesting to note that, later, the King's agents for Massachusetts, Joseph Dudley and William Stoughton, wrote a letter to the Earl of Sunderland, the English Secretary of State, in which they throw a little doubt on Knepp's trustworthiness. 'We hope he [Knepp] will give you a true information, though we were never particularly advised of the cause of the breach.'[4] It is also interesting that Edward Randolph made no comment on unusual conditions during his voyage across the Atlantic in the *Rose*. When he reported his arrival in a letter to the Governor of New Plymouth he confined himself to conventional thanks for his safety. 'I am very glad I can advise you that, God be thanked, I arrived here [Boston] fryday last.'[5] All the same, it seems unlikely that the whole of Knepp's journal was fabricated. Phips's habit of exceeding his powers by forcing other ships to strike their colours is confirmed by other testimony.[6] It also seems fairly certain that Phips behaved rather badly in Boston in an attempt to show off to his fellow-countrymen. Later events also confirm that Phips had picked rather a wild bunch for a crew, but they also demonstrate that he could control them when he had to. Knepp criticized Phips for making 'every sailor his companion' and for not imposing his authority on them from the start. This does indeed seem rather foolish behaviour for the captain of a royal ship, but we must take notice of Phips's own reason for his lack of authority, the fact that the men were unpaid volunteers and so not amenable to naval discipline. There were never any discipline problems on Phips's later voyages, when the men were on wages and not shares.

Be that as it may, the crew continued to behave extremely badly after leaving Boston, if we can believe Knepp. A report was brought in of the landing of seven of the *Rose*'s crew at Pemberton's Island where they made the wife of the island's only inhabitant drunk and then raped her one after the other in the presence of her children. The *Rose*'s men also killed sheep and pigs in various places, behaviour which was perhaps only to be expected, since they had to pay for their own food and no doubt had very little money left after so long drinking in Boston. There was also an ominous report that many of the crew had declared that 'if Phips did not make them a voyage upon the wreck according to their expectations . . . they would goe and take the first Spaniard they met withall'. This must have seemed only too likely. The reports became less regular as the *Rose* left the American coast for good and sailed south towards the Bahamas. She arrived at New Providence on 9 February, only three weeks after the Spaniards had sailed in from Cuba and sacked the settlement, and the place must still have looked rather a mess, while most of the inhabitants were packing up in preparation for seeking greater security in Jamaica. William Warren, Phips's new partner, had actually been in the harbour at the time, but had slipped his moorings and sailed away, making no attempt to stop the Spaniards from landing.

Phips seems to have spent some time fitting out in New Providence, once more making a nuisance of himself by forcing ships to strike, and he did not actually arrive at the well-known wreck-site until 16 March. Here he discovered a man called Welch already at work. Phips told him to clear off and threatened to shoot any of his divers who was sent down. Phips and Warren then set to work to do some fishing. We do not know whether they expected to make much money by the exercise. There was every indication that by the spring of 1684 there was not much silver left in this wreck which had been worked for years by a succession of ships well-equipped with divers and Bermuda tubs. Back in November, when Phips had been in Boston, a ship had arrived in port after six months' working at the wreck. Her captain, Peres Savage, told Knepp that there were six ships working there, with eighty divers between them, and that 'they had shared but $7\frac{1}{2}$ pounds of plate a man'. At five shillings an ounce this would have been worth £30 a head, which would have been good money for six months' work by contemporary standards, but, of course, it would have been considerably reduced by the need to pay for the ships, divers, provisions and equipment. Anyhow there was not much left. Savage said that 'he would not give five pounds for any man's share that goes to make a voyage now, for said hee if there had been any hopes of getting any thing more he would not have come off the wreck having soe many of such good divers'. Savage incidentally gave an extremely good description of the method used by the salvagers to remove debris with dredges so as to clear the silver. 'He had made ten severall paths from stemb to stern athwart her and found but thirty sowes* of silver in all and doth verily believe that there is but very little more left in her, for he took as much paines in clearing of her with his drudg as possible a man could and that hee had brought up severall peces of her kelson and some of her hooks before and some of her transums abaft.' Savage's gloomy predictions of the chances of finding much more in the wreck were confirmed by Welch, who said that he had been diving for ten months and had got very little. He had little hope of success for Phips, especially as he only had three good divers and they were sick with smallpox, and he re-

---

* Sows and pigs are contemporary words for bars of silver of various sizes.

ported that Phips and Warren had got nothing at all in their first fortnight of diving on the wreck. It looked as though Captain Phips was
going to have quite a job getting working capital together for his search
for the much bigger prize in the Abrojos.

John Knepp sailed for England on 13 May, and, with the end of his
reports, we lose touch with Phips for the next five months. The last
Boston entry in Knepp's journal records the arrival of two ships from the
wreck, who reported that smallpox was rife on both the *Rose* and the
Good Intent, and that Phips was so short of good divers that he had taken
into partnership yet another ship which happened to have 'very good
ones'. How long Phips remained at the wreck after this we do not know.
Indeed, the only evidence we have for Phips's activities at the wreck off
the western Bahamas, apart from the reports received by Knepp in
Boston, is some later correspondence about a pig of silver and a delightful chart drawn by Charles Salmon.[7] This 'description of the Bahama
Bancks', which is now amongst the manuscripts of Sir Hans Sloane in the
British Library, is the only record kept by Salmon of his long voyage
with Phips which has survived. It shows the location of three wrecks –
the Genoese wreck, the copper wreck and the plate wreck, which was
the one Phips worked – and has some useful information for the mariner,
such as good places to anchor in smooth water when it was rough at the
wreck site. But it gives no indication of how long Phips spent working
on the plate wreck, or how much silver he managed to recover from it.

For the next part of the voyage of the *Rose of Algeree* we have to rely on
the biography of Phips published in 1697 by his contemporary and
admirer, the famous puritan divine Cotton Mather. Where Mather's
account of Phips can be checked he is usually quite accurate in regard to
bare facts, but he was determined to make his subject a hero, and so
usually exaggerated his descriptions and added considerable colour,
while leaving out anything discreditable to him, such as his behaviour
while the *Rose* was in Boston.

What Mather records as happening in this five-month period of
official silence is so much what one would expect from the crew of the
Rose after a long period of unsuccessful 'fishing' in the Bahamas that it is
easy to believe. We will leave Mather to describe it. The men 'approach'd him on the quarter-deck, with drawn swords in their hands,
and required him to join with them in running away with the ship, to
drive a trade of piracy in the South Seas'. But it was not to become a buccaneer that Phips had made his journey to Whitehall. 'Captain Phips,

though he had not so much of a weapon as an ox-goad or a jaw-bone in his hands, yet like another Shangar or Samson with a most undaunted fortitude, he rush'd in upon them and with the blows of his bare hands fell'd many of them and quell'd all the rest.'[8] So much for naval discipline! Phips sailed on but he was soon to have fresh trouble:

One day while his frigot lay careening, at a desolate Spanish island, by the side of a rock from whence they had laid a bridge to the Shoar, the men, whereof he had about an hundred, went all, but about eight or ten, to divert themselves, as they pretended, in the woods: where they all entred into an agreement which they sign'd in a ring that about 7 a clock that evening they would seize the captain and those eight or ten, which they knew to be true unto him, and leave them to perish on this island, and so be away into the South Sea to seek their fortune.

Phips was warned in time by a carpenter who had been privy to the conspiracy. While the mutineers were still in the woods, the loyal men went across to the island and turned round the guns which had been landed to guard the stores taken out of the ship while she was careening. They then came aboard again, took up the planks that made a bridge to the shore, loaded and ran out the rest of the ship's guns and waited for the rather incompetent and short-sighted mutineers to return. When the mutineers came out of the woods they quickly saw what had happened and cried out 'We are betrayed.' To which the Captain replied in good clean Matheresque prose: 'Stand off, ye wretches, at your peril.' He then made arrangements to reload the stores, intending to maroon the mutineers as they had planned to maroon him. But when they went down on their knees and humbly begged his pardon, he relented and, after taking the precaution of disarming them, took them aboard and so to Jamaica, 'where he turn'd them off'.[9]

Where and when all this happened we do not know, but that Phips went to Jamaica is corroborated by our old friend Colonel Hender Molesworth, who, in a letter of 18 November 1684, discusses Phips and comments, incidentally, that he had 'put in here accidentally for relief', which seems to confirm at least part of Cotton Mather's story. Judging by this letter, Phips had already been in Jamaica some time, but was now just about to sail again. It comes as no surprise to learn that Molesworth had no better an opinion of Phips than Governor Bradstreet in Boston. 'This man never had better than a carpenter's education, and never before pretended to the title of captain; but now he assumes it, tho he cannot yet show a commission for it, and takes more to himself than any other of the King's captains.'

Phips's main offence, apart from his low birth and his bombast, was not one to endear him to the Jamaican Governor, though Molesworth saw him as a tool rather than as the instigator of his evil actions. Phips had been led on by a party on the island opposed to that clandestine trade with the Spanish colonies of which Molesworth was the keenest advocate. Most of the opponents of trade with Spain were planters, who objected to slaves being sold to Spanish factors because the trade would raise the prices of the slaves that they themselves bought. But there were many who had objections in principle to any friendliness towards Spain and wanted a return to the old freebooting, buccaneering days. What Phips had actually done was to fire at a Spanish ship in the harbour, which, in celebration of some festival of the Church, had been flying a flag to which Phips objected. Later, 'Captain Phips, meeting the Spanish captain in the street, with a rabble at his heels, told him that if he did not pay him for his shot he would take his sword from him. The Spaniard was unwilling either to give up his sword or to pay the money, and the rabble was ready to have laid hands on him if a gentleman passing by had not taken ten shillings from his pocket and paid it for him.' The Spaniards were so angry that their two biggest ships left the island, a triumph for Phips and the anti-trade party. Molesworth was furious but, like Bradstreet in Boston, he was reluctant to discipline Phips lest he hinder his voyage and thus do damage to the King's private business.[10]

It is worth noting that on the one day when we are absolutely certain that Phips was at Port Royal, 18 November 1684, Captain Edward Stanley was also in the port.[11] In fact he had been there for five days, and it is probable that they coincided on other occasions as well. Did they meet each other and discuss the venture which they were separately conducting for the King? There is no evidence, though it seems highly probable that the captains of two royal ships both in Port Royal at the same time would have met, and what else would Phips and Stanley have had in common to talk about? Sir Richard White was also in Jamaica at this time, and later claimed that he had provided Phips with some vital information about the location of the wreck.[12] However, White seems to have been a consummate liar, and there is no good reason to believe that his claim was true. But even if Phips learned nothing from either Stanley or White, he must have been able to acquire considerable information of interest to his venture from the general gossip in the Jamaican port. A little money passing hands or a few drinks would have told him many things. He must have learned that the Abrojos were a dead loss. He probably learned that there were supposed to be other reefs to the eastward and also that there were survivors of the shipwreck still living in Hispaniola. He may have learned many other things, such as the details of the Spanish directions. All of which must have seemed very useful, as he sailed out of Port Royal some time in late November with his handful of loyal men and a fresh crew picked up off the Jamaican waterfront. At some stage, either before or after he left Port Royal, Phips acquired two consorts. One of these was the same sloop commanded by William Davis which had accompanied him from Boston. The other, also a sloop, was commanded by Abraham Adderley, who is variously described as coming from Jamaica or New Providence. Both these men seem to have been old friends of Phips, presumably acquired in the days when he had been trading out of Boston.

We now lose track again of the details of Phips's movements for the next few months and have to rely on the rather vague information in Cotton Mather's biography. It is clear that Phips was a jump ahead of Stanley, who did not leave Jamaica for his first voyage to search for the eastern reefs until the end of January 1685. It is also clear that Phips did very much what Stanley did, without apparently getting into such trouble with bad weather. According to Mather, he sailed from Jamaica to Hispaniola, 'where, by the policy of his address, he fished out of a very old Spaniard, (or Portuguese) a little advice about the true spot where lay the wreck . . . that it was upon a reef of shoals a few leagues to the northward of Port de la Plata'.[13] We can assume that the New England divine was not too sure of his compass directions and meant north-east when he wrote 'northward', as it seems unlikely that Phips would have wasted time sailing due north from Puerto Plata to search the Abrojos. So Phips sailed from Puerto Plata and, like Stanley, found 'a new banck',[14] which was almost certainly the Silver Bank. Phips was to provide the new bank with a name, the Ambroshia or Ambrosian banks, and it was by this name that the bank was to be known for the next few years. Here he spent some time searching for the wreck but did not 'exactly hit upon it'.[15]

Phips and Stanley must have been very close during these early months of 1685, maybe one each side of the Silver Bank, but they did not see each other. Stanley must also have heard of Phips's enquiries in Puerto Plata when he anchored in the Hispaniolan port on 6 May on his way back to Jamaica after his abortive voyage. It will be remembered that, when Molesworth reported back to England on Stanley's voyage, he urged the need for haste because he had 'a certaine account of two others, ye one from New England, and one from this porte, that are set out upon ye same designe'.[16] It seems more than likely that the ship from New England was the *Rose*, and that it was this ship which had the Spaniard aboard 'who was cast away in ye wrack', that same 'very old Spaniard' whom Phips had fished out of Hispaniola by the 'policy of his address' and no doubt a fair sum of money. The ship from Jamaica could well have been the sloop of Abraham Adderley, which, as we have seen, was in consort with Phips during this part of his voyage.

Phips had no more luck than Stanley in searching the reefs in the early months of 1685, but he was nonetheless confident that he was looking in the right place. He was, however, not too sure of the men that he had picked up in Jamaica. They seemed 'too ill a crew to be confided in' and rather too likely to mutiny if his venture should prove successful.[17] He therefore decided to return to England and come back later with new men, better divers and equipment to finish off the job.

The last call in Captain Phips's odyssey was at the island of Bermuda, the only one of the four English colonies which he visited where he had no complaints from the Governor. There was a good reason for this. Bermuda was in a state of near rebellion and the Governor, Richard Cony, was ready to welcome anything that looked remotely like a royal ship. He had almost completely lost control before the arrival of Phips. There were many reasons for Cony's problems. There was no English colony where the governor could enjoy the goodwill of all the settlers, either for political reasons or because of the personality of the particular governor. In this respect Cony seems to have been disliked more than most. But there were also more serious difficulties. The island had recently been brought under direct royal rule after being governed since its first settlement by proprietory companies. This was the general royal policy at this time and had caused political unrest in many colonies. In Bermuda such unrest had been aggravated by the recent death of King Charles II and the succession to the English throne of his papist brother, James II. The radical elements in the island were preparing to adopt the same revolutionary attitude to this situation as their brethren in the West Country of England, who erupted into rebellion under the flag of James, Duke of Monmouth, at about the same time as Phips sailed from

Bermuda. Meanwhile, many of the islanders challenged Cony's right to rule. 'The clamour of the country is that I have no power to govern but through the Duke of York [James II], a Papist', wrote Cony to the Earl of Sunderland. And, lest that was not sufficient to bring help from England, he claimed that the Bermudans were planning to turn the island into a pirates' refuge or even sell out to Spain.[18] These were standard claims for a governor in trouble and probably did not mean much.

Phips's role in Bermuda, where he spent the months of April and May 1685, was to show the flag and his guns and reinforce the shaky authority of the Governor. When he sailed, early in June, he carried with him two of Cony's main opponents, Henry Bysshe, 'a great incendiary', and Sarah Oxford, his 'principal abettor'. But there are always at least two sides in a political quarrel, and Phips's intervention in Bermudan politics was to result in his arrest at Bysshe's instance when he arrived back in England after his long voyage. In fact, the first letter in Phips's handwriting which can be found in the State Papers was written while he was in custody. His script, incidentally, was quite good for a man who 'never had better than a carpenter's education'. 'I am now in custody in the bailiff's hand in the liberties of the Tower; whereby I am kept from the King's business. Pray issue some order for my discharge. Signed W. Phips from the Nagg's Head on Little Tower Hill.'[19] He was out the next day, 4 August, when the King gave orders 'that bail be given on his behalf for so much as relates to Capt Phips transportation of the prisoner'.[20]

The words 'for so much as' strike an ominous note in the King's order for Phips's release. He had got a lot of talking to do to explain away the dossier collected by Knepp. There was also a matter of accounting. The late King had not lent a royal ship to the Boston captain for fun. Back in February 1684, when King Charles had first received reports from Knepp, he had given orders to the royal agents in Massachusetts to arrest Phips 'if it appears that Phips or his seamen have a design to defraud the King of the ship with the plate and bullion thereon'. Phips had already sailed for the Bahamas and there was nothing the agents could do.[21] Shortly after King Charles's death, a year later, there were fresh enquiries on behalf of the new King who was interested to know on just what conditions one of his ships had been lent to such a man as William Phips. Samuel Pepys, the Secretary to the Admiralty, who had been in Tangier in 1683 when the negotiations were carried out, wrote to the Navy Board for details, and was referred to Sir Richard Haddock and Sir John Narborough, the other members of the Board not 'haveing been privy to the designe'.[22] But, despite these general suspicions regarding Phips, no action was taken against him when he returned to England just under six months later. He was clearly able to talk himself out of trouble.

The accounts for the voyage did not have such a happy conclusion. Pepys ordered the Navy Board to survey the *Rose* when she returned to England. The survey disclosed wear and tear which would cost just over £700 to put right, a heavy charge on the meagre profits of the voyage. Just how much the profits were was to give rise to much discussion in the course of the following year. Phips was summoned to attend the Lord Treasurer on 30 March 1686 and again on 15 May to discuss his accounts. The final statement disclosed that the King was entitled to receive only £470 19s 8½d., not even enough to cover the repairs to the ship, although it comes as some surprise to learn that there were any profits at all.[23]

Such disappointing results were hardly likely to encourage the new King to back Phips for the fresh voyage to the reefs which he was so desperate to make. James II was a man who watched his money carefully. He was also a shrewd investor, who was quite happy to place royal money in private projects if they showed a good chance of turning a profit. But Phips looked a bad bet. The Boston captain was going to have to look elsewhere for a backer.

CHAPTER TWELVE

Captain Phips's Wreck Project

The projector, that too enthusiastic man with an idea but no money, was a familiar figure in late seventeenth-century England, flitting from person to person at Court or the Royal Exchange, rather desperately trying to persuade the incredulous that the improbable was not only possible but a downright certainty. Captain William Phips was now to join this circle of eager, sleeve-clutching men, as he sought to raise cash to equip a new ship to follow up the discoveries made on his recent voyage. Phips's record in the *Rose* might be disappointing, to say the least, but he could be quite hopeful of ultimate success in his quest. For England was a good place for the projector. There were many wealthy men, but a distinct lack of exciting-looking investment opportunities, especially of the type which might attract the courtier or the wealthy man-about-town rather than those for whom business was itself a profession. A story of a fabulous treasure lying beneath the seas in a place known only to this impressive, fast-talking Boston sea-captain might well tempt money out of hands that would otherwise have spent it at the races or on the backgammon board. Nevertheless, progress was slow, and 'this project went a begging for a great while'.[1] It was too fantastic for most. 'Bless us! that folks should go three thousand miles to angle in the open sea for pieces of eight.'[2] And Phips himself must have looked a poor prospect to those who had had the opportunity of studying Knepp's report or the accounts which were being made up by the Treasury. Phips was to need all his patience to overcome the disappointments of the first few months after his return to England. It seemed that no one was interested in making a fortune, while many were openly hostile to the former captain of the *Rose of Algeree*. But, 'he who can wait, hath what he desireth', as Phips's biographer rather optimistically avowed,[3] and in this case it was certainly true.

Phips had originally hoped that the King would once more back his venture but, as we have seen, King James was a different man from his brother and was certainly not prepared to risk another royal ship on such an unpromising expedition. This was sad news for the man who had so enjoyed exercising what he conceived to be the powers of a captain of a man-of-war, but it was not of course the end of the road. Failing the King, Phips needed to get a man of very high rank who was close to the King to back him, for he was worried about the possibility of competition and felt that it was necessary to get an exclusive royal grant to search for the wreck. Only an accomplished courtier would be able to obtain that. Phips always aimed high, and the next man he approached was the King's most powerful subject, the Earl of Sunderland, King James's Secretary of State. But neither he nor many other great men whom Phips approached were prepared to concern themselves in his project or 'to venture any money upon it'.[4]

The first real break came some time early in 1686. Once again, as so often in this story, Sir Richard White appears as the contact man. Sir Richard, it will be remembered, was the rather mysterious Irishman who, in 1682, had first tempted the Commissioners of the Navy and King Charles into entering the treasure-hunting business. He sailed with Captain Churchill in the *Falcon* on the first voyage to the Abrojos and then stayed in Jamaica to carry on his business as a middleman between Spanish slave-dealers and the English Royal African Company. While he was in Jamaica he tried to double-cross both his partner, Captain Harmon, and King Charles II. He wrote to Don Pedro Ronquillo, the Spanish ambassador in England, offering to find the *Concepción*, 'not asking for more than 12,000 *escudos*, with the assurance that he knew the place [where the wreck was] as he had discovered it while in America on the King's frigate [the *Falcon*]'. Ronquillo passed the offer on to the King of Spain, but it was turned down.[5] White's claim seems to have been completely fraudulent. As we have seen, the *Falcon* was only present during Stanley's first voyage to the Abrojos and there is nothing that White could have learned about the correct location of the treasure while he was aboard the English frigate. The truth is probably that he had come to the same conclusion as Stanley, that the wreck must lie on reefs to the east of the Abrojos, and hoped to cash in on his deduction.

Now, back in England in early 1686, he was hoping to cash in once again for, according to a later report, he was the first to encourage Captain Phips, whom he had already met in Jamaica. Indeed he went farther and drew up a document by which he agreed to 'be at ye charge of 1/8 of ye adventure'.[6] There was a good reason for a fresh interest being shown in Phips at this time, for it must have been some time in

February that Captain Stanley's log-book arrived in England, together with the letter from Colonel Molesworth describing Stanley's last treasure-hunting voyage, and it seems more than probable that White, who had first promoted Stanley's voyages, should have been allowed to see these documents. If this is so, it is easy to see why White should have been prepared to encourage Phips, for the log-book provided independent confirmation of much of what Phips was saying and, in particular, confirmed his description of the general location of the wreck. In addition, Molesworth's letter reported that Stanley had had such a bad time on his last voyage, 'as wholly discourages him from prosecuting it further'.[7] In other words, the project was hopeful and the field was clear.

It was not long before Phips found further support from that high-ranking milieu which he had so far solicited in vain. Late in March he proposed the matter to the Duke of Albemarle and Sir John Narborough and 'they agreed to join therein'.[8] The Duke consented to head the syndicate and put up one quarter of the capital and Sir John came in for one-eighth. At this point the mysterious White decided for some reason to withdraw his subscription and we hear no more of him in the matter.[9] What his role had been is not clear. He probably acted as a commission agent and took an introduction fee from Phips. This may well have also been his role in relation to Captain Harmon. Sir Richard White comes across in the documents which have survived as the classic crooked middleman. He never put up any capital for any of the projects he promoted, simply milking them for as long as he could and then moving on to some other scheme.

Christopher Monck, second Duke of Albemarle, was a great catch, wealthy, distinguished and extremely well connnected. There would be no problem in raising the rest of the investment with his name behind the venture. His motives for involving himself in this gamble are classic, for this immensely wealthy man, with lands in eleven counties and in Ireland, was in serious financial difficulties. Ever since he had come into his inheritance at the age of seventeen, he and his Duchess, the former Lady Elizabeth Cavendish, had spent and spent in a mad attempt to compete in ostentatious consumption with King Charles, throwing away their money with both hands in a gay whirl of gambling and lavish entertainment at their great houses in London and at New Hall in Essex. Not even Albemarle's income could pay for this for ever. In 1682 he had had to sell the massive Albemarle House in London, the house being pulled down and the grounds divided into streets, of which Albemarle Street on the north side of Piccadilly is all that remains to remind us of the Duke's former glory. By early 1686 he was again in financial trouble and was contemplating the sale of more property. The long career of high living had had its effect on both the Duke and his Duchess. She was slowly going mad, while he suffered intermittently from the jaundice which was eventually to kill him. His physician, Hans Sloane, has left us an unflattering pen-portrait of his employer.

His Grace the Duke of Albemarle aged about 33 of a sanguine complexion, his face reddish and eyes yellow as also his skin, accustomed by being at Court to sitting up late and often being merry with his friends whence he eat very little and what he did eat was crusts of bread drinking great draughts of Lambeth ale after it, had been very much about six or seven years before given to hunting, fowling and other exercises of that kind but now loves a sedentary life and hates exercise as well as physick.

He drank too much sherry, could not sleep at night and often found 'his head somewhat out of order'.[10]

To add to his other troubles the Duke was out of favour early in 1686. The previous year had been a sad and frustrating one for him. In February he had lost his friend and master, Charles II. In June he had hoped to make a name for himself by snuffing out Monmouth's Rebellion in one whirlwind campaign. But everything had gone wrong. The militia troops which he had commanded as Lord-Lieutenant of Devonshire had run away at their first sight of the rebels. Worse still, his patent as Commander-in-Chief had been ignored by King James who had promoted the Earl of Feversham to command the royal army sent down to combat the rebellion. When Albemarle complained, the new King said that his patent 'ended with my brother, his life'.[11] Sulky and angry, Albemarle resigned his remaining military commission as commander of the Guards, and the King in his turn relieved him of his position as Lord-Lieutenant of Devonshire. It was, then, a disappointed, comparatively broke and heavily drinking duke whom Phips approached in March 1686.

Albemarle seems to have leaped at the opportunity which Phips offered. He had always been interested in the West Indies and in the possibilities of making money and a name for himself there. He was one of the Lords Proprietor of Carolina and the Bahamas and took a personal interest in the development of the new colonies. He had been a strong

advocate of Henry Morgan, when official displeasure forced the buccaneer to leave the West Indies for London in the early 1670s, and
his support was vital in getting Morgan knighted and reinstated as
Lieutenant-Governor of Jamaica. Now in 1686, Albemarle seems to have
devised a master plan for putting himself firmly on the political map and
at the same time making a new fortune. His support of Phips was simply
part of a much wider vision. In April Sir Philip Howard, the man who
had replaced Molesworth as Governor of Jamaica but had never taken up
his post, died, and Albemarle successfully petitioned the King for his job.
Everyone assumed that he would simply pocket half the perquisites and
appoint a deputy to do the work for him. But, to the general amazement,
Albemarle made it clear that he intended actually to go to Jamaica himself. It seemed unthinkable that a duke, let alone a duchess, should be
prepared to commit themselves to the heat and disease of Jamaica, not to
speak of the appallingly low-bred manners of the colonists. Petitions
were got up to persuade the Duke not to go, friends remonstrated with
him, his servants prayed that his illness would 'continue without danger',
so as to prevent his voyage.[12] But the Duke was adamant. He would go to
Jamaica. He would be a new and greater Morgan, and he took good care
to ensure that his patent as Governor included full rights over such things
as the gold and silver mines in America. All the same, he was in no hurry
to go, and it was not in fact until eighteen months after he first got the job
that he actually set sail for the West Indies.

The motives of Sir John Narborough in associating himself with Phips
could hardly have been more different. He was certainly in no financial
difficulties. He had been commander of three successful expeditions to
the Mediterranean against the corsairs of Tripoli and Algiers and had
amassed considerable prize money. When his active career finished in
1679 he became a Commissioner of the Navy, with special responsibility
for the victualling department, an absolute goldmine even for an honest
man. Finally, he had married as his second wife an extremely rich lady
called Elizabeth Hill, whose father left the enormous sum of £100,000
to Sir John's successor as her husband.[13] Sir John was then a very rich
man, with none of the crazy social ambitions of the Duke of Albemarle.
His interest in the wreck project was the result of the fact that he had
always been interested in the wreck of the *Concepción* and felt that Phips
had a very good chance of finding it. As we have seen, he was involved
in the earlier voyages of both Stanley and Phips and would have had
ample opportunity to study all their reports. He was quite happy to

invest in a one-eighth share, a modest sum for such a man, on the chance that Phips might be as successful as he promised he would be.

The most immediate requirement of the adventurers was a ship. Phips was commissioned to find a suitable one and discovered that the *Bridge-water* of 200 tons and 23 guns was up for sale and seemed 'fitt for said design'. Narborough surveyed her and found her satisfactory, and so the partners purchased her for £860, changing her name to the *James and Mary* in honour of the King and Queen. Meanwhile Albemarle and Narborough had drawn in two more investors, Francis Nicholson and Isaac Foxcroft, who each took an eighth share. Nothing much is known about these two men. Foxcroft was a lawyer of the Inner Temple and Nicholson was simply described as 'of Hatton Garden Esquire'. On at least one occasion they were involved together in the profitable business of the speculative builder.[14] They seem to have had no connection with either Albemarle or Narborough and were probably simply attracted by the gamble and the fact that such a great man as the Duke of Albemarle was prepared to lend his name and his money to the project. A fifth partner was acquired when it was decided to buy a sloop to act as consort to the *James and Mary*. Phips discovered a suitable ship, the 40-ton *Henry*, and her owner, John Smith, a merchant with interests in the Low Countries, agreed to credit the purchase price of £230 to the account of the adventurers in return for a one-eighth share in the enterprise.[15] The last two one-eighth shares were taken up by two wealthy and very well connected men. Anthony Cary, fifth Viscount Falkland, was Treasurer of the Navy from 1681 to 1689 and so must have known Narborough very well indeed. His step-father, Sir James Hayes, a former Secretary to Prince Rupert, was one of a syndicate farming most of the revenue of Ireland, a business that was only a little less of a gamble than looking for a forty-year-old wreck in the open sea.[16]

Arrangements were now made to secure the interests of Phips and the seven partners. On 18 July the King, in his role as Lord High Admiral, gave Albemarle an exclusive warrant 'to search for, seize and take-up all such wrecks as shall bee by him or them [his substitutes] found in ye seas to ye windward of ye north side of Hispaniola or about the islands or shoales of Bahama near the Gulf of Florida in America', on condition that one-tenth of all proceeds should go to the Crown. Orders were sent out 'strictly forbidding all our aforesaid officers and loving subjects to molest or interrupt ye said Duke of Albemarle or his substitutes in ye execution thereof'.[17] Narborough and Foxcroft felt that this warrant did not give them sufficient protection, since it could be countermanded as soon as the ships left the river, and Albemarle later got a grant under the Great Seal to confirm it.[18] On 31 July articles of agreement between the partners and Phips were drawn up and signed. The partners agreed to fit out, man and victual the two ships at their own cost and to bear losses as well as gains in proportion to their investment. It was also agreed that any new grants which the Duke of Albemarle received were to be shared with his current partners. Phips was to command the expedition to search for the wreck and was to use 'his uttermost skill for the owners' benefitt and advantage'. He was to keep 'bookes for entry of all the doeings dealeings and proceedings in the said voyage' and to oblige himself in the sum of £20,000 to carry out the agreement and not swindle the partners. In return he was to receive one-sixteenth of the treasure, 'one-tenth part of the whole being first taken out for the King's Royalty and the whole charge of the voyage being first paid and satisfyed'.[19] So once again Phips did not stand to get a very big share of the treasure for all his efforts.

In order to reduce the cost of a potential failure it was decided to spend about £500 on a small cargo to barter with the Spaniards in Hispaniola. The proceeds from this, together with what they could hope to get from re-selling the ships, ought to insure that they lost very little if everything went wrong. John Smith, as 'the only person that was a merchant among them', was given the task of organizing the cargo and got together a fairly standard mixed lot of trade goods, such as textiles, hardware and pottery and a good quantity of hard liquor. Smith also seems to have done much of the necessary purchasing for the ships themselves, though Narborough and Phips were also involved in this.

The complete accounts for the fitting-out of the two ships have survived and give an interesting picture of the realities of equipping such an expedition.[20] The purchase price of the two ships and of the cargo which Smith assembled made up only half of the total initial cost of £3,210 which was laid out on the venture. A quarter of the total was paid out to suppliers and craftsmen in the dockyard to fit the ships out, with particularly big bills being sent in by the ropemaker, blockmaker, sailmaker and anchorsmith. The ships not only needed to be freshly rigged for the voyage. It was also necessary that they should be totally independent of colonial dockyards, in order to preserve the secrecy of the expedition. There would be no one to help them on the reefs, a good reason for spending plenty of money on anchors, chains and cables. Then there were big bills from the butcher, the baker, the cooper and the brewer, who, it is nice to know, was a Mr Whitbread. The men needed heat and light as well as food and drink, and so we find the accounts of tallow-chandler, oilman and coal-merchant, all these bills together coming to about half of the cost of fitting-out the ship. Alongside all these other bills, the 'saylors bill of half-pay', £73 16s 8d or about £1 per head which was paid out on board the ships at Gravesend, looks very small indeed, especially when it is realized that much of this money came back into the partners' accounts as a result of selling the crew goods from the cargo. Finally, of course, there were special items of equipment needed for the salvage operations. These are not specified, presumably being included under 'Captain Phips bill of disbursements', but we can tell from later accounts that Phips took diving tubs, dredges, rakes and grapples with him as well as the normal lifting equipment which one would find on any ship. Right at the bottom of the accounts for the voyage there is rather a nice item, £13 5s 0d paid out for an iron chest especially bought 'to bring home the treasure in'. Altogether, looking for treasure was quite an expensive business, and once one looks at the accounts it is easy to see why Phips needed backers and did not just get on and find the treasure for himself. An expedition to the lawless and totally unprotected waters off the north coast of Hispaniola needed to be powerful enough to defend itself against all comers, whether they be pirates, French privateers or Spanish patrol-boats. It also needed to be completely self-contained in order to maintain secrecy for several months. For these reasons it was bound to be expensive. The six men with one-eighth shares had to pay out £400 and the Duke of Albemarle £800, a lot of money in 1686, especially for a mere project which was later described as 'a lottery of a hundred thousand to one odds'.[21]

There were about seventy men in the crews of the two ships, and we know the names of forty-five of them from the accounts which Phips kept in accordance with his articles of association.[22] Only five of these men had sailed on the *Rose* before the attempted mutiny: Francis Rogers who was to command the sloop *Henry*, William Covill who was second mate of the *James and Mary*, and three others, two of whom had joined the *Rose* at Boston. Presumably these five were among those loyal 'eight or ten' whom the mutineeers knew to be true to Phips. The crew seems to have been well chosen, and there is no evidence of the sort of trouble witnessed by John Knepp on the *Rose*'s voyage to Boston. Some of the officers seem to have had expectations of an unspecified share of any treasure which might be found, but the crews were on wages, as we have seen. Phips had no wish to repeat the experience of sailing with men 'that paid for their owne victualls and received no wages'. In addition to the crews, Phips took four divers[23] with him, which seems an incredibly small number when we remember that Peres Savage reported that there were eighty divers on the six ships working the wreck off New Providence when he was there.[24] One source suggests that Phips's divers were East Indian pearl-divers,[25] but this seems very unlikely, since there is no other evidence to suggest that Phips had ever had any connection with the Indian Ocean. The divers would be much more likely to be some of those whom Phips had taken on in the Bahamas or at Port Royal, a supposition which seems to be supported by the names of the two who appear in the ship's accounts, Jonas Abimeleck and John Pasqua, or Sasqua, names which suggest christianized American Indians rather than Asians. The only other extra man whom Phips carried was Charles Kelly, a former page of the Duke of Albemarle, who kept the accounts. But Kelly does not seem to have been a second Knepp, and he caused no trouble.

By late August everything was nearly ready, and on the last day of the month Phips's final instructions were signed by the seven partners. On 12 September the *James and Mary* and the *Henry* left the Downs and 'set sail for the Fishing-Ground, which had been so well baited half an hundred years before'.[26] The partners crossed their fingers and hoped for the best.

CHAPTER THIRTEEN

Shipwreck Refound

The historian who writes the story of the most fantastically successful commercial project of the seventeenth century can hardly complain of a lack of sources. For today, nearly three hundred years later, it is still possible to read the journals of both the ships which set out from the Downs with such high hopes on 12 September 1686. The journal of the *James and Mary*, which was probably kept by Captain Phips's servant, Thomas Waddington, a cockney judging by his spelling, was retained by the Duke of Albemarle after the voyage and later got into the hands of his physician, Hans Sloane. The journal of the *Henry* was kept by William Yarway and ended up amongst the papers of Sir John Narborough. Waddington and Yarway were clearly men who did not like to waste paper, for both journals were written in the back of old log-books recording previous voyages, a matter of some confusion for the student who finds entries relating to the Hispaniola venture side by side with entries relating to a voyage to India and back in 1683.[1]

Neither journal is quite complete. The journal of the *Henry* starts on 24 September 1686, with 'ye lighthouse of Silley bearing north-east, six leagues distant', and ends on 16 March 1687. This journal is beautifully kept and has a boldly written title-page which reads as follows: 'A journal of our voyage intended by divine assistance in the ship Henery, Francis Rogers Cmdr., bound for ye Ambroshia Banks on ye north side off Hispaniola, in company with ye James and Mary, Capt. Wm. Phips Cmdr. Both in persuite of a Spanish wreck, in which search God bee our Guide.' The journal of the *James and Mary* starts much later, on Saturday, 11 December 1686, with the ship already in Samaná Bay at the east end of Hispaniola. From this date the journal is continuous and ends on 4 June 1687 with the *James and Mary* in the English Channel. So, between them, the two journals cover the whole expedition from England out to Hispaniola and back again.

The first thing one learns about the *Henry* is that she was a poor sailer compared with the *James and Mary*. The two ships lost contact on

4 October, ten days out from the Scillies, and the *Henry* was to fall farther and farther behind during a period of foul weather in which she shipped a good deal of water. Nevertheless, the reader has confidence in Francis Rogers's seamanship, and so probably did his small crew when they sighted the island of São Miguel in the Azores on 12 October. On 1 November Rogers, judging himself to be 'in ye lattitude of Barbadoes, steard down west for ye island', and nine days later he dropped anchor in Carlisle Bay alongside Phips, who had arrived in Barbados ten days previously. The two ships watered and took on some fresh provisions, paying with £13, which they took up on a letter of credit, which had been arranged by the merchant John Smith, and then set sail again for the Mona Passage between Hispaniola and Puerto Rico. On 22 November they anchored off the island of Mona, an island which 'produceth plenty of beefe, goates and hoggs wilde, but noe inhabitants'. The *Henry* lost an anchor here, when her cable fouled a rock, and this provided an opportunity to employ one of the divers who successfully brought it up. Next day they sailed through the Mona Passage, and on 28 November anchored near the entrance of Samaná Bay, a place which Phips thought might be suitable both for the purpose of trade and as a base from which to set out to search for the wreck.

Phips and Rogers spent a fortnight in Samaná Bay, a place which 'aboundes with all necessary provission fitting for man, as beefe, hoggs, plenty of fish, turtle, mannatee, very goode fresh water, orringes and lymes'.[2] Here they found the evidence of a recent drama, 'a wreck in 4 fathom water, and burnt down to her gundecke, judgeing her to bee a ship about 400 tonns. Likewise found two or three iron shott which had ye broade arrow [the device of the Royal Navy] upon them and severall firelocks'.[3] This was the wreck of the *Golden Fleece*, a pirate vessel commanded by Captain Joseph Bannister, which had been upsetting the authorities at Port Royal for many years. Five months before Phips arrived in Samaná Bay, Bannister had been caught by two English frigates while careening the *Golden Fleece* and her smaller consort. However, he had rigged up two shore batteries from the ship's guns and was able to give the navy a warm welcome. 'The frigates stood in, though they were warmly entertained for two hours from the batteries and with small shot from the ships, and, bringing all their guns to bear, sunk and beat almost to pieces the buccaneers' ships.'[4] Bannister abandoned the *Golden Fleece* when she caught fire. Her consort had not quite been beaten to pieces and he was able to escape in her, but not for long. On

28 January 1687 Colonel Hender Molesworth was delighted to see Captain Spragge of the frigate *Drake* sail into Port Royal harbour, 'with Captain Bannister and three of his consorts hanging at his yard-arm, a spectacle of great satisfaction to all good people and of terror to the favourers of pirates, the manner of his punishment being that which will most discourage others'.[5]

Captain Phips's main priority in Samaná Bay was to make contact with the local hunters who, it was hoped, would be able to tell him if there was any chance of trading with the Spaniards. This was not too easy. The north coast of Hispaniola was not a place where men instinctively trusted newcomers. Phips saw a canoe full of men and sent his pinnace after them with a flag of truce, hailing them in Spanish. But the crew of the canoe were taking no risks and paddled away as fast as they could. Several days later, more friendly relations were achieved, and the hunters, who were French, agreed to get some meat for Phips. They brought aboard eleven wild hogs which they bartered for a case of spirits and six gallons of brandy from the ship's trading cargo.[6] The hunters told Phips that there was little hope of trade in Samaná Bay. The nearest Spanish settlement was at La Vega de Concepción, fifty miles from the head of the bay and sixty or seventy from where Phips was anchored. The Spaniards had completely abandoned this part of the island to foreign hunters and corsairs, maintaining just a few armed lookout posts on the major headlands to give warning of a foreign landing which might threaten La Vega or the other inland settlement at Santiago de los Caballeros. Seeing that there was no hope of trade, Phips and Rogers stocked up with water and firewood and prepared to set sail again. Rogers's orders were to head for 'ye windewarde [i.e. eastern] banke', but to make for Puerto Plata if the weather was unsuitable for searching the reef.

Rogers lost touch with the *James and Mary* on the second night out of Samaná Bay and headed north towards the bank to see if he could find her there. After a week spent tacking to and fro looking for Phips, he sailed into Puerto Plata to discover that Phips had been there since the afternoon after he lost him, 'finding ye weather not convenient' for the bank. Every day that Phips lay in Puerto Plata he fired three guns 'to give ye Spanyards notice of our being here'. But no one came. Puerto Plata had had a brief period of occupation during Villavicencio's attempts to locate and salvage the wreck, but now it was as deserted as Samaná Bay, especially in winter, and it looked as though the trading

venture designed to cut the costs of the expedition would be a total failure. This was a nuisance, because, apart from the financial loss involved,
Phips was not too keen to go on the banks for a few weeks yet, when the
worst of the rainy season would be over and there would be less danger
of being caught unprotected on the reefs by a 'norther', which, with
gusts of sixty knots or more, was terrifying enough on the open sea, let
alone in a boat anchored alongside a coral reef. But if there was no
trade, there was no point in staying in Puerto Plata, so, after firing the
guns for five days with no result, Phips ordered the ships to load with
wood and water and get ready to leave for the bank as soon as there was
the likelihood of a prolonged spell of good weather.

However, their presence had been noticed by the lookouts, and on
28 December, after Phips had been in the harbour for a fortnight, four
Spaniards arrived from Santiago, thirty miles away across the mountains
to the south, with instructions from the Governor to find out who they
were. Phips 'treated them very kindly' and sent them back with a roll of
cloth and a case of spirits as a present for the Governor and a letter which
'was to lett him understand that wee were Englishmen and friends and
that wee came for noe other intent then to gett wood and water and provisions for our money, soe makeing much of them which is the only way
to gaine on the hearts of those people. They went away, very well satisfied, with a promise to bee downe againe in three dayes.'[7] Since trade between Englishmen and Spanish colonists was in fact illegal, Phips did not
of course embarrass the Governor's emissaries by saying that he had
come to trade, but everyone knew what he meant when he repeated the
standard formula that he had only come for wood and water. Trade now
seemed probable, and Phips, expecting to receive large quantities of
meat and hides in exchange for his cargo, sent Rogers to the Turks Islands
to see if there was any salt made in the islands' famous natural salt-pans.
Rogers's departure was delayed for two days by a norther, and he set sail
on New Year's Eve, while Phips prepared to open shop.

Captain Phips's first customers were some Spanish hunters who bartered wild pork for hessian, canvas and the inevitable spirits. A few days
later the *alferez* of Santiago, 'who is as wee understand the ensigne bearer
of the towne', arrived. After he had been treated 'very nobly' by Phips,
to the tune of half a case of spirits, he gave a more or less official blessing
to the trading operations of the *James and Mary*. A number of Spaniards
came down to the port and bought a wide variety of goods – coats and
breeches, hats, stockings, buttons, pewter and earthenware plates and

mugs, chocolate cups and gunpower and, of course, spirits – which they paid for partly in cash, but mainly in cow-hides, tobacco, meat and rice. Phips said later that he had taken in £200 worth of Spanish cow-hides,[8] not much to set against the £500 that John Smith had laid out on the cargo, a 'small matter of trade . . . not at all to answer our expectation'.[9] Small or not, the trade did have the advantage of furnishing the crew with meat sufficient to last for several weeks on the reef. It also provided a satisfactory excuse for Phips's presence on the north coast of Hispaniola. No one guessed the real objective of the *James and Mary*.

On 8 January 1687 Rogers returned from the Turks Islands. He had visited three of the islands, including Salt Key, with its great salt-pan 'half a mile broad and a mile long', but the recent rain had wrecked the salt, and he had to be content with shooting a few seals and 'goannoes'. There was nothing for the *Henry* to do at Puerto Plata, so Phips decided to send her out to make a preliminary search for the wreck. Rogers fitted a new set of sails, stocked up with salt pork, wood and water, and prepared to sail again. On 12 January he welcomed aboard three of the Indian divers and William Covill, the second mate of the *James and Mary*, who had been his shipmate in the *Rose* on Phips's previous voyage to the banks. In the evening, 'with a fine land brease at south-west', he set sail 'with orders if they could gett a slatch of faire weather to goe on ye bank and make a search for the wreck'.[10]

Once Rogers was clear of the harbour's mouth, he steered east along the coast. The weather was not encouraging, with very heavy rain and variable winds. At dawn on his fifth morning out of Puerto Plata, the white perpendicular cliff of Cape Cabron bore south-east by south. about nine leagues distant, and Rogers 'steard away due north for ye banke'. There is no doubt that he knew exactly where he was going. At nightfall he reduced sail, and, at midnight, he tacked south and then north for the rest of the night to hold his position. At dawn on 18 January, 'judgeing our selves in ye lattitude of ye southernmost part of ye banke', he steered due west and at 8 a.m. the lookout could see the bottom and shortly afterwards they saw the east end of the reef. This reef, now known as the North Riff, forms the northern edge of the Ambrosian Bank (i.e. Silver Bank). It is about forty miles long, running from south-east to north-west between 20° 30′ and 21° north. When Rogers refers to the 'southernmost part of ye banke', he means the southern part of the North Riff. He did not yet know that the North Riff was not the only reef or bank on the Ambrosian Bank. The North Riff was later described by the mathematician John Taylor, who visited it from Jamaica. 'This is a bank of flat broad rocks, come on level with the water, and called boylers whereon the water seems to boil, between the rocks is 9 and 10 fathom of water.' Elsewhere he described the rocks, which were the heads of coral formations, as 'craggy, thick and visible, quite level with the water which seems to foam and boil like a furnace'.[11] It was a fearful place.

By one in the afternoon Rogers had come up to the eastern end of the reef. 'Then began to meet with ye boilers very thicke, being 10, 8, 6 and some not 4 foot under water, soe that wee were forct to keep a man att topmast heade to conn her through.'[12] But, later, the wind dropped, and Rogers was unable to prevent the current driving him on to one of the boilers, which they struck 'once or twice'. Fortunately, no harm was done, and the *Henry* was towed to safety by her boat and anchored in ten fathoms of water about three-quarters of a mile south of the reef. The weather was very calm, but it must have been an eerie night. Rogers was anchored in between three boilers, each one only a hundred yards away from him, and the peace of the night was occasionally disturbed by the blowing of the sperm whales who made their home in the vicinity of the reef.

Next morning Rogers began to search the reef. He went in the ship's boat with one diver, and William Covill went in the canoe with the other two divers, to the east end of the reef and they then 'searcht downe alongst ye north side'. They returned about ten hours later, 'haveing searcht att least 6 miles in length, from ye east end towards ye west-warde, not soe much as passing one boyler without a dilligent inspec-tion'. Visibility through the water was good, but there was nothing to be seen, except the beauty of the coral.

At eight on the following morning, 20 January 1687, Rogers weighed anchor 'with a fine small brease' and sailed west along the southern edge of the reef until he was opposite where they had left off searching the day before. Here he anchored about noon and, soon afterwards, the canoe and boat set off to continue their search. Only two hours later the boat returned,

bringing us happy and joyfull news of ye cannew's findeing ye wrecke, their being in her Mr Coule [Covill], Francis and Jonas, ye 2 dieverrs. For which blessing wee returne infinite praise and thankes to Almighty God. Our boate carryed [away] with her a chaine and grapnell, a new buoy rope, a new buoy, with severall wooden buoyes, and 2 longe oares, to fix uppon ye wrecke that wee might the better finde her when wee came on ye banke next. She lyes in ye midst of reife betweene 3 large boylers that ye tops of them are dry att low water. In some places upon her there's 7 fathoms, which is the largest depth, 6 and 5, ye shoallest [shallowest]. Most part of her timber is consum'd away, and soe over growne with curlle [coral] that had itt not been for her guns shee would scarce ever been founde, itt being at least 45 yeares since shee was lost and ye richest ship that ever went out of ye West Indies.

It was in fact forty-five years and eighty days since she was lost. William Covill and his two divers had found the wreck of the *Nuestra Señora de la Concepción*.

Further details about the initial discovery of the wreck can be gleaned from two accounts written after the event by people who were not there, but who knew the participants well. One is by Hans Sloane, physician to the Duke of Albemarle, and the other by Cotton Mather, Phips's contemporary and biographer. Sloane's account is the more unlikely.

After having been a long time on the rocks without finding any remainder of the ship, or signs of the money, at length one of the divers in a canoa found out by a piece of stick that stood over the place, that there there was treasure, they being East Indians, and used to fish for pearls in their native country. One of them immediately dived, and found under a rock on which grew vast quantity of coral, first an enamelled pair of silver stirrups with coral growing on them to a pretty length, and coming up told his fellows the good news, and desired they would give him an iron crow to break the coral, which having done he found vast numbers of pieces of eight, which they brought up by thousands, sticking together, the sea water having dissolved some of the alloy or copper next with the silver, and made it into verdigrease, which has fastned them together.[13]

Sloane provides a good description of the way in which silver coins which had been under water a long time clump together, but it is a description which is based on later salvage from the wreck. On this first occasion the boat and canoe brought back to the *Henry* just five bars of silver and eighty-two silver coins. There is no mention of silver stirrups, and the divers were not East Indians, which does not leave much of the description, except Sloane's delightful prose.

The description by Mather is more likely, but also suffers from the unnecessary desire to over-dramatize an occasion which is sufficiently dramatic in the words of the journal of the *Henry*.

This periaga [canoe], with the tender, being anchored at a place convenient, the periaga kept busking to and again, but could only discover a reef of rising shoals thereabouts, called the boilers, which rising to be within two or three foot of the surface of the sea, were yet so steep, that a ship striking on them would immediately sink down, who would say how many fathom into the ocean? Here they could get no other pay for their long peeping among the boilers, but only such as caused them to think upon returning to their captain with the bad news of their total disappointment. Nevertheless, as they were upon the return, one of the men looking over the side of the periaga into the calm water, he spied a sea feather [i.e. coral] growing, as he judged, out of a rock; whereupon they had one of their Indians to dive and fetch this feather, that they might however carry home something with them . . . . The diver, bringing up the feather, brought therewithal a surprising story, that he perceived a number of great guns in the watry world where he had found his feather; the report of which great guns exceedingly astonished the whole company; and at once turned their despondences for their ill success into assurances, that they had now hit upon the true spot of ground which they had been looking for.[14]

This is a nice story and it could just possibly be true, although they could hardly have been all that desperately disappointed, since they had only spent just over a day 'peeping among the boilers'. It is really much more likely that Covill and the divers saw the guns from the canoe, as the journal suggests. There were patches of white sand between the boilers and bronze guns would show up well. 'The said rocks are all under water and appeare of a blackish colour, the sand is as white as snowe which makes it so transparent.'[15]

All writers who describe the wreck stress that practically all the superstructure of the ship had been washed away or eaten by shipworm and what was left was covered by a growth of coral, a 'growing stony sea' as John Taylor aptly described it. What is not clear in the account given in the journal of the *Henry* is that the stern, which it will be remembered was lodged between two underwater rocks at the time of the wreck, was now completely enclosed in coral so that it was a rock itself, a rock which was far too thick for the divers to break into, armed as they were with nothing more powerful than a pickaxe.[16] It was, then, on the forward part of the wreck that Rogers's three divers worked for the next two days, raising another three bars of silver and nearly three thousand silver coins of different denominations. But then, towards the middle of the morning of Saturday, 22 January, the sky 'begann to looke suspicious' to the north and Rogers reluctantly ordered the boats to be taken back on board and set sail for Puerto Plata, lest a norther catch him on the reef before he could tell Phips the good news.

Rogers was to have far more trouble getting back to Puerto Plata than he had in finding the wreck. The weather kept fine as he steered south towards Hispaniola but at four in the afternoon, to his surprise, he began to see boilers again and, by six, they were thick about them. Just then the wind died. Rogers turned the *Henry*'s head to the north and quickly lowered the boats to tow him back out of trouble. At nightfall he anchored a little to the north of the thick cluster of boilers. He sent the canoe astern to see what clearance he had, if a norther should get up in the night, and found to his horror that there was a boiler standing proud of the water less than a cable's length from his stern. The canoe was then sent away to the north in the darkness to see if it was possible to warp away a further cable's length from the dry boiler, 'but they founde ye soundings soe uncertaine that wee were forct to ride still where wee were'.[17]

This was the first that Rogers knew that there were other reefs between the North Riff and Hispaniola. 'This *unexpected* place of danger', the journal says, 'lyes south from ye wrecke att least seven leagues.' The use of the word 'unexpected' helps us to get a rather better idea of where Rogers and Phips had been the previous year. They clearly knew exactly where the North Riff was, but did not realize the full extent of the Ambrosian Bank. Where Rogers was now was later called the South Bank or South Ambrohos Bank,[18] and it seems more than probable that it was here that the Stanley brothers had nearly come to grief on their last voyage, only about twenty miles from the wreck but once again on the wrong reef.

Rogers was luckier than Stanley. There was no thunderstorm that night, no lightning to illuminate the waves breaking on the boilers which surrounded them. 'All last night, God bee praised, wee had fine faire weather with very little wind.' Next morning the boat found a clear channel through the reef to the south and, with a 'man att our topmast heade to conn her through', the *Henry* was clear of all the boilers by noon. 'For which wee returne infinite thankes and praise to Almighty God for his safe deliverance from soe great a danger.'[19] But Phips still had a long time to wait before he would know the success of his gamble.

On 25 January, as Rogers stood in for Puerto Plata, he saw a sail to the west of the port. As he got closer, he 'perceived her to bee a great ship and to sail very well, which occassion'd us much to suspect her'. This was no time to be captured by a corsair, who would soon realize what they were up to when he discovered the silver and would surely torture them to reveal where the treasure lay. Rogers headed away from land but, next morning, when he returned towards Puerto Plata, the strange ship was still at the harbour's mouth and he prudently decided to sail for the Turks Islands. They were going to need salt in any case to preserve the meat brought in by the hunters as provisions during the long period of salvage in the reefs that lay ahead.

Phips had continued to trade with the Spaniards, while Rogers was out searching for the wreck, and he had heard about the strange ship from the men on the lookout post to the east of Puerto Plata. It was said to be a French corsair who had landed a party to surprise the town of Santiago. Later he had seen two ships at sea, presumably the Frenchman and the *Henry*, and had sailed out to investigate. At dawn on 25 January the lookout saw a sail. 'Wee chased him. At first we thought it to be Mr. Rogers but, when wee came up with him, we haild him and found him to be a French merchantman come from France with passengers, but where he was bound wee could not rightly understand.'[20] Satisfied that the ship would cause them no trouble, Phips returned to Puerto Plata the following day.

Rogers spent three days in the Turks Islands, but again there was no salt. On 30 January he was on his way back to Puerto Plata, but the winds were so contrary that it was eight days before he managed to weather the harbour's mouth and get into port. It was not till three in the afternoon of 7 February that he dropped anchor, an incredible sixteen days after he left the wreck to sail the eighty miles back to port. One writer says that Phips was so worried at Rogers's long absence that he was just about to sail for Jamaica, 'having made all things in a readiness'.[21] But there is no indication of this in the journal of the *James and Mary*. They were still trading with the Spaniards and had not yet taken in wood and water, which they would have done if they were preparing to sail. In any case the *Henry* had been seen just outside the harbour's mouth three days before she at last came to anchor, so they knew she was not lost on the reefs.

We know very little about the character of Francis Rogers, except that he must have been a very loyal man whom Phips could trust absolutely. But, at the moment of his arrival in Puerto Plata with his stupendous news, he was to show that he certainly had a sense of humour. The entries in the journal of the *James and Mary* for 7 and 8 February 1687 tell the story. '[7 February] This day towards 4 a clock Mr. Rogers came in who gave us to understand that they had been on ye banck and told us they had don as much as any men could doe . . . [8 February] This morning our Captain sent our long boat on board Mr. Rogers which in a shoart time returned with what made our hearts very glad to see which was 4 sows, 1 bar, 1 champene, 2 dowboyes,* 2000 and odd dollars by which wee understood that they had found the wreck.' Cotton Mather also records Francis Rogers's little joke, and this time there is no reason to disbelieve him, since the journal confirms his story.

They went back unto their Captain whom for some while they distressed with nothing but such bad news as they formerly thought they must have carried him. Nevertheless, they so slipt in the sow of silver on one side under the table, where they were now sitting with the Captain, and hearing him express his resolutions to wait still patiently under the Providence of God under these disappointments, that when he should look on one side he might see that odd thing before him. At last he saw it; seeing it, he cried out with some agony, Why? What is this? Whence comes this? And then, with changed countenances, they told him how and where they got it. Then, said he, Thanks be to God! We are made; and so away they went, all hands to work.[22]

At this point it seems worthwhile to speculate a little as to why Rogers, or rather Covill, was able to find the wreck so easily after so many other men had failed in the previous forty-five years. The most obvious suggestion would be that Phips had learned something from the 'very old Spaniard (or Portuguese)' whom he had found in Hispaniola the previous year. Or perhaps he learned something from the one man with a Spanish name on the *James and Mary*, John de la Cruse, who was possibly one of the divers.[23] This, of course, is the same surname as Andres de la Cruz, the Indian servant who was the last man off the *Concepción*. Unfortunately, it is a very common surname, and we must treat this simply as coincidence. In any case, what could Phips have learned from selfstyled survivors living on Hispaniola, or indeed from any Spaniard?

One thing that one would expect Phips to have learned was the name of the ship for which he was searching. But it is quite clear that Phips never knew this. The name, *Concepción*, does not appear in a single English document relating to the wreck. All that Phips knew was that she was an Almiranta which had sunk between forty and forty-five years

* Names for various types of silver bullion.

previously. And the most widely publicized name for the wreck in England and the English West Indies was the *Golden Lion*. This would have been a most unusual name for a seventeenth-century Spanish galleon, which were nearly all named after saints or the Virgin Mary, and there is certainly no record of a Spanish ship of this name being wrecked at anything like the right date. And yet, directly the Spanish government heard of Phips's success, they knew that it was the *Concepción* that he had found. Would it have been possible for a survivor to have forgotten the name of his own ship?

The second problem with the hypothesis that survivors provided Phips with his information is even more obvious. If survivors, or indeed anyone else, knew where the wreck was, why did they not go and find it years before? One has a shrewd suspicion that both Phips and Stanley were conned by so-called survivors who knew a sucker when they saw one. Old men living in the north of Hispaniola had found a profitable new business.

What seems a much more likely explanation of the *Henry*'s success is far more prosaic. This is that the Spanish directions were basically correct, but that everyone assumed that they referred to the northern reef on the Handkercher Bank, that is the bank which was generally known as the Abrojos, which, of course, was the name used by the survivors for the place where they had been wrecked. When one looks more carefully at some of the directions given by Harmon to Stanley, then it seems probable that this hypothesis is correct. On his very first voyage to the Abrojos, Captain Harmon was clearly looking for a reef in the northern part of the bank which bore south-east to north-west and, when he found one, he got very excited. He then ordered Stanley to anchor close to '3 great spotts which appear'd to have but little water . . . Captain Harmon judged the wrack to ly among these rocks'.[24] Disappointment was to lead Harmon to change his mind, to Stanley's annoyance, but it is interesting that, on their second voyage to the Abrojos, Harmon should want to return to the same place. 'Captain Harmon desired that I would bring him in sight of ye breakers which lay about two leagues to the west of the southern point [of the reef] . . . the breakers wee fell with all in Captain Churchill's time.'[25] So Harmon was trying to find a wreck which he understood to lie between three nearly dry rocks which were about six miles west of the southern end of a reef which was on the north of the Abrojos and bore south-east to north-west. This description fits the place where Covill found the wreck almost exactly, except of course that it was on the North Riff of the Ambrosian Bank and not on the Handkercher Bank. Phips's success, therefore, lies in the fact that, unlike Stanley, he found the North Riff, and he found it in sufficiently good weather to be able to see that this reef fitted the Spanish directions far better than did the reef on the Handkercher Bank. It was simply a question of sending Rogers and Covill and the divers to search. There are still one or two problems. What about the marker rock mentioned in the Spanish directions, which 'apeares like a boate keele up', for which Harmon and Stanley searched so long? There was no such rock where Covill found the wreck. Indeed there were no rocks standing high above the water at all, and none are mentioned in the accounts of the survivors. The absence of this lone rock has always worried writers and treasure-hunters. One possibility is that the rock was not standing proud of the water at all. It might well have been a coral formation below the water that looked like a boat keel up. Many of these formations rise at least fifty feet from the sea bottom, the height that the sailor Thomas Smith mentioned, and they are easily visible through the clear water.[26] The last problem relates to the silver on the flat rock. The three large boilers that surrounded the wreck were flat and the tops of them were dry at low water, but there was no silver piled up on them when Rogers and Covill arrived. Had there ever been? Had it been washed off? Or had it been seen and removed by a passing ship's crew who little realized how close they were to a much greater fortune? We shall never know.

All the above is pure conjecture. There is no conclusive evidence as to why Phips was successful where so many had failed. Perhaps he was just lucky. Phips himself knew who to thank for his good fortune. 'Then, said he, Thanks be to God! We are made; and so away they went, all hands to work.' It is time that we rejoined them.

CHAPTER FOURTEEN

Salvage

'All hands to work!' The armchair treasure-hunter is at first amazed at the coolness of Captain Phips. Here he was, with the dream of a lifetime come true, with a fortune in silver just waiting to be picked up, and yet he did not sail out of Puerto Plata until nine days after he had seen 'that odd thing', a sow of silver under the cabin table. How could he bear to wait so long? But, of course, there was a lot that had to be done if Phips was going to be able to spend weeks, or even months, in continuous salvage work on the reef. Both ships had to be careened, their bottoms scrubbed clean and the *Henry* coated with tallow, 'to make her iff possible to saile better'. More hogs and bullocks had to be acquired from the Spanish hunters who 'came on board and cutt out ye bones and salted them for us after their way'. Casks had to be hauled out and carried ashore to be filled with fresh water. Wood had to be cut and brought aboard. Meanwhile Phips still had quite a bit of his trading cargo left which he proceeded to sell to the crew for bargain prices. Cases of spirits which had been sold to the islanders for twenty-four shillings were sold to crew members for only nine. They also acquired a fair amount of cloth and the remainder of a consignment of knives which they bought up for threepence each. When Phips eventually set sail from Puerto Plata on 17 February, the crew had bought between them twenty-three whole cases of spirits and five and a half anchors of brandy, promising a lively expedition.[1]

Once again the *James and Mary* lost touch with the *Henry*, but, although progress was slow with the wind in the north and the east, there was no problem in finding the reef with William Covill back aboard as pilot. At 3.30 p.m. on 21 February the *James and Mary* 'came to anchor, ye wreck bearing of us north-east a half east, about four or five miles, the reefe makeing like to a halfe moone'. The patient Phips was quite happy to make the ship snug for the night and wait for the morning to peer down at his good fortune. But Mr Covill could not bear to be so close and not check that the wreck was still there, so by his 'persuasions wee hoysted out ye pinnace. Mr. Covell and Mr. Strong [mate] and two of ye divers went in her to ye wreck and just as day light began to shutt in they came on board bringing with them out of ye wreck 84 whole dollars, 51 halfe dollars.'

Next morning Phips himself went to the wreck with all four divers. There is no record of his reactions. We do not even know if he could swim, let alone dive. Still, it seems improbable that a man brought up on the coast of Maine, who had been for many years a wreck-hunter, could be incapable of diving to thirty or forty feet. We must imagine Phips diving down to survey the wreck and later discussing the many problems of salvage with his four professional divers. That afternoon the *Henry* arrived, and Rogers was ordered to anchor between the wreck and the *James and Mary*, 'as near the reef as conveniently he could without danger'. This was not very close. Rogers eventually anchored about two miles south-west of the wreck, about half the distance between the wreck and the *James and Mary*. Both ships made themselves snug, lowered their topmasts and yards, took enormous trouble to prevent their anchor cables snagging or rubbing against the coral heads, and got in a posture 'fitt to receive bad weather'.

Everything was now ready for a long season of hard work and a routine was soon established. Each morning the pinnace, and sometimes the long-boat, took the divers and a party of sailors to the wreck ready for many hours of work before returning to the mother ship at some time in the afternoon. Then the day's take was hauled aboard, counted or weighed, and divers and sailors could relax, wash some salt pork down with Mr Whitbread's beer, or the brandy acquired from the ship's cargo, and rest before the next day's arduous labour. On the seventh day they rested. 'This day being ye Lordsday and soe consequently a day of rest wee did not try for ye wreck.' Captain Phips, a good New Englander, was not prepared to risk the wrath of God by worshipping Mammon on a Sunday. Altogether the *James and Mary* was fifty-eight days on the reef, including the day she arrived and the day she set sail, and the men worked on the wreck on forty of them, losing eight Sundays, nine days of bad weather and one day when the divers were too ill to go on the wreck. Collecting a fortune is hard work.

How did the divers go about their work? We do not have any detailed descriptions of their method of operation, but two things seem quite clear from the log-books. There is no mention of anyone but the four divers actually diving. And there is no mention of the use of a Bermuda tub until the third week of salvage. This would have made the divers' task far less arduous, but for the tub to be used, it would be necessary to anchor one of the ships directly above the wreck, a very dangerous man-oeuvre which Phips was not prepared to risk. Later events will show that he was right. So one has to imagine the four divers doing all the underwater work in the brief period during which they could hold their breath and then coming back up for air and a rest. John Taylor has left an interesting description of their method of doing this:

And I observed that the Indian divers, when they rise up out of the water, as soon as they put their heads above the same, would in an instant duck their head under water and there keep it about a quarter of a minute, and then rise up and recover the boat; for they said if they should at first receive too much of the land air it would destroy them, but by the concoction of the first received air they got strength to enable them to receive the benefits of the air fully like others which dived not.[2]

At first there must have been considerable crow-bar and pick-axe work, breaking off coral and clearing a route to the forward treasure chambers of the ship. 'And 'tis further remarkable that the silver had so remained under water, as to petrify a congeal'd substance into white coral-trees growing thereon, some with mighty spreading branches, even to a great height.'[3] The divers would be assisted in this preliminary work of clearance by the sailors in the boat above who would use long-handled rakes and dredges to strip the wreck clear of débris. Once a passage was clear, the divers' task was to fill baskets with loose coins or pieces of plate or else fix ropes to larger items which could then be hauled up by the sailors with their tackle. Much of this would be done in a congested space where the manhandling of a large piece of bullion, such as a 'sow' which weighed about sixty pounds, presented fairly obvious problems.

We must remember, too, that, although the wind was normally from the east or north-east, and so the wreck was in the lee of the reef, the divers would frequently be working in rough water, having to brace or even belay themselves to provide sufficient purchase for their heavy work. The time that Phips could stay working on the wreck was severely limited by his supplies of provisions and water, and he kept the divers at it, making them work in some pretty rough weather, 'a fresh brease notwithstanding, our boats went to worke on the wreck'. Some days work was impossible, the worst period being four continuous days of gale-force winds from the north-east, during which 'ye sea ran very high on ye reefe'. On the fifth day the wind dropped, and the boats went to work, 'but ye sea rann soe high on ye reefe that they dared not to venture on ye wreck'.[4]

It was no joke being a diver. Every morning the boats left the mother ship early and generally returned between three and five in the afternoon. Allowing for the time that it took to cover the considerable distance between the *James and Mary* and the wreck, the divers must have been working at least four and often several more hours a day for six days a week in good weather. It is not surprising that on several occasions the journals have entries such as, 'the divers proveing very ill wee made a bad day's worke'. However, they kept going and only one day was lost to human frailty. 'This day [10 March], although it was very fine weather, our captain would not lett ye divers worke by reason he see that some of them were nott well', or, as the journal of the *Henry* put it, 'our dieverrs being out of order and tired with all did not worke'. They must have been very tough men indeed.

One consolation for the hard work must have been the beauty of the underwater scenery. A modern writer has described what she could see through the glass bottom of her boat as it travelled through the reefs of the Ambrosian Bank:

great towering coral cliffs, honeycombed with caves, rising from a white-sand floor, topped by pinnacles bizarrely fashioned like something from the Arabian nights. There were vast outcroppings of every kind of coral – tangled jungles of branch coral like berry bushes in a pasture, solid beds of lettuce coral, waving Gorgonia and sea fans, and topping all, the lovely yellow-brown stag coral, forming shady parasols for the teeming, colorful small fish beneath it. Not only were the reefs a tumbled mass of coral, but the whole ocean floor was scattered with these formations, some close to the bottom but many towering thirty and forty feet.[5]

It was between three of these towers that the wreck of the *Concepción* lay, a place of beauty and a place of excitement as each day more treasure was hauled up by the sailors of the pinnace and the long-boat.

It was certainly exciting to count the coins brought back to the *James and Mary* each evening but, after the first flush of enthusiasm, Phips must have begun to be a little worried by the slow progress of the salvage. Four divers were not really enough for the job. On that first Sunday, riding at anchor on the Ambrosian Bank, Phips was at leisure to do a little arithmetic. In the first five full days' work on the wreck, the divers brought in a total of just over 20,000 pieces of eight in dollars and half-dollars,* about 1,000 pieces of eight per diver per day. They also raised about four hundred pounds† weight of bullion and three guns. This may sound a lot, and indeed it was a lot, since it was sufficient to cover the complete costs of the expedition. However, if Phips was to salvage the wreck completely, and that was clearly his intention, he had to think in terms of tons of silver, not thousands of pieces of eight. The very smallest estimate of the silver on the ship – that given by Pedro de Medina, the silver-master, in his evidence to the enquiry held at Santo Domingo – was just over a million pesos, equivalent to about thirty-five tons of silver. And it is certain that Phips would have laughed at the idea of a fabulous Spanish galleon carrying only one million pesos. Three or four million would be what he expected, in other words well over a hundred tons of silver. But twenty thousand pieces of eight weighed less than one ton! At this rate it would take the divers more than two years of constant work to raise the treasure, if they survived, even if no account were taken of Sundays and bad weather. It was not good enough.

Phips was never to raise quite as much silver as he may have promised himself, but the rate of salvage was soon to get very much faster. At noon on that first Sunday on the bank two sails were seen to the west tacking laboriously towards them. It must have been a disturbing moment. Had they lost the benefit of secrecy so soon? Phips nervously clutched the royal order 'strictly forbidding all our aforesaid officers and loving subjects to molest or interrupt the Duke of Albemarle or his substitutes' in their search for treasure. As the ships came nearer they were identified as a sloop and a shallop, too small to hurt them, but too fast to catch if they should turn and run to spread the news of two strange ships anchored on the Ambrosian Bank. But the sloop and shallop kept tacking towards them and soon could be recognized as the ships belonging to Abraham Adderley of Jamaica and William Davis of Bermuda who had sailed together with the *Rose* the previous summer, when the North Riff had been first located. They came to anchor under the stern of the *James and Mary* and announced that they had come 'up here to spend away ye summer in search of ye wreck'. They also said that a small ship of ten

---

* i.e. pieces of eight reales = one dollar; pieces of four reales = half-dollar.

† These are pounds avoirdupois. Later, in London, the treasure was weighed in pounds troy, which has caused some confusion.

guns had been fitted out in Barbados for the same purpose.

It is possible that these two ships had arrived by pre-arrangement, though there is no real evidence for this. Whether their arrival was by accident or not, it was followed by a couple of days of very keen negotiation. The two ships, with their unknown number of divers, were a real godsend to Phips, a fact which must have soon become apparent to Adderley and Davis. There was no question of their working for shares. Phips had an exclusive grant from the King, and this time he was not going to spread it around. It was also obvious that Phips had the firepower to enforce any contract that was made. All the same, Adderley and Davis were in a strong position, and there is no doubt that they made a good bargain for the hire of their ships and divers. Unfortunately the contract has not survived, and we do not know the details, but Phips could afford to be generous. Whatever it cost, the extra help was invaluable and the rate of salvage was soon to accelerate.

More divers meant more hands underwater, but there was another factor involved which was to increase the productivity of each individual diver enormously. During the first few days of salvage the day's take normally consisted mainly of loose coins, a few pieces of bullion and various pieces of broken or damaged wrought silver, such as spoons and forks. Collecting all this was obviously slow work. But, on 4 March, two days after the contract had been made with Adderley and Davis, the divers started to move into a real treasure chamber. 'Our boats went to work on ye wreck and in ye evening brought on board 2,399 pounds weight of coynd silver which we suppose were in chests which wee putt in 32 baggs'; over a ton of silver in one day. From now onwards, coins were no longer counted but weighed. Next day the weather was not very good and 'the divers could not make noe great hand of their work, nevertheless they brought on board 13 baggs of coynd money weighing 1,139 pounds, one dowboy and a quarter of a dowboy gold', incidentally the only pieces of gold recorded as being salvaged on this expedition. As for silver, half a ton was now a bad day. How quickly horizons change! What had happened was that the divers had now got into one of the main storerooms of the *Concepción* and were able to fasten their ropes to 'whole chests of 2,000 dollars together, for although the chests were rotted off and consumed, yet the dollars, with rust, were so grown together as one lump – although the middlemost of the chest was bright and sound – and not many of them was much wasted by the water'.[6] Exactly the same experience is recorded by treasure-hunters today.[7] In four days' diving, from 4 to 8 March, Phips's divers raised three and a half tons of coins and two more brass guns. Then, beneath the chests of coin, they got into a section rich in bullion. There were only seven working days between 9 and 22 March, the period which saw the worst weather of the whole expedition, but when the divers could work they did well and raised over five tons of bullion, together with a fair bit of coin. Next they moved into a section rich in coin, and so it was to go on. On the twenty-four working days between 4 March and 11 April they never raised less than half a ton of silver; on eight different days they collected over a ton, and on two remarkable days at the end of March they brought up nearly three and three-quarter tons, mainly in bullion.

This was certainly rather more like it, but, even so, Phips would have liked to have worked faster still. On 7 March, a day of fair weather and smooth water, Phips determined to try using the Bermuda tub to increase the divers' productivity. William Davis was persuaded to take his sloop right into the reef and anchor her 'heade and sterne with two chaines and grapnells' directly over the wreck. The tub was then lowered and the divers got to work. Conditions were very much more pleasant. The tub was a big one, fitted with a seat where the divers could rest, breathe, talk to each other and even take a dram from a bottle of brandy that they had taken down with them. Every half an hour or so the air would become foul and the tub and divers came up to the surface. Rigging the tub took time, but it was a good day and over a ton of silver and two brass guns were recovered. Towards evening, 'ye clouds did ryse in ye northward board very suspitious and likely to blow hard'. Blow hard it did, and soon the sloop was in trouble, as recorded by the journal of the *Henry*.

About 10 last night ye sloope begann to fire guns very fast, itt blowing fresh northerly. Uppon which our boate was immediately man'd and sent to see what was ye meaning of ye fireing, doubting some disaster had befalne them. As soon as they perceiv'd ye boate comminge they left of fireing, kept ye boate with them till morn, then came on boarde, and inform'd us that when they fir'd soe quicke last night, att ye same interim of time ye heade fast gave way, so that they drove uppon a shoal, but happening to be high water they beate over itt without any great dammage, onely looseing ye rudder, and broake away some part of their gripe. This morning ye wind vear'd to ye southwarde of east, with fine faire weather all ye day. In ye afternoone ye sloop lett slipp, and went off to ye James and Mary and there to repaire her dammage.

We hear no more of the tub being used. Presumably neither Davis nor Phips was prepared to take such a risk again.

The twelfth of April was the first working day for over a month when the take had been less than a thousand pounds' weight of silver. On the following day the divers completely emptied the great storeroom which they had mined so effectively, and only 295 pounds were raised. Next day was a day of exploration. 'Having clear'd ye roome where they workt before, our dyvers spent their day in finding a new one, wherefore they brought aboard but a small quantity which being inconsiderable wee left ye weighing off itt alone till another time.' The search for a new treasure chamber was not immediately successful, and the next three days saw takes of only 144, 257 and 171 pounds, which must have seemed chicken-feed after the bonanza of March and early April. It was time that Captain Phips did some thinking.

He had now raised over twenty-five tons of silver, seven guns and a few bits and pieces, including a little gold. It was obvious that this was only part, perhaps only a relatively small part, of the total treasure, but it was still worth an enormous amount of money in seventeenth-century England. Finding a new treasure storeroom might take days, or it might take weeks, and he was getting rather short of provisions, since the lack of salt in the Turks Islands had meant that he had not bought as much meat in Hispaniola as he would have liked. The divers were also tired, and, although they had worked well in the last few days, they were probably not up to the particularly arduous task of hacking their way through to a new storeroom. Then there was the weather. He really had been extremely lucky to spend nearly two months on the banks and have practically no trouble at all, except for a few lost days when the divers could not work. Should he chance his luck any longer?

Finally there was the problem of security. A fortnight previously, on 29 March, Davis's sloop had been sent to Jamaica to get rid of the hides acquired in Hispaniola and to see if the Duke of Albemarle had yet come out to take up his post as Governor. The Duke's former page, Charles Kelly, had been sent with Davis to tell Albemarle the good news if he were there and to arrange for letters to be sent to England to inform the other partners of the success of the venture. Phips was now getting worried about the non-return of the sloop. What if she had been captured? Even now there might be a couple of 30-gun French corsairs on their way from Tortuga to seize his hard-won treasure.

Phips was also worried about his own crew. They were certainly quite

different from the gang of roughs who had sailed on the *Rose*, and there
had not been a hint of trouble, despite the brandy, but no seafaring man
could have been all that happy to work day after day raising fabulous
quantities of silver of which he had no expectation of a share. Phips could
see the look in their eyes, and he did his best to assure them that they
would be well rewarded. They seem to have believed him.

There was one extraordinary distress which Captain Phips now found himself
plunged into [wrote his biographer Cotton Mather]. For his men were come
out with him upon seamens wages, at so much per month; and when they saw
such vast litters of silver sows and pigs, as they call them, come on board them at
the Captain's call, they knew not how to bear it, that they should not share all
among themselves, and be gone to lead a short life and a merry, in a climate
where the arrest of those that had hired them should not reach them. . . . And he
then used all the obliging arts imaginable to make his men true unto him, especially by assuring them that, besides their wages, they should have ample requitals
made unto them; which if the rest of his employers would not agree unto, he
would himself distribute his own share among them.[8]

Phips may have had a silken tongue, but he was taking no more
chances, and, on 19 April, he and Rogers got up their yards and topmasts and weighed anchor to set sail for the Turks Islands. Adderley and
his shallop were left behind with the divers to continue salvaging the
wreck for a week, while he waited to see if Davis's sloop would return.
Then he was to rendezvous at the Turks Islands. Phips's second day at sea
with the treasure aboard was to be somewhat alarming. A gale got up,
and, as usual, he parted company with Rogers in the *Henry*. At one point
Phips skirted dangerously close to the north-east part of the Handkercher
Bank, those Abrojos which we have got to know so well, but all went
well and 'presently wee found ye depths to deepen'. The same night they
anchored off Cotton Key in the Turks Islands where the *Henry* successfully found them. A week later the shallop turned up with the divers and
just over half a ton more silver. There was no sign of Davis's sloop. It was
time to be gone. Adderley was paid off, 'but before they went, Captain
Phips caused Adderley and his folk to swear that they would none of
them discover the place of the wreck or come to the place any more till
the next year, when he expected again to be there himself'.[9] Phips and
Rogers wooded and watered and, on 2 May, set sail for England. They
soon lost company with each other.

It was an uneventful voyage home for the *James and Mary*. They spoke with only one ship the whole way, the *Lisbon* from Barbados on 31 May. Phips boarded her with 'some peeces of eight in a bagg to the value of about £10 . . . and a dough-boy of silver and bought . . . some provisions and some liquors'. Then they were off again. They sighted the Scillies three days later, and anchored in the Downs on Monday, 6 June, a nine-month round trip which was to make Phips famous for ever and keep England buzzing with excitement for years into the future. The word soon got round. 'Letters from Deal of the 7th advise the arrival of the *James and Mary*, Captain Phipps, from the West Indies, who went in search of the Spanish galleons that were cast away 42 years since, one of which she found and got treasure to the value, it is said, of £250,000.'[10] A quarter of a million pounds sterling! It was unbelievable.

CHAPTER FIFTEEN

Good News for the Mint

The news of Phips's success rippled outward from Deal, where he had gone ashore to send letters to his partners, and soon excited letter-writers all over England were sending somewhat exaggerated accounts of the astonishing story to their correspondents at home and abroad. 'My Lord Duke of Albemarle has had a lucky bout . . .' wrote Charles Bertie to his niece, the Countess of Rutland.[1] 'Tho' its near on 11 at night, and I fear the post is going, I cannot forbear to send you a peice of news, odd and unusuall. There was a Spanysh ship . . .' wrote Sir Edmund King to Viscount Hatton.[2] For those who had no well-informed correspondents there were news-letters, broadsheets and the *London Gazette* to tell them the news.[3] England loved the story. There is no jealousy expressed in any of the accounts, simply pleasure at the unexpected success of their fellow-countrymen and a certain atavistic sense of well-being that the Spaniards had been done down once again. And, of course, where Phips had led others could follow. 'The money fished up has caused great excitement and has awakened the spirit of many to engage in similar enterprises, which were previously thought impossible', wrote the Tuscan envoy to his masters in Florence.[4] The great treasure-hunting boom had begun.

Meanwhile the King's officers were making sure that Captain Phips's treasure actually got safely into the Thames so that it could be weighed and the King's tenth removed to the Mint. A naval guard was placed on the *James and Mary*, and an escort saw her to Deptford where she was anchored alongside the King's ship, the *Rising Sun*. Here the naval guard was replaced by 'the most trusted officials' of the Customs who were ordered to remain aboard until the arrival of the officers of the Royal Mint.[5] The Duke of Albemarle and the other adventurers came down from London to see for themselves the result of their gamble, and a good time was had by all as casks were broached and the crew drank a health to their lucky employers.

The crew had good reason to be happy, for the Duke had honoured Phips's pledge to his men and a portion of the treasure had been set aside to be shared between them. The crews of the *James and Mary* and the *Henry* got over £8,000, after paying the King's tenth.[6] If it had been shared equally between the seventy men in the two ships it would have come to nearly £120 per man, but it is probable that the ships' officers, the divers and the senior ratings, such as the carpenter and cooper, got considerably more. One source suggests that Rogers and Covill got £1,000 each, which seems only reasonable, since their loyalty had been so abundantly proved. The ordinary seamen probably got about fifty pounds each, a small share of the total treasure, but a very pleasant bonus in an age when the annual earnings of seamen were estimated at only twenty pounds. How much more the men in the two ships managed to hide away we do not know, though it would have been a miracle if none of the silver and other treasure bought up had stuck to their hands. There was a suspicious £1,200 worth of silver which was 'overlooked' at the first weighing, and, over a year later, five of the officers of the *James and Mary*, including John Strong, the first mate, and William Covill, were taken into custody after information had been laid against them for 'being concerned in defrauding His Majesty of about 1000 [pounds] weight of silver which was runn privately on shoar out of the *James and Mary*'. Mr Hawthorn, a tide-waiter in the London customs, was examined at the same time, which may suggest the method of the running, but nothing was proved against them, and they were soon discharged. There was also talk of a gold hat-band and a yard-long chain of gold which were seen adorning the person of Captain William Phips, but nothing more was said of this. Phips was too much of a national hero for anybody to bother about such trifles.[7]

On 14 June 1687 the Warden and other officials of the Mint were ordered to make their way down river to Deptford to weigh the treasure and remove the King's tenth. They set up their great beam on the *Rising Sun*, and the sailors hoisted the silver out of the hold and swung it across to the King's ship where every item was carefully weighed. It came to a grand total of 68,511 pounds troy and seven ounces.[8] The silver was generally reckoned to be worth five shillings per ounce, despite the fact that 'by reason of the wetnesse and rusting thereof the same is subject to considerable wast',[9] and so was valued in all at £205,536. Then there was the small parcel of gold which weighed 25 pounds, 7 ounces and 15 penny-weight, a few pieces of jewellery and some precious stones which were considered to be of 'very inconsiderable' value and one copper and six bronze guns, whose value was not determined and which were sent to the Tower where they were discovered to be still in working order.[10] Altogether, the treasure was probably worth about £210,000, rather less than the quarter of a million pounds which was being bandied around by popular opinion, but a very large treasure for all that.

It is almost impossible to translate seventeenth-century values into modern terms. Simply to say that the bullion value of the silver salvaged by Phips would be £2,367,740 at the time of writing does not help very much, since silver bullion prices have only risen by a multiple of less than twelve since 1687, whilst the wages of a labourer, for instance, have risen by a multiple of over three hundred. Perhaps the easiest way to demonstrate why Englishmen were so excited by Phips's success is to compare it with other notable windfalls of the day. The obvious point of comparison is the treasure seized by the buccaneers. Phips's treasure was worth more than twice the loot shared out by Henry Morgan after the most sensational exploit of the buccaneers, the sack of Panama. And Morgan had to share his loot with fifteen hundred men. Indeed Phips brought home almost as much treasure as Morgan shared on his three most famous and successful raids – Porto Bello, Maracaibo and Panama – and he did this without the loss of a single man at a cost of £3,200.[11] No wonder contemporaries were excited. Here was a cheaper and easier, less dangerous and less vulgar way of taking Spanish money.

Once the treasure had been weighed the division could begin. King James was pleased with his windfall gain, although he must have kicked himself for turning down the chance to finance the whole expedition. His total royalty was £20,872,[12] a nice present for any seventeenth-century King of England, less than one per cent of his total revenue, but still enough to pay his growing army for a few days. The King was grateful to the provider of this bounty. Phips was invited to Windsor to tell his story for himself, and on 28 June was knighted for his loyal additions to the royal exchequer and his important contribution to the ailing English money supply. William Phips, ex-shepherd-boy and ex-ship's carpenter, was now Sir William. He had arrived, and nothing would ever stop him again. 'He had the offers of a very gainful place among the Commissioners of the Navy, with many other invitations to settle himself in England, [but] nothing but a return to New-England would content him.'[13] Phips's desire to go home was respected, and on 4 August he was granted the post of Provost-Marshal of New England, just one step away from the summit of his astonishing career, the governorship of Massachusetts.

Phips's financial reward was more modest. His biographer said that
'he had less than sixteen thousand pounds left unto himself'.[14] But in fact
Phips's share was considerably less than this. He received exactly what he
had contracted to receive, one-sixteenth of the treasure after the deduction of the King's tenth, which worked out at just over £11,000.[15] In addition, as an acknowledgement of his honesty, the Duke of Albemarle
'made unto his wife, whom he never saw, a present of a golden cup, near
a thousand pound in value'. This may seem a poor return for the man
who, after several years' effort, had located and recovered a treasure
worth over £200,000, but Phips was a man who sought honour just as
much as money, and there is little reason to doubt that he was satisfied
with this reward for following his dream. The man who could return to
Boston, after three years' absence, as a knight and provost-marshal was in
a strong position to strut a bit and humiliate his former enemies. And
£11,000 was a lot of money in New England, quite sufficient to buy that
'fair brick-house in the Green-Lane of North-Boston' which he had
promised to his sceptical but loving wife so many years before, quite sufficient to provide a decent income to support his new status for the rest of
his days.

When the King and Phips and the seamen had been paid off, the rest of
the silver was divided into eight piles to be distributed to the adventurers. Each pile contained 6,901 lbs 7 oz,[16] worth £20,703 15s 0d, an attractive return on an investment of £400. No one had ever made such a
profit on an investment before, and, as some small expression of their
gratitude to the men who had laboured for them, the adventurers gave a
great dinner at the Swan Tavern in London, 'where they gave the Captain a gold medal and chain, and to every sailor silver ones; the medals
have the King and Queen's picture'.[17] On the reverse the medals were
engraved with a picture of the *James and Mary* riding at anchor with, in
the foreground, three sailors in a small boat fishing on a wreck with a
rake. We must hope that the sailors were pleased with this memento of
their sensational achievement.

Not everyone shared the general euphoria at the success of Sir William Phips. The most persistent complaints of England's new wealth
came from a predictable source, from Don Pedro Ronquillo, the Spanish
ambassador, who was of the opinion 'that his master might let his
money lie as long at the bottom of the sea as he pleased'.[18] He first heard the
news that an English ship had arrived from America with a great amount of
silver from a sunken Spanish galleon on 9 June, three days after Captain

Phips's arrival in the Downs. He immediately sent a memorial to King James claiming the silver and cannon for the King of Spain, and he was supported by the Spanish Agent who requested the High Court of Admiralty to sequester the treasure.[19] On 13 June he wrote to his master and to the Council of the Indies to tell them the news.[20] Ronquillo was well informed about wrecks and the problems of salvage, and was very impressed by Phips's achievement in discovering a ship, 'which sank more than forty years before in the high seas, seventeen leagues distance from land'. If there had not been 'such a visible demonstration of the truth', the story 'would, on all accounts, have been taken as ridiculous and as the hoax of this age'. However, admiration for Phips made no difference to the fact that the treasure belonged to Spain and not England, and Ronquillo's main aim in his letter was to impress upon the King the need to claim the silver, if only to prevent the English from getting any more. Ronquillo emphasized that probably only about one-third of the silver in the wreck had yet been salvaged and suggested that the total contents of the galleon were at least four million pesos (£1,000,000).

The ambassador urged his master to take prompt and positive action, reminding him that he had already thrown away one chance of discovering the wreck by turning down Sir Richard White's proposal of 1684. Nor was this the only opportunity lost.

Later I sent a proposal from another man to salvage artillery and merchandise from lost ships and, at the end of many months, you replied that it was not possible to undertake anything of this nature. . . . This is not the first opportunity that we have lost, as a result of disregarding information and advice, and refusing to accept that . . . the times and people have changed. . . . In this case, our carelessness has made us a laughing-stock, which cuts me to the heart. On other occasions, we have lost islands and riches to our enemies, particularly in America. They have risked little or nothing to gain a great deal, as they have the opportunity to act upon proposals.[21]

This forceful condemnation of the Spanish system of bureaucracy and the philosophy of *mañana* was to have little effect. Spanish officials identified the wreck as the *Concepción* on receipt of Ronquillo's letter and a file was prepared, demonstrating the more or less continuous attempts made by Spain to locate the wreck, evidence which could be used to persuade the English that the treasure had never been abandoned and so still belonged to its original owners.[22] Ronquillo was instructed to continue to press the Spanish claim in England, but not to press too hard. He must realize the importance of 'maintaining our rights without forcing them in a manner which could become damaging'.[23] This last comment brings home the dangerous situation in Europe in 1687 when the entire Spanish Empire was threatened by the bellicose ambitions of an over-mighty France. Spain dared not antagonize England by pressing too hard for the treasure.

In any case it must have been obvious to Ronquillo that he was wasting his time. No one in England was going to give up such a treasure now. Ronquillo's memorial was simply ignored by King James, and the request for the treasure to be sequestered was refused. The Tuscan envoy, Francesco Terriesi, reported the activities of the Spanish ambassador and pointed out that 'there is no doubt that the Spanish ministers do not expect to succeed in their enterprise'.[24] Protests have to be made, and Ronquillo was still protesting in December, but the Spaniards never received a penny from the wreck of the *Concepción*.

The Spaniards might have no hope of acquiring any of the treasure already found, but there was nothing to stop the King of Spain sending out an expedition to compete for the salvage of what remained in the wreck. There was no shortage of treasure-hunters who were prepared to seek commissions to fit out such an expedition. However, the first petition to reach the King of Spain came from a man who seemed to know nothing about Phips's success, despite the fact that it was dated two months after the much trumpeted arrival of the *James and Mary* in the Downs.[25] The petitioner was Captain Gaspar Romero Maldonado, an old man who had been a passenger in the *Concepción* in 1641 and now, forty-six years later, was seeking to locate the wreck. He gives no reason why he had waited so long to do so, and, since his name does not actually appear in the list of survivors from the wreck, it is probably wise to treat his petition with some suspicion.[26] Maldonado emphasized his unique qualifications for the task in that he had been on the ship himself. Other Spaniards who had hunted for the *Concepción* only 'had half the [necessary] information and did not have the detailed inside knowledge which I have given in my memorial'. All of which was standard stuff for such a petition. The big joke comes on the fifth page of Maldonado's petition in a passage which must have brought a smile to the faces of the officials who read it. 'It is certain that all the silver and artillery brought in the said ship is still there, as it would not be easy for anyone to ascertain its position who had not been on it.' At the end of the petition there is a postcript in another hand which says that the petitioner had just received word of the arrival in England of the successful expedition. However, Maldonado still remained sceptical and 'could only be persuaded that the news was correct . . . if another ship had been lost in the Abrojos in the same place'. The ship could only have been found by luck, not 'by the practical experience which this petitioner possesses'.

The King of Spain was soon to have some other petitions to consider. On 25 July Don Pedro Ronquillo sent a letter from Windsor, in which he outlined proposals from two subjects of the King of England who wished to work for Spain.[27] The first was from a well-known treasure-hunter and inventor of diving equipment, John Poyntz, who asked for a general commission to search for sunken galleons. He had instructed Ronquillo 'to inform His Majesty that if he would like, and with the permission of God, I will attempt to recover these lost riches if they can be found in up to twenty fathoms of water'. He asked for one-third of the goods recovered and hoped to salvage a million pesos' worth of treasure in a short time. The reader may well be able to guess by now who was the author of the second proposal. Yes, it was Don Ricardo de Vite, better known to us as Sir Richard White. White told Ronquillo that he knew of many other ships full of precious cargo which had been lost. He also knew where a great quantity of silver belonging to the *Concepción* was located. This information was not known to Captain Phips. White once again asked the King for 12,000 *escudos* and said that he would give the Crown one-fifth of whatever he found. He never gave up. However, despite pressure from Ronquillo, all these proposals were turned down, and there were no treasure-hunting expeditions sent out that year under the commission of the King of Spain.

Sir Richard White was determined to get something out of the treasure from the *Concepción* and this same letter from Ronquillo contains an account of an extraordinary accusation which White made against Phips.[28] Ronquillo reported that White had presented two witnesses to King James II who 'claimed that Captain Phips had told them upon his return that he had found the place where the silver was located because Sir Richard, who had been in Jamaica for four years, had written a letter which contained the secret [of the location] for Phips to take to London and deliver to his brothers, in the event that he [White] died during the voyage. Imagining what this letter would contain, Phips opened it and took advantage of the secret, although he tried to deny it later.' One would certainly have expected Phips to have done this if there had ever been such a letter. But this is surely just another of Sir Richard White's little tricks. There is no evidence that he really knew where the wreck was. If he had known, it seems extremely unlikely that he would have trusted Phips with a letter describing its location. The obvious way to communicate with his brothers would have been to send the letter in the normal way on a merchant ship, not to entrust it to a potential competitor who in any case was not travelling direct to England. However, nonsense as it may seem to us, Sir Richard's story impressed King James II. Ronquillo reported that the King was so shocked that he wanted to give White his own tenth. This is difficult to believe, but it is interesting to note that, on 9 September 1687, the King ordered the officials of the Treasury to pay out '£1,000 to Sir Richard White bart., as royal bounty, without account . . . to be issued out of moneys (now in the Exchequer) of the wreck which was taken out of the sea near Hispaniola'.[29] No reason is given for the King's bounty, but it looks as though Sir Richard did receive some reward for the five years that he had spent intriguing in Spain, England and the West Indies to make a little profit out of the wreck of the *Concepción*.

Don Pedro Ronquillo's complaints were made simply because he would have looked a fool not to make such complaints. Sir Richard White complained because he never missed a chance to make some money. But another man had a real cause for feeling bitter at the events which followed the arrival of the *James and Mary* back in England. This was John Smith, the merchant who had been the former owner of the *Henry* and had been accepted into the Duke of Albemarle's adventure for a one-eighth share. Late in October 1686, about six weeks after the *James and Mary* had set sail for the West Indies, Smith had gone to Flanders on business, having first made up his accounts with the other partners. He was still in Flanders when the *James and Mary* returned and his wife had gone on the ship at Deptford to request that Smith's eighth 'be preserved and care taken thereof'.[30] We do not know how she was treated by the other partners but, as we have seen, the treasure was divided into eight parts, after the King's and Phips's share had been deducted, so she must have expected her husband to receive his one-eighth share as soon as he returned from Flanders. But when Smith arrived in England five days later, he discovered that his share had been deposited with a London goldsmith and the other partners 'doe now deny him to have any share or interest therein and pretend a right among themselves to the said whole treasure . . . notwithstanding the aforesaid agreements of all the said partyes, all along whyle the said designe was only hazardous, that they should all be gayners or losers thereby'. In other words Smith was to get nothing.

Smith was dumbfounded by this apparently dirty trick and, after a few weeks of fruitless argument, he petitioned the Privy Council who referred his case to the Court of Chancery.[31] The proceedings in John Smith *v.* the Duke of Albemarle *et al.* have proved a very valuable source for the business side of this book. The procedure in Chancery was for the plaintiff or complainant to submit a written Bill of Complaint in which he set out in detail the nature of his grievance and asked the court for relief. The defendants then submitted answers demonstrating their complete innocence and the deceit of the complainant. In this case we have Smith's Bill of Complaint and the separate answers of the Duke of Albemarle, Sir John Narborough and Sir William Phips.

In his answer to Smith's complaint the Duke claimed that when Smith made up his accounts in October there were several discrepancies and that the merchant had not paid up his share of the cost of fitting out the expedition. When Smith was 'pressed to produce his vouchers and to adjust his accounts he pretended businesse into Flanders for three weeks or a month and went thither'. In the early months of 1687 several letters were sent to Smith in Flanders, but he still did not pay his share or justify his accounts. Finally, on 6 May 1687, another letter was 'sent and safely conveyed to the Complainant, whereby he was againe admonished and required forthwith to justify his said account or pay the balance thereof within fifteene days ... or else he should be excluded from the said partnership'. Smith did not do so and for this reason he had been cut out, since it was a condition of his sharing any treasure that might be forthcoming that he 'should beare, pay and discharge his one-eighth ... which the Complainant did not doe'.

Smith's view of the matter was obviously very different. His share had been fully paid up and there were no discrepancies in his accounts. The accounts had been cleared with the auditor, Mr Monteage, in October, and there were no objections, nor did Monteage send the particulars of his objections in the New Year. Smith claimed that there had been a deliberate plot to defraud him. When the letters which Phips had sent via Jamaica announcing his success arrived in London, the other adventurers had intercepted the letter addressed to Smith. They decided to cut Smith out. 'To that purpose and designe Mr Monteage upon examining your Orator's accounts framed an account as if your Orator was £922 in debt to them upon account of his share of the money to be advanced and errors pretended to be in his accounts.' The letter sent to Smith in Flanders on 6 May was 'an artfull contrivance', since the other partners knew that he would never accept that he was £922 in debt to the partnership and so they would be able to use the letter as grounds for excluding him from his rights. Now they were endeavouring to bring him 'to accept of some meane and low composition'.

Bills and answers in the Court of Chancery were deliberately phrased in a way which exaggerated the truths and falsehoods of the real situation which they purported to describe, and there is no way that we, nearly three hundred years later, can be sure of what really happened. Nevertheless, it does look as though Smith was the victim of a very nasty piece of sharp practice by his aristocratic and well-connected partners. John Smith, merchant, was very much the odd man out in this company. What the court would have made of Smith's complaint we do not know, for he never put it to the test. However good his case, and it was by no means beyond dispute, Smith knew as well as any other merchant that justice is expensive and always uncertain, especially in the Court of Chancery. He was therefore prepared to listen to the arguments of Francis Nicholson, who pointed out that 'he had great persons to contend with and . . . they had six to one and had the money in their hands and that the law was chargeable and he might be kept out twice seaven years'.[32] Smith could see the truth of this and agreed to settle out of court. There is no record of how much he received, but it seems probable that he got about £13,000, which is the difference between what was left over after Phips had been paid and what was shared between the remaining six partners. If this is correct, Smith's compensation was hardly 'meane and low', but it was of course considerably less than the share of the other partners who now got one-seventh of what was left. Smith was also cut out of any further share of the treasure that was left in the wreck.

Since this whole business of the division of the silver is rather complicated, it may help the reader if the result of these calculations is presented in tabular form.

DIVISION OF THE SILVER

	Weight to nearest pound troy		Value at £3 per pound troy
Total[1]		68,512	£205,536
The King's tenth[1]	6,851		20,553
The sailors' share[1]	2,763		8,289
Remainder		58,898	
Captain Phips's $\frac{1}{16}$	3,681		11,043
Remainder[2]		55,217	
Smith's compensation	?4,429		13,287
Remainder		50,788	
Duke of Albemarle[3] $\frac{2}{7}$	14,512		43,534
Sir John Narborough $\frac{1}{7}$	7,255		21,766
Viscount Falkland $\frac{1}{7}$	7,255		21,766
Sir James Hayes $\frac{1}{7}$	7,255		21,766
Isaac Foxcroft $\frac{1}{7}$	7,255		21,766
Francis Nicholson $\frac{1}{7}$	7,255		21,766
			£205,536

Source:

[1] For total, King's tenth and sailors' share see T 52/12 p.345.

[2] For remainder after Captain Phips's share see C.10/227/63. The Duke of Albemarle's Answer. 'His Majesty's officers haveing taken his Majesty's tenth of the silver . . . and the said Sir William Phips' parte being delivered to or set out for him . . . and the share which the officers claimed being delivered . . . this Defendant sayth that . . . an eighth parte of the sayd silver did then amount to 6,901 lbs 7 oz', i.e. 55,212 lbs 8 oz in all, a slight discrepancy with my figure.

[3] For Albemarle's share see the declaration of his accountant in C.24/1177/30.

The other figures are calculated on the basis of the existing data and the adventurers' contract.

The five one-seventh adventurers thus got £21,766 each, a return of about forty-seven-fold on their investment. Invested in land, at the normal rate of twenty years' purchase, this would have produced an income of over £1,000 per year, enough to live a very comfortable and leisured life in the late seventeenth century, the income of a very rich country gentleman or a rather poor lord. The Duke of Albemarle's dividend of £43,534 was simply enormous by contemporary standards, sufficient to pay even his vast debts and still leave something over for a good time in the future. People assumed that he would now forget his former intention of going to Jamaica to serve as Governor, but they were wrong. The Duke was determined to use his new-found wealth as the basis of even greater things.

The adventurers tried to squeeze a little more out of their treasure by melting it down in their back gardens, it being believed 'that the former proprietors might mix their gold and silver to defraud the King of Spain of his customs'.[33] There is, however, no evidence as to whether this belief proved true. But the fact that there were no further visits from the officers of the Mint to collect extra tenths for the King suggests that it was not.

The six partners might now be very rich men, but they had by no means had enough. Sir William Phips would have agreed with the estimate of the Spanish ambassador that he had only salvaged about one-third of the treasure, if that, and no sooner had he arrived in England than arrangements were started to organize a second voyage. On 14 June the King received the adventurers at Windsor Castle and an agreement was drawn up, 'concerning the further search for plate, bullion and other treasure castaway on the north coast of Hispaniola'. The King agreed to provide a frigate for the protection of the salvage team from the numerous predators who might be expected to want to grab some of the treasure for themselves. The adventurers were to be responsible for the men's pay and victuals. The King also agreed to 'hinder, as much as by law he may, any of his other subjects' searching for treasure in the same place. In return for this increased assistance, the King expected a larger share of the treasure. He was to receive one-fifth of all that was found up to the value of £150,000, 'and for what soever they shall find above £150,000 the King shall have a cleare third part'.[34] The Spanish ambassador naturally opposed this fresh example of English perfidy. 'His Majesty cannot give patents for fishing up things that belong to the Spaniards.' King James excused himself by saying that the patent granted to Albemarle was a general one for fishing up lost goods and did not specify any particular wreck.[35] Meanwhile, the adventurers set to work to get ships ready to return to the North Riff.

It can be imagined that the partners were now besieged by applications from people anxious to buy their way into the syndicate, but of course they had no need for fresh capital. It therefore comes as rather a surprise to learn that three-quarters of Smith's former share, in other words $\frac{3}{32}$ of the total equity, was sold in October to Thomas Neale, the Duke of

Albemarle adding the other $\frac{1}{32}$ to his existing quarter share.*[36] No reason was given for this apparently generous move, and we do not know what price Neale had to pay. However, two good reasons can be suggested. Thomas Neale was Master of the Mint, a rather useful officer to have as a member of a treasure syndicate. He was also the most famous of all projectors in an age famous for projecting, and there was no telling what other fabulous adventures he might introduce to his new partners in return for their favour.

With so much money behind them, and with the prospect of a certain treasure before them, the adventurers were able to organize this second expedition on a far more lavish scale. Altogether, there were to be five ships in the wreck squadron. The frigate promised by the King was the *Foresight*, and the command was given to Sir John Narborough himself who was at last to get the chance to see the wreck which he had sought and dreamed about for thirty years. Sir John repaid the compliment by inviting Edward Stanley to be his first lieutenant. One wonders what *his* thoughts had been when he heard of Phips's success. It was certainly kind of Narborough to give him this opportunity to go and see for himself where the wreck really was. Then there was the strangely named *Good Luck and a Boy*, a 400-ton merchantman which was to be commanded by Sir William Phips. The *James and Mary* and the *Henry* were also refitted for this second voyage and finally there was a ship called the *Princess* to be commanded by Francis Rogers. Diving equipment, boats and divers were provided on a similar generous scale. The total cost was estimated at £16,000, five times the cost of the first expedition.[37]

It was arranged that the wreck squadron should sail with the Duke of Albemarle, who was at last going to Jamaica to take up his position as Governor. Everything was ready by the middle of July, which was extremely good going. On 18 July the Tuscan envoy reported that the Duke of Albemarle had paid his debts 'and purified his estate and was preparing to leave in a few days, having taken leave of his friends in the last week at a very sumptuous banquet'.[38] The Duke's manner of leave-taking had a predictable effect on a man suffering from jaundice, and he fell dangerously ill. The departure of the wreck squadron was postponed. It was not till 3 September that Narborough and Phips eventually set sail from the Downs, and it was over a month later when the Duke

* The equity was thus shared as follows: the Duke of Albemarle $\frac{9}{32}$; Sir John Narborough $\frac{4}{32}$; Viscount Falkland $\frac{4}{32}$; Sir James Hayes $\frac{4}{32}$; Francis Nicholson $\frac{4}{32}$; Isaac Foxcroft $\frac{4}{32}$; Thomas Neale $\frac{3}{32}$

and Duchess of Albemarle, after continuous delays, sailed from Plymouth in the *Assistance*.[39]

It was soon apparent that this six-week delay in the departure of Sir John Narborough's wreck squadron might have serious consequences for the success of the venture. Early in July rumours reached London that unlicensed ships from the colonies were fishing on Phips's wreck. Nothing could have seemed more likely. Within days of the first news of the success of the expedition reaching London, there had been reports of ships being fitted out in England, France, Holland and Spain to engage in the same activity. It was only too obvious that colonial ships would get there first. A man called William Constable had the bright idea of cashing in legally on this bonanza. He petitioned the King for a patent to collect the tenths from 'divers of His Majesty's subjects being in all probability imploying themselves on the galleon lately discovered . . . desiring only the tenths of such tenths for his troubles, pains and charges in the said undertaking.'[40]

The King reacted favourably to Constable's petition. He was always interested in collecting his due rights. But was he entitled only to one-tenth of treasure salvaged from 'wrecks of the sea'? He had only received one-tenth from the Duke of Albemarle and his partners, but that had been the result of a special agreement. It is perhaps not all that surprising that there should have been some confusion about the rate of the King's royalty on wrecks, since the total receipts from this branch of the King's prerogative in the twenty-seven years since 1660 had been thirteen shillings and sevenpence collected in 1662.[41] The King had received absolutely nothing from the long line of wreckers who had been working in the Bahamas and Bermuda.

King James referred the matter to the judges of the Admiralty Court, and on 11 July they gave him the answer that he sought. The King's right to things taken up from the bottom of the sea was not a tenth but a half, 'and the variation of proportions from this at any time hath proceeded from Grace and Pleasure'.[42] The King was delighted and, on 23 July, gave William Constable a warrant 'to repair to the place where the said treasure was lately taken up and demand . . . one moiety or half part of all gold etc. recovered by any of the King's subjects, other than the Duke of Albemarle or his partners.' Colonial governors were to give him every assistance.[43]

Constable had no trouble in raising the money to fit out his expedition. Now was the chance for those moneyed men in London who had been unable to share in the Duke of Albemarle's good fortune to invest in this new way of acquiring some of the treasure from the *Concepción*. On 2 August a joint-stock company, with thirty-two shares and a capital of £6,400, was established 'to support the charges and expences of the Hon. William Constable esq.' Dealing in these shares seems to have been brisk and they were soon selling above par. Later, the capital was doubled and the investors also became involved in a different but closely related business, 'an adventure with the Lord Mordaunt and partners for the taking up of wreckt silver in America'.[44]

The appearance of Charles, Viscount Mordaunt, in the story is a sharp reminder that we are now talking about the years 1687 and 1688, the years which saw King James II so alienate his subjects that they were to make virtually no attempt to prevent his nephew, William of Orange, from invading England in November 1688 and driving the legitimate king from his throne. Lord Mordaunt had opposed James II ever since he became king in 1685, and he was said to have been the first to press the Prince of Orange 'to undertake the business of England'.[45] Now, late in 1687, he had obtained a patent from the Prince of Orange to fit out a well-armed expedition in Holland to get what he could from the wreck of the *Concepción*. When the official English wreck squadron set out on 3 September, it must have seemed as though they were likely to have some company on the North Riff. It also must have seemed quite possible that they would require rather more naval protection than a single frigate.

CHAPTER SIXTEEN

Unhappy Return

Sir John Narborough must have been a frustrated man when the frigate *Foresight* dropped anchor before the town of Funchal in Madeira on 13 October 1687. It was imperative to reach the Ambrosian Bank as quickly as possible, before the *Concepción* was picked clean by unlicensed wreckers from the colonies, but everything seemed to conspire to delay his passage. It had been bad enough to lose six weeks as a result of the Duke of Albemarle's over-indulgence at his sumptuous farewell party. But that had only been the start of his troubles. Contrary winds and bad weather had made his voyage from England so slow that he had been forced to make this unscheduled call at Madeira to take on fresh provisions and water. And he had lost two ships from his wreck squadron on the way. The *Good Luck and a Boy* had lost the head of her foremast in a storm, and Captain Phips had taken her back to Plymouth to refit. Sir John could only hope that the work would be done quickly, since Phips had all the diving equipment on board, as well as four months' provisions for the squadron. A few days later the *Foresight* had lost touch with the *James and Mary*, a hundred miles off Cape Finisterre. Would Captain Strong have the good sense to make his way to the rendezvous at Barbados? Sir John must have been a gloomy host to the English merchants of Madeira whom he invited aboard to celebrate the King's birthday on his second day at the island.[1] But perhaps things would look a little better when he sailed into tropical waters.

Sir John reached Barbados on 16 November and was happy to find the *James and Mary* anchored in the harbour. But there was to be further delay, for he had promised the Duke of Albemarle to wait some days in the island 'in hopes of kissing your Grace's hand'. This meant waiting nine days, a period which was enlivened by shipping aboard '600 odd gallons of rum to be served to our ship company in lew of brandy'. So began a famous naval custom, for a few months later the Admiralty ordered that rum should be issued instead of brandy on all ships in the Jamaica service. Captains were instructed to take care 'that the good or

ill effects of this proofe, with respect as well to ye good husbandry thereof, as the health and satisfaction of our seamen, be carefully enquired
into'.² Let us hope that Sir John enjoyed his rum for he was to receive bad
news in Barbados. On 29 November he wrote to Sir James Hayes in
London. 'I heare that severall vessells are at worke on ye wreck and have
taken up all the upper silver to a considerable value, soe that what is to be
got is with great labour.'³

The arrival of the Duke of Albemarle at Barbados was well worth
waiting for. No one of his rank had ever come out to the islands as
Governor before, and he got a splendid reception as he sailed into Carlisle Bay in the frigate *Assistance*, with his very own yacht following in
her wake. Captain Stanley described the Duke's disembarkation in his
log-book. 'About 11 this forenoone ye Duke and Dutchess of Albamarl
[sic] went on shoar. Wee saluted him with 15 guns. All ye merchantmen
in ye roade saluted him. At his landing all ye forts fired. Hee was
received by all ye gentlemen belonging to ye island and a regiment of
horse and another of foot, ye streets being covered with green baize from
ye landing place to the Governors House.'⁴

His duty done, Sir John could now leave the Duke to make a stately
progress to Jamaica, calling at all the other English colonies on the way,
while he set sail for Samaná Bay in Hispaniola, where he anchored on
5 December. Two days later, Sir William Phips arrived from England,
and the wreck squadron was at last complete. But this happy reunion was
spoiled by a visual confirmation of the bad news they had received in
Barbados. For, also in Samaná Bay, were several sloops which had been
working on the wreck and were now filling up with water, wood and
provisions prior to returning to the North Riff to bring up some more of
the treasure. The master of one of the sloops told Captain Stanley that
'they left 25 saile at ye wreck'. He was soon to discover that this was no
exaggeration.

On 15 December Lieutenant John Hubbard of the *Foresight* got his
first sight of the Ambrosian Bank. 'At noone saw the ships and sloops
riding at the wreck.... At 3 anchored.... Saw the boats at the wreck
plaine. They bore of us N by E 4 miles off.' It was an amazing sight.
Those dangerous waters which had so long been shunned by the seamen
of all nations were now simply swarming with ships from almost every
one of the English colonies in North America and the West Indies. The
wreckers were quick to realize what the presence of a royal ship meant.
Those who had already made a good haul quickly weighed anchor and

sailed away before a boarding-party should come to search them. Only those who had arrived late and 'had noe money' remained behind to salute the *Foresight* and see what the future might bring.

According to Stanley, there were altogether eight ships and twenty-four brigantines, sloops and shallops anchored in the clear water to the south of the reef, one small shallop anchored directly over the *Concepción*, working the wreck with a diving-tub, and about twenty boats and canoes full of divers also working on the wreck. And this was just the number of vessels that were actually at the wreck site when Sir John Narborough arrived. There had been a Dutch pink anchored off Mona Island, 'intending for the wreck' and five sloops from the wreck in Samaná Bay. No doubt there were others in Puerto Plata. At least nine ships had returned to Jamaica and another nine to Bermuda before the arrival of the *Foresight*.[5] And of course there were still ships on their way from the remoter colonies, where the news had taken longer to arrive. It seemed as though all the men and all the ships in the English colonies were either on the Ambrosian Bank or on their way there. The Governor of Bermuda was seriously worried by the danger of an invasion while there were so few men on the island, and Nevis could only raise a guard of honour of boys to greet the Duke of Albemarle on his arrival. All the men had gone to the wreck.[6]

Captain Phips's attempt to preserve the secret of the wreck's location had been a total failure. Sir John Narborough said that it was 'the Burmudoes men which Sir William Phips left behinde him [who] discovered ye wreck into all these parts'.[7] Cotton Mather as usual tells the story in more detail. Captain Phips 'left so much behind him, that many from divers parts made very considerable voyages of gleanings after his harvest. Which came to pass by certain Bermudians compelling of Adderly's boy, whom they spirited away with them, to tell them the exact place where the wreck was to be found.'[8] Adderley and Davis seem to have returned to Bermuda on 23 June, and the news of the wreck was certainly known in Jamaica by 6 July, so this swarm of colonial fortune-hunters had been gleaning Phips's harvest for at least five months and possibly longer. No one has left a description of what happened during those months of unlimited private enterprise, but it must have been a fairly horrific scene, particularly under water. On some days there must have been well over a hundred Indian divers, working on shares, struggling to grab the biggest pieces of silver for themselves. Neither was it likely to have been a very friendly party on the anchored ships. There was no one in command, and most of the Jamaican sloops were manned by former buccaneers, while the Bermudans had a reputation as wreckers equalled only by the Cornish. The treasure of the *Concepción* would have been fiercely won.

When Sir John Narborough arrived, he ordered Captain Stanley and Lieutenant Hubbard to go in the *Foresight's* boats and take possession of the wreck. There was no trouble. Stanley searched the men working at the wreck, 'but found little money on board them'. He then 'put them off' and they returned to the anchored sloops and shallops. Stanley's own divers spent the rest of the day searching the wreck for themselves, but they could not find any treasure. Everything that could be easily salvaged had been taken already. Prospects for the adventurers from London did not look too good. Sir John hired some of the sloops and divers to help in the salvage work. The rest soon left the banks and returned to their homes with their treasure.

Colonial governors now had the difficult, if not impossible, task of collecting the King's royalty on the treasure recovered by the crews of the sloops. Hender Molesworth, the Lieutenant-Governor of Jamaica, had issued a proclamation on 6 July permitting vessels to go to the wreck and return to the island with their treasure, on condition that they paid the King's dues, which he thought were a tenth. It was not until 17 November that he realized that the King had granted the Duke of Albemarle the sole right of fishing on the wreck, and not till the Duke himself arrived on 19 December that he was told that he should have collected a half and not a tenth. He later explained the reasons for his error to the Lords of the Treasury. 'No orders had been issued as to the matter in my time, so I collected these tenths by advice of the Council on the precedent of the King, who, we hear, took the tenths from Sir William Phips as Sir William did from the Bermuda man who was fishing at the wreck. Our law books know no better.'[9] Before the Duke arrived in Jamaica, Molesworth had collected from eleven sloop captains a total of 1,829 pounds troy of silver in pieces of eight and broken plate as the King's tenths and had pocketed a ten per cent commission for his efforts. Altogether, the Jamaica men actually declared treasure worth over £57,000.[10] But how much more had they concealed in Jamaica or in the Bahamas? How much more had they shipped to foreign colonies whose governors demanded no royalty? The Duke of Albemarle recognized the problem in a letter of 11 February 1688 when he asked the King to accept only a tenth on any new wrecks discovered. This would encourage 'the trade of wreck fishing, [and] may withal hinder the carrying to foreign parts what shall be so found upon new discoveries'.[11]

The Governor of Bermuda, Sir Robert Robinson, had made exactly the same errors as Hender Molesworth. He, too, had given permission for ships to sail to the wreck and he, too, had thought that the King's royalty was a tenth. On 21 October 1687, the King wrote to Robinson explaining his error. 'You will therefore take care to collect that half, not only from ships that return from the wreck at Hispaniola in future, but also from the two ships that are already come in.' These were the sloop and shallop belonging to Abraham Adderley and William Davis who had already paid their tenths on over £27,000 worth of silver. The King informed Robinson that he had 'appointed Henry Horzdesnell to be our Chief Judge in Bermuda, and you will give him all assistance, and send back our share of the treasure in H.M.S. *Swan* which we have appointed for the purpose. If you have any difficulty in enforcing our rights, you will give notice to Captain Frederick Frowde of the *Swan* and to the commander of our foot soldiers on board that ship.'[12]

The *Swan* anchored in Castle Harbour, Bermuda, on 15 January 1688 and Horzdesnell, Robinson and Frowde tried to carry out the King's orders. The job was not an easy one, and the fact that Horzdesnell suspected Governor Robinson of having taken a fair bit of the treasure for himself did not make it any easier. On 28 January Horzdesnell reported that they had seized twelve guns which had been raised from the wreck and had collected £5,555 on silver which had been brought in by the Bermudan wreckers. But nearly all of this was in tenths. Trying to get a man who had already paid a tenth to pay a half was virtually impossible. 'The money is dispersed by their expences and buying of necessaries for their wives and children all over the country and now, by way of trade, in the hands of those who were never concerned in the getting of itt.'[13] The three officials continued their examinations, but met either declarations of innocence or poverty or an insolent silence. Horzdesnell believed there to be 'a combination against His Majesty's profitt; itt being here a maxim that a man can never gett an estate by being honest'. On the last day of February a final grand effort was made by the King's officers. Arrangements were made for a search of every house occupied by a man who had been at the wreck. A party of thirty soldiers and sailors was landed from the *Swan* to do the job, while Captain Frowde rode on horseback 'from house to house to see good order'. Needless to say, such a well-advertised search produced practically no silver. Two months' hard work by Horzdesnell and Frowde resulted in the collection of only £600 more than had already been collected by Robinson before their arrival in Bermuda. They estimated that they had received in all only about one-fifth of the treasure owed to the King.[14]

Meanwhile what of William Constable, the man who had got a commission in London to collect the King's moiety? We do not have a full record of his movements, but he certainly spent a considerable time on the North Riff and his name appears fairly regularly in the correspondence of the colonial governors, as he or his agents sailed round the West Indies and the North Atlantic seaboard trying to collect the King's dues. No one seems to have trusted him very much. In August 1688 he accounted to the Treasury for the silver that he had collected in the West Indies, nearly 2,000 pounds weight in all, but most of this was treasure already collected by Molesworth in Jamaica which Constable took home on the orders of the Duke of Albemarle.[15] Constable's backers got a very poor return on their investment. He had arrived far too late to seize a moiety from the really successful wreckers, most of whom had already left the wreck-site before Sir John Narborough arrived, which gives a fairly good idea of what they thought of the official adventurers' chances of making a profitable voyage.

How much treasure did the sloop captains take out of the *Concepción*? Sir John Narborough thought that they had taken a quarter of a million pounds sterling, more than Phips had brought home on the first successful voyage.[16] This estimate was based on the wreckers' own gossip, and may well have been near the truth. The men from Jamaica and Bermuda actually declared a treasure of over £100,000, and smaller amounts were declared by men from New York, New England, Barbados and other islands in the West Indies. It does not seem at all unlikely that what was actually taken was twice what was declared. Men who came back from the wreck had to declare something, or life would have been rather uncomfortable at home, but one would hardly expect them to declare everything. A man could never get an estate by being honest.

If Sir John's estimate was right, it did not necessarily mean that his expedition would be a disaster. Maybe half a million pounds sterling had been taken out of the wreck, but that was still only half the treasure, if the Spanish ambassador had been right, and there had really been four million pesos (£1 million) shipped at Vera Cruz in 1641. Of course, it was very annoying to lose so much treasure to the small fry of the islands, but there was still a job to be done. Sir John Narborough's wreck squadron settled down to do it.

Sir John had no shortage of hands for the work. There were nearly four hundred men on the five ships of his squadron, and, in addition, he was employing about two hundred divers, some brought out from England and some hired from the sloops.[17] The divers were encouraged to work hard by being offered a quarter of everything that they brought up. They were not to get very rich. For the first few weeks work was concentrated on the forepart of the wreck. It was from here that all the treasure so far raised had been taken, and the work was laborious, boring and unprofitable. Day after day the divers hacked away with their pick-axes to clear the ship right down to her bottom, while the sailors in the boats above them hauled up not treasure, but planks and timber and tons and tons of ballast and pieces of coral. There was some silver scattered about in the wreckage or encased in the coral which was smashed on board the ships with hammers, but it was a good day when fifty pounds was raised, and 17 February was marked down in Lieutenant Hubbard's log-book as a red-letter day when they took up 275 pounds weight of silver. 'The best days worke since our being at the wrack.' Phips had often taken up ten times as much in a day on the first expedition. The men from Jamaica and Bermuda had done their work too thoroughly. After two months on the wreck, Sir John had raised only twelve hundred-weight of silver; after three months just over a ton. By now the divers had completely cleared the forepart of the wreck from the stem to the foot of the mainmast; most of the ballast and floor planks and timbers had been taken up, and the whole area had been thoroughly searched for scattered pieces of silver.

On 15 February Sir John received news that he must have been expecting. Lord Mordaunt's Dutch squadron was at anchor in Samaná Bay. There were three Dutch men-of-war, two of fifty guns and one of forty, a galleot hoy and an English merchantman. A ripple of excitement ran through the wreck squadron. There might not be much treasure, but it looked as though there would be a fight. Sir John sent word to the Duke of Albemarle in Jamaica and asked for the frigates *Falcon* and *Assistance* to be sent directly. 'I hope ye ships are on there way unto me or will be speedily dispatch'd . . . to secure ye wreck. Otherwise, it will be a loose-ing voyage to your Grace and ye gentlemen concerned.'[18] A week later, one of the Dutch ships was reported at anchor to the south and the *Fore-sight* cleared for action, 'not knowing his design'. On 22 February Lord Mordaunt in the 48-gun *North Holland* and the Dutch galleot hoy dropped anchor some distance from Sir John's squadron, and the ships watched each other suspiciously. Nothing happened for two days, and then Mordaunt sent his officers over to the *Foresight* to ask permission to view the wreck. Among them was a man very well known to Narborough and Stanley, Captain Harmon, the Dutchman who had led Stanley such a dance on the Handkercher Bank five years previously.

Relations were very friendly, and Narborough let Stanley take the Dutchmen across to the wreck in the pinnace, but the sea was so rough that they were unable to see anything below the water. The disappointed Dutchmen returned to their ship, and that was that. Five days later, Mordaunt returned to Samaná Bay, where the *Assistance* was already on patrol.[19] Later the Duke's yacht and the *Falcon* arrived at the North Riff from Jamaica, and the *Swan* from Bermuda, so that practically the entire English naval strength in the West Indies was guarding the wreck.[20] But there was no need of them. Mordaunt made no further move, although he was still reported to be in the vicinity of Hispaniola in early May. What had he been up to? It has been suggested that he wanted to sound Narborough as to his loyalty to King James II.[21] This is a reasonable hypothesis. Narborough would have been a great catch for William of Orange. However, our records show that Lord Mordaunt remained aboard the *North Holland* and never spoke to Sir John. Perhaps he was simply waiting to see whether Narborough raised sufficient treasure to be worth seizing. What he had got by the last week of February was certainly not worth an international incident.

Sir John Narborough quickly forgot the curious antics of Lord Mordaunt and got on with his work on the wreck. He had by no means lost heart. There might be nothing much left in the forepart of the *Concepción*, but there still remained the stern in its thick case of coral. They had still to uncover the poop with its great cabins full of who knew what marvellous treasure. And then there were the after plate rooms. Sir John's Spanish informants on the island of Hispaniola had said that most of the *Concepción*'s silver lay aft of her mainmast,[22] and he still felt that 'there is more treasure in ye wreck than what hath binn taken up'.[23]

The problem was to get at it. The stern was so overgrown with coral that the divers could not get down to it. Only in one place was there a break in the solid coral, a cave under the rocks into which the divers could swim underwater, but the cave was so dark and so encumbered with debris that they could find very little in there.[24] There was only one answer. The great weight of coral which had grown on to the stern of the *Concepción* would have to be removed. Sir John had sixty divers working below at a time, 'as many as cann work on ye after part'. Some of the coral rocks could be loosened with pick-axes and hauled up with the tackle of the ships' boats above. This early success encouraged the underwater salvage team. They could see three guns and then they came to part of the ship's cargo of indigo and beneath that found some scattered pieces of eight. 'Most here take it for a good signe to have stowed silver under ye indigo', wrote Sir John on 15 March.[25] But they were still just scratching at the great mass of rock. Soon there was no more that the Indian divers could move. It was going to take more than brute strength to break into the after treasure rooms. They tried everything. The long-boat was equipped with a spar forty feet long with an iron crow-bar attached to its end, but this was no more effective than the divers working with pick-axes below the water. They tried to break off the coral by fixing grapnels to the rock and hauling on the long-boat's tackle, but the strain was too great and the grapnels broke. There was only one answer. They would have to blow the coral up with explosives.

The technical problems of using explosives underwater in 1688 were simply enormous. Gunpowder was the only explosive available. Electricity had not been invented. Waterproof metal piping did not exist. Now was the chance for Sir William Phips to show that he really was a master of underwater salvage. He waited for a completely calm day, 9 April, to make his attempt.[26] The fuse was led down through forty feet of cane tubing to a waterproof chest packed with gunpowder. The divers placed the chest under the coral and quickly swam away, while Phips's gunner lit the fuse in the long-boat above. The flame raced down the cane tubing but, before it had got half-way to the chest, the heat split open the cane and water poured down, 'soe that ye powder in ye chest was damnafied'. They never tried again. God knows what would have happened to the long-boat crew and Sir William Phips himself if the explosion had worked.

The salvage team returned to their old methods of trying to break up the coral, but with no more success. On 20 April Lieutenant Hubbard reported despondently that 'our divers doe not take up a pound weight of silver a day'. Everyone was getting very depressed. The weather had been exceptionally bad ever since they had arrived on the reef, and conditions were very uncomfortable in the wreck squadron, especially when the men were reduced to half rations. All this could have been borne if they had been raising plenty of treasure. As it was, the crews were getting restless. No treasure; no fight with the Dutch; indeed the only exciting moment in the log-book of Captain Frowde, who spent some time at the wreck site in early April, was itself a reflection of the men's frustration and boredom. 'About 10 of ye clock my master and purser comeing a board in my boate from ye foresight, the purser in a quarell bitt off a great piece of his nose.'[27] By early May Sir John had to report to Lord Falkland that the divers were fed up too. 'Ye divers we carried out of England are most of them tired and cannot or will not hold ye worke . . . saying there is noe treasure remaining.'[28] Worse still, disease had struck the squadron. Men started dying on 1 May and on the 4th Captain Stanley reported that 'wee have a sickley shipp'.

However, Sir John was still unwilling to give up. There must be treasure in the stern, and it must be possible to break in and get it. Any little thing like the discovery of a single gold coin was sufficient to keep him going. He was also worried that what he left might be taken by others. 'Though we lye at great charge, I am unwilling to leave off till I have more reason to believe there is no more treasure of value. It would trouble me if treasure should be found by others after we leave it.'[29] Narborough's confidence was not shared by others. On 8 May Sir William Phips sailed for New England 'to entertain his lady with some accomplishment of his predictions',[30] and the last of the escorting warships left the wreck site. On 20 May three of the sloop captains came on board the *Foresight*, cleared their accounts and declared their intention of going home. 'What they had got was not worth their longer stay.'[31] The rest followed their example in the next few days. Now even Narborough had to admit that he was beaten. On 18 May, he had caught the fever that was raging through the *Foresight*, and on the 26th, now very sick, he admitted defeat in a letter to the Duke of Albemarle. 'We are findeing very little silver on ye wreck and have used all our endeavours to gitt up ye rocks abaft, but find them too strong for us.'[32] He had commissioned two sloop captains to take possession of the wreck in King James's name and intended to set sail for England that same day

Sir John never went home. His last conscious action was to order the divers to recover an anchor which had fouled on a piece of coral as the *Foresight* set sail. At three in the morning of 27 May 1688, he died. Stanley and Hubbard sent for all the surgeons of the fleet to ask if it would be possible to embalm him and bring his body home to England, but the surgeons declared that they had not got the proper ingredients for the job. So, at five in the afternoon, Captain Stanley took the admiral's corpse in the pinnace and rowed towards the reef, followed by all the sloops and boats in the fleet. As Stanley struck the pinnace's flag and lowered Sir John's body into the sea, the *Foresight* fired three volleys of musket shot and forty guns, at which signal all the other ships and boats honoured their dead admiral with a salute.[33] And so, Sir John, who had sought the treasure of the *Concepción* since he had been a boy of seventeen, was buried on her wreck site. The *Concepción* had made him a rich man but, on this last voyage, she had denied him even greater riches. He was forty-eight years old.

Captain Stanley took the *Foresight* home. On 14 July he met a small ship from London bound for Newfoundland whose master told him that 'there was a Prince of Wales borne and the Quene recovered againe from her lying in. To rejoyce at which we first fiered 21 guns and then 19.'[34] The news had not been greeted so loyally in London. The birth of a male and Catholic heir was to be that last straw that finally determined King James's Protestant subjects that their King must go. Ten days later, the *Foresight* was off the Gunfleet where a boat brought a letter from Narborough's father-in-law, asking Stanley to deliver 'that part of Sir John as we had presarved home'. As the relic was handed over, Stanley struck his colours 'and fiered 3 vollois of small shot and 48 guns'.[35]

On 2 August Foxcroft, Nicholson and the officers of the Mint came aboard in the Thames to receive the treasure. It weighed 3,213 lbs 10 oz, out of which a fifth was taken for the King.[36] This left the adventurers with silver worth just over £7,500, less than half the initial cost of the expedition. And they still had to pay over a year's wages to the crew of the *Foresight*. It had been a losing voyage.

CHAPTER SEVENTEEN

The Treasure-Hunters

If this had been a work of fiction, it would certainly have been appropriate to finish the book with the death of Sir John Narborough and his dramatic burial on the wreck-site. But life is not as simple as that. Sir John's letters, which survive to this day, were to form a legacy that was to inspire many other men to try to salvage what was left of the treasure of the *Concepción*. The first to try were his own partners, who organized a third expedition to test the truth of Sir John's report 'that great store of treasure might be recovered . . . if engines and proper instruments were sent.' Three ships were fitted out and set sail late in 1688 under the command of one William Robinson, who was to be the adventurers' agent during the voyage. No log-books survive for this last expedition, and all we know is that it was a complete failure.[1] After this, the official adventurers gave up, but there is no doubt that many other men sailed to the Silver Bank to try their luck. But there was no engine known to man in the late seventeenth century which was sufficiently powerful to remove the coral from the stern of the wreck, and so eventually the waters of the North Riff were again abandoned to the whales which bred there. The very site of the *Concepción* was forgotten, and what remained of the wreckage became an integral part of the reef, only to be rediscovered by a modern adventurer armed with the proper instruments of the twentieth century.

The adventurers lost over £19,000 on the second and third expeditions, a very big sum for the day, but not sufficient to make more than a small hole in the enormous dividends that they had received from the first successful voyage.[2] They remained very rich men. It may however please those who wish no good to capitalists and fortune-hunters to know that, for the most part, this wealth did not bring its possessors long life and happiness. Sir John Narborough enjoyed his new fortune for less than a year before his death on 27 May 1688. He was to be followed in the same year by the Duke of Albemarle, who, after a fairly disastrous career as a colonial governor, died in Jamaica on 16 October. His end, as described by his physician Hans Sloane, was typical of his life. He 'made merry on occasion of the newes of the Prince of Wales his birth, and was taken ill with his usuall jaundice, constipation etc. where all things were given which he usually took in such circumstances, without successe'. He was only thirty-five.[3]

Albemarle's death was to lead to an extremely protracted lawsuit, for his executors refused to pay the Duke's share of the costs of the third expedition on the grounds that he had never personally given his consent to it, and that his heirs could not be bound by the actions of the Earl of Bath, his agent in London. Was the Earl of Bath's signature to the agreement for the third expedition conditional on the Duke's approval? Would the Duke have approved if he had lived? Such delightfully tricky questions were to ensure that much of the treasure of the *Concepción* would end up in the hands of the lawyers, as hearings and rehearings in Chancery were interspersed with appeals to the House of Lords, and the case dragged on well into the eighteenth century, long after every one of the original adventurers was dead.[4]

Two of the remaining partners, Lord Falkland and his stepfather, Sir James Hayes, were to die before the very first hearing of the cause in June 1696. Falkland remained in favour after the Revolution of 1688 and was appointed a Commissioner of the Admiralty. However, his career was brought to an unfortunate end in February 1694, when he was severely reprimanded by the House of Commons and committed to the Tower for bribing Members of Parliament out of Admiralty funds. He was released from the Tower after only three days, but died a few weeks later, aged thirty-eight.[5] His stepfather died soon after. This left just two of the original adventurers, Isaac Foxcroft and Francis Nicholson, to carry on the legal battle in conjunction with the formidable widows of their dead partners.* Nicholson was to survive another ten years, but on his death, in July 1705, the Duke of Albemarle's executors claimed 'that upon the deaths of . . . the only surviveing co-partners . . . the said cause abated'.[6] In other words the widows would have to start the whole business all over again.

Early death, disgrace and expensive lawsuits might be the fate of the six men who had most profited from the treasure of the *Concepción*, a fate

* Rebecca, Dowager Viscountess Falkland (Falkland's widow); Rachell, Dowager Viscountess Falkland (Falkland's mother and Hayes's widow); Dame Elizabeth Shovell (Narborough's widow who was to marry his protégé Admiral Sir Cloudesley Shovell, who was himself to be drowned in a famous shipwreck in the Scilly Isles in 1707).

which many might consider to be the just reward of those who meddled with dead men's silver. But what was the fate of the man who had been most responsible for the success of the venture; what was the fate of Sir William Phips, 'whose noble mind, impell'd by angels, did those treasures find'?[7] At first sight, the rise of William Phips is like a fairy story, so incredible does his elevation seem in the status-ridden world of the late seventeenth century. He was knighted in 1687. In 1688 he returned to New England as Provost-Marshal, and two years later he was to command a successful expedition against the French in Nova Scotia. He returned to England in 1691 and was then appointed the first royal Governor of Massachusetts. What shepherd-boy or ship's carpenter had even dreamed of success like that? But Phips's governorship was not to be a happy one, and he was to die early in 1695, aged only forty-four.

Phips arrived in Boston in May 1692 to find his native land in the grip of mass hysteria. 'On my arrival, I found this province miserably harassed by a most horrible witchcraft or possession of devils, which had broke in upon several towns. Some scores of poor people were taken with preternatural torments; some were scalded with brimstone; some had pins stuck into their flesh; others were hurried into the fire and water, and some dragged out of their houses and carried over the tops of trees and hills for many miles together.'[8] Phips had arrived in the middle of the notorious affair of the Salem witches, best known of the witchcraft scares which periodically broke out in Europe and America in the seventeenth century. Many men and women had already been accused of being witches and had been found guilty at a preliminary hearing. It was the task of the new Governor to decide what should be done with them.

Phips was hardly well qualified to make such a decision. Indeed it would have taken a very remarkable man to have made the right decision in the summer of 1692, a time when nearly everyone in Massachusetts thought that those accused of being witches were really witches and deserved to die. By the 1690s many people in England no longer believed in the existence of witches. But in puritanical New England there were very few complete sceptics, and Sir William Phips was certainly not one of them. He believed that there were witches, and he knew that 'thou shalt not permit a witch to live'. But how does one know if a person is a witch? Phips did not know, and, on the advice of lawyers and divines, he handed over the trials of the accused witches to a special commission whose president was Judge William Stoughton, the Lieutenant-Governor. Phips then set off to fight the French and Indians who were invading the eastern parts of the colony. In his absence, twenty men and women were found guilty and hanged. Practically the only evidence brought against them was so-called 'spectral evidence', based on accusations made mainly by hysterical children that they had seen the spectres or spirits of the accused behaving in a witchlike way. No alibi, indeed no defence at all, was possible against such evidence. In the end the children were to go too far and accuse people whom even the most credulous could not believe were really witches. Amongst the accused was Phips's own wife, a fact which quickly brought him to his senses. 'I found that the devil had taken upon him the name and shape of several persons who were doubtless innocent', he wrote in October, 'for which cause I have now forbidden the committal of any more accused persons.'[9] No more witches were hanged, and the use of spectral evidence was banned. Since there was no other evidence, the sad affair came rapidly to an end.

Although nothing so dramatic was to occur during the rest of Phips's short governorship, it was soon seen that a successful treasure-hunter was not necessarily the best person to be a colonial governor. No doubt many of the complaints made against Phips were simply the product of jealousy or dislike of a bumptious upstart, but Phips certainly did not help himself. His bursts of bad temper were notorious, and he quickly added many new enemies to those who had disapproved of him for personal or political reasons on his first appointment. His enemies were soon intriguing for his recall, and in 1694 he was summoned to London to answer a number of charges of maladministration. Phips remained self-confident and sure of his innocence. When he arrived in London in January 1695 he petitioned the King for an early date to be fixed to try the false accusations made against him, but his sudden death on 18 February, probably from influenza, prevented his case being heard. So ended the strange career of Sir William Phips, the archetypal treasure-hunter, the archetypal self-made man. His example was long to be remembered.

What one man could do, others could try to emulate. From the moment that the *James and Mary* returned to England in June 1687 the country was to be gripped by a treasure-hunting fever which was only to die down after more than two decades of repeated and expensive failures. Never had there been so many seamen who knew the exact location of a sunken Spanish galleon. Never had there been so many projectors ready to persuade the seamen to repeat their stories to the rich and mighty. Never had there been so many gullible investors so eager to part with their money for a dream. Phips had just started the first stock-market boom in English history. The Crown was besieged by petitioners seeking exclusive rights to search for wrecks in any area not yet granted to someone else. Inventors rushed to secure patents for new methods of working underwater or raising shipwrecked goods. Scores of expeditions, some backed by massive accumulations of capital, scoured the bottom of the seas for Spanish silver. One or two old wrecks, long worked out by Spanish salvors, were actually found. But no one found much treasure. There was not to be a second William Phips.[10]

So many failures at last persuaded Englishmen that there was no future in searching for treasure beneath the sea, and they turned their attention to other ways of making money. The achievement of Sir William Phips was seen to be unique, something that could never be emulated. The story remained attractive and was often repeated, especially in America where the rise of Phips could be seen as a prime example of the reality of the American dream. But it would have taken a dreamer indeed to believe any longer that it was possible to locate and salvage the wreck of a Spanish galleon.

Such at least was the situation for more than two hundred and fifty years after William Covill found the wreck of the *Concepción* in January 1687. But dreams have a pleasant habit of sometimes coming true. It was suitably enough a Bermudan, Teddy Tucker, who demonstrated in 1954 that it was not impossible to raise treasure from a sunken Spanish galleon, when he located and salvaged a wreck, later identified as the *San Pedro*, which had sunk in 1595. 'Tucker had accomplished the first major salvage of Spanish treasure in the Western Hemisphere since the days of William Phips', writes a modern authority on treasure-hunting.[11] Tucker's discovery was to start a treasure-hunting boom which was soon to outpace even the frenzied efforts of the 1690s, a boom which was of course to benefit enormously from the advances made in submarine technology since the Second World War. Most people were to be disappointed in the 1960s, just as they had been in the 1690s, but there were sufficient discoveries to keep interest alive and to ensure a steady flow of venture capital into the treasure-hunting business. The most sensational affair of the 1960s was the salvage, not of a single wreck but of a whole fleet which had sunk off the coast of Florida in 1715. This was the achievement of Kip Wagner and the Real Eight Corporation, so far the most successful of all the modern treasure-hunters.[12]

It is perhaps inevitable that this new breed of treasure-hunters should be interested in the *Concepción* and in Sir William Phips, for Phips is

almost the patron saint of the modern treasure-hunter, and his achievement is the yardstick by which they measure their own successes. 'We
had thousands of gold coins, tens of thousands of pieces of eight, 40-odd
discs of precious metals, a dozen or so silver wedges . . .', wrote Kip
Wagner in his fascinating description of his search for the wrecks of the
1715 fleet. 'Not even Sir William Phips could top this!'[13]

Given this interest, it is not surprising that many men have tried to re-
locate the wreck of the *Concepción*, or Phips's wreck as it is often called.
The first man to try really hard was Alexandre Korganoff, a French law
student of Russian extraction, who after many years of research set sail
for the Silver Bank in 1952. He had many adventures but no luck. He
was followed a few years later by Ed Link in a better equipped and better
organized expedition and, in 1968, Jacques Cousteau, best known of all
the modern popularizers of the underwater world, set out to search for
Phips's wreck in his famous *Calypso*. Link and Cousteau found some interesting things at the bottom of the sea, including some wire left behind
by a previous dynamiter, but they did not find the *Concepción*.[14] Others
have followed them, including Melvin Fisher, self-styled king of the
modern treasure-hunters, who operates from Key West. But he was to
have no more luck than his predecessors.

Why should it be so difficult to find the *Concepción*? Lengthy research
in Spanish archives and sophisticated technology have enabled many
other famous seventeenth-century wrecks to be discovered in recent
years, but the *Concepción* presents some very special problems. Most
wrecks are located in fairly well-charted, shallow, off-shore waters, a
fact which means that the arduous preliminary task of locating the wreck
can be done relatively cheaply in small boats operating from dry land. It
also means that the treasure-hunter can choose his weather. But the
Concepción lies in international waters on an extremely dangerous reef
which is over eighty miles from the nearest land. Simply to search for the
wreck demands a major expedition in a ship which is large enough to be
self-sufficient for several weeks, a costly business which is likely to
become even more so when rough weather prevents the crew from operating their equipment for several days at a time. And just to make things
a little more difficult, the reefs of the Silver Bank are poorly charted.
Both the American and British charts of the area are based on what
appears to have been a very inaccurate survey done by the officers of the
British ship HMS *Blossom* between 1829 and 1832. Since few people
choose to sail to the Silver Bank, there has been no reason to revise this

survey with the aid of modern equipment. Sailors are simply warned to keep well clear of the area.

A poor chart makes navigation on such a dangerous reef a hazardous operation. It also makes the interpretation of research data almost impossible. But in any case, research on the *Concepción* has been hampered by a rather paradoxical fact. There are few wrecks so well-documented as the *Concepción*, and there are certainly no Spanish wrecks of the seventeenth century which are so well-documented in English. It has, however, been the tradition of the modern American treasure-hunting business to do its research in Seville, for fairly obvious reasons. It is in Seville that one can find detailed accounts of Spanish shipwrecks and, even more important, detailed accounts of the operations of Spanish salvage teams. But, of course, for the *Concepción*, this material is of little use. The survivors of the shipwreck did not know where they had been wrecked, and no Spanish salvage team ever found the wreck. It is in England that one has to look to find out where the wreck of the *Concepción* lies. But the researchers who work for American treasure-hunters do not know their way round English archives as well as they know the archives of Seville, and every expedition that has searched for the *Concepción* has relied heavily on the English documentation collected by Cyrus H. Karraker for his book *The Hispaniola Treasure*, which was published in 1934. This documentation is impressive and includes the logbooks of the *James and Mary* and the *Foresight*, together with a chart probably drawn by Lieutenant Hubbard of the *Foresight* showing the reef and the wreck-site. As we shall see, there was one vital document which Karraker missed, and was therefore unknown to the treasure-hunters who based their research on his book. Even so, one might think that these two log-books and a chart drawn by a man who had spent several months on the wreck-site would provide enough information to locate the wreck with the aid of modern search technology. But, in fact, none of these documents give the precise location of the *Concepción*. They give the latitude and they give the bearings to various prominent points on the north coast of Hispaniola. But both latitude and bearings vary slightly from one document to another, and, in any case, modern ships do not have sufficiently tall masts for anyone to be able to see Hispaniola from the Silver Bank, however clear the weather. The net result is to present the searcher with a dauntingly large area to search, an area composed of thousands of individual coral heads, any one of which might conceal what remains of the *Concepción*. The problem is simply compounded by the absence of an accurate chart. Most expeditions have concentrated on trying to find a section of the reef which looks, as Phips described it, 'like unto a half moon'. But there are a lot of half moons on the forty-one miles of the North Riff. There are also a lot of wrecks, and much time, effort and money has been wasted blowing up sections of coral which turned out to be the last resting place of other, more recent wrecks.

Since searching for the *Concepción* is such a difficult and expensive business, it is not surprising that many people have wondered whether the wreck was really worth looking for. It would certainly be a feather in anyone's cap to repeat Phips's achievement, but the aim of the treasure-hunting business is to make money, and there are those who consider that there is not much money to be made out of the *Concepción*. They feel that the ship must have been picked clean in the seventeenth century. This is an opinion which it is difficult for the researcher to refute entirely. He knows what Phips took out, but he does not know how much was loaded in Vera Cruz or how much was extracted by the sloop captains who worked the wreck between June and December 1687. All he can say is that Narborough thought there was plenty left when he gave up in May 1688; indeed, he thought that there was as much left as had been taken out. Was he right? Did the whole stern section really remain covered by coral? If he was right, then there was a fortune lying beneath the North Riff. And, if there was a fortune there, the technology existed to locate it. Such, at least, was the opinion of Burt D. Webber Jr. of Annville, Pennsylvania, and it is to his story that we must turn for the final episode in the strange history of the treasure of the *Concepción*.

CHAPTER EIGHTEEN

The Second Captain Phips

History may not repeat itself, but similar situations often call forth similar men and this is certainly true of the two sensational discoveries of the wreck of the *Concepción*. Burt Webber may not be the twentieth-century reincarnation of Captain Phips, but he has many of the same attributes and these have perhaps been heightened by the many years which he has spent reflecting on the achievement of his seventeenth-century predecessor. Webber, like Phips, is a man of almost superhuman energy, enthusiasm and single-mindedness, a man who cannot be deterred by failure and the ridicule of the world, an egotist whose obsession is fed by a strong sense that God is on his side. Webber, like Phips, is a supreme individualist, irresponsible by the standards of his age and completely indifferent to danger, a man who has many of the characteristics of the mercenary, just as Phips had of the buccaneer. Phips was 'tall, beyond the common set of men'; Webber is a stocky man of medium height, but he is an immensely powerful man whom one can easily imagine quelling a mutiny with his bare hands and the force of his personality.[1]

Webber was born in 1942 of Pennsylvania 'Dutch' stock, and he has a strong sense of his German ancestry. Indeed, he is thought by many to be typical of the German-American, and such disparate characteristics as his stubbornness, seriousness and love of guns are cited by his friends as sure signs of the German in him. But Webber's choice of career was certainly not typical in the intensely respectable bourgeois community in which he was brought up, and now that he has been successful, he takes enormous pleasure in the thought that he has shot ahead of his careful, unadventurous classmates with their mortgages and steady jobs. The new house which Webber is building for his wife in Berks County, Pennsylvania, is the answer to twenty years of local ridicule. Once again the parallel with Phips in Boston is only too obvious.

Webber says that he always wanted to be a treasure-hunter, an obsession fed early by children's books and sustained ever since. A boy with his head full of nonsense who liked to dive in local stone quarries might be forgiven by his family and friends even in a small Pennsylvania town, but it was a different matter when he left school at eighteen and refused to do the conventional thing and go to college. Webber announced that he would go to a divers' training academy and that is what he did, graduating as a first-class commercial deep-sea diver in 1961. It was then just a question of accumulating the experience which would enable him to find the treasure he knew must one day be his.

There are only a few men who have the motivation and the ability and can command the resources needed to become full-time professional treasure-hunters. Webber was soon to become a member of this strange, select community who consider themselves to be the last bastion of free enterprise in an increasingly bureaucratic America. Such men respect each other, but there is an intense rivalry among them which manifests itself in continuous disparagement of their competitors' character and ability and in continuous spying on their latest activity. What makes this rivalry even more intense is the fact that, although there are hundreds of sunken Spanish galleons concealed on the sea-bed, there are just a few which earn for their finders far more stars than the others, not just because they are thought to be fabulously rich but also because so many people have tried to find them and failed. These are the great prizes in the American treasure-hunting world, prizes which will earn their finders fame as well as fortune. Most prized of all are the wrecks of three *almirantas*, all of which were wrecked in the seventeenth century: the *Nuestra Señora de Atocha* which sank in 1622, the *Nuestra Señora de las Maravillas* which sank in 1656 and the *Nuestra Señora de la Concepción*. All treasure-hunters worth their salt have tried to find at least one of these wrecks; most have tried to find all three, and Burt Webber was no exception. For nearly ten years he searched intermittently for the *Atocha*, and he has also looked for the *Maravillas*, that very same wreck which served almost as a bank for the Bahaman treasure-hunters of the early 1680s. But, sadly for Webber, both these prizes fell to rivals in the early 1970s.[2] There was nothing left but to seek the greatest prize of all, the *Nuestra Señora de la Concepción*.

Webber's years of failure may have made his name a byword for folly in Pennsylvania, but they also gave him enormous experience in the arts of the treasure-hunter. They also demonstrated where his greatest strengths lay.

Webber had shown on many occasions that he was a leader who could persuade people to follow him even when all hope had been lost. He had also shown himself to be a first-class practical technician and had made enormous improvements in the design of the electronic wizardry with which the modern treasure-hunter works, in particular, the design of special underwater housings for magnetometers, instruments which measure anomalies in the world's magnetic field and hence will indicate the presence of ferrous material such as anchors, iron guns and other large fittings on wrecks. Webber's technical ability was to be crucial to his success. Equally important was his ability to communicate his enthusiasm to men with enough money to back his dreams. Webber once had to sell encyclopedias to support his family, and this episode has been much publicized by the American press, but what is really far more remarkable is that, for most of his career, rich men have paid him salaries to search for wrecks, despite his record of continuous failure.

Webber was at first doubtful of the value of the *Concepción* as a target. It would give his reputation a great boost to repeat the achievement of Captain Phips, but was there enough treasure left to justify the expense? He was persuaded that there was by an old friend and rival, Jack Haskins, an independent treasure-hunter who operates from Islamorada in the Florida Keys. Haskins, a man who is as Irish as Webber is German, is a former commercial pilot who now supports himself and his treasure-hunting ventures by dealing in coins. He has taught himself to read with ease the difficult Spanish manuscripts which provide the American treasure-hunter with his main research tool and is now far the best researcher in the treasure-hunting community, as well as being an extremely competent technician and a superb diver with an eagle eye for the underwater clues to sunken treasure. He had been fascinated by the story of the *Concepción* and Captain Phips since childhood and had already collected a file of material on the wreck. He agreed to put this at Webber's disposal and to continue to do research on the location of the wreck in return for a share of any profits in the venture.

Webber was now all set to raise the money necessary to locate and salvage the wreck of the *Concepción*. He decided to do this in a revolutionary way. Most treasure ventures are financed casually and, as a result, are normally seriously under-capitalized. Searching for treasure is a lengthy, expensive and normally unsuccessful process. But, even when he is successful, the treasure-hunter faces many problems. Salvaging wrecks is even more expensive than searching for them. But perhaps the most serious problem of all is the long time that the treasure-hunter has to wait between his first successful discovery and the eventual realization of the value of his treasure. This period of frustration, heavy bills and steeply rising interest charges is often made worse by lengthy legal quibbles with states claiming royalties and individuals claiming to have some right to a share of the treasure. And then, even when all other problems have been solved, the successful treasure-hunter shares with other successful citizens the sad necessity of having to hand over a large share of his gains to the tax man.

Webber's view was that the research skills, the documents and the technology existed to find large numbers of Spanish wrecks in general and the *Concepción* in particular. It was his view also, which he could buttress with evidence from Spanish documents, that several of these wrecks carried treasure which could pay their finders fabulous dividends. All that was needed to find them was to buy the best research brains, the best technology and equipment and the best crews and divers. And all that was needed to keep a reasonable share of the treasure that was found was to buy the best lawyers, accountants and tax experts. All that was needed, in other words, was money.

Webber's dream of a massively financed treasure-hunting business run on similar lines to the oil-prospecting business became potential reality on the day in 1976 when he was introduced to Warren Stearns, the young, dynamic and very hard-headed chairman of a Chicago firm of investment bankers. Webber had met his Duke of Albemarle. The wealthy Stearns was educated at Amherst and the Harvard Business School and gained his early business experience with Procter & Gamble before moving into investment banking. He knew nothing about treasure-hunting or magnetometers, but he knew a lot about men, risks and financial ventures and was impressed both with Webber himself and with the plans Webber laid on his desk. He was particularly impressed with the technology which Webber claimed to possess, but, before committing himself, he asked the advice of Professor Richard M. Foose, an expert in marine geology with a world-wide reputation. Foose told Stearns that Webber was the world's expert in the design of housings for magnetometers and in their use underwater. Stearns was persuaded. Treasure-hunting would be transformed by Chicago finance into just another branch of big business, drawing on the risk capital of extremely rich men who knew that American law on tax losses would protect them from the normal penalties of failure, and who would gain in return for their investment vicarious excitement, expenses-paid vacations to the West Indies and a real possibility of fabulous dividends. Webber got his money, and Foose became scientific adviser to the partnership. An expedition was planned to search for the *Concepción*. Its code-name was Operation Phips.

The first step was to obtain an exclusive search licence, which was harder than it sounds as it is by no means clear which country has sovereignty over the Silver Bank. The great powers define the region as 'high seas', but this definition finds no acceptance in the three countries which lie nearest to the bank. The Dominican Republic, Haiti, and the Turks and Caicos Islands all lay claim to the area. The partners decided to negotiate with the Dominican Republic, the country which was nearest by some thirty miles and which also had the potential naval strength to enforce its claim. A team composed of Webber, his lawyer, Tim Lowry, and Stearns' valued Spanish-speaking assistant, Stan Smith, set out for Santo Domingo to make a deal.

The Dominican government struck a much tougher bargain with Webber than did the government of James II with Phips. They demanded a royalty of fifty per cent and insisted that a representative of the Dominican Navy 'remain on board to observe any operations being carried out, with the faculty to audit the company's logs and to inspect and inventory all materials salvaged'.[3] The Dominicans are a charming people, but they had no intention of making a present of the wealth of the Indies to a syndicate of *gringo* businessmen. From the treasure-hunters' point of view, these generous terms were an exercise in international goodwill as much as anything else. Too many treasure-hunters have lost everything by trying to be too tough with the governments of small countries. Good relations with the Dominican Republic should lead to good relations with other countries in the future. The partners saw this venture as just the beginning of a vast and profitable business. 'This isn't the Holy Grail, you know', Stearns said after the discovery of the *Concepción*. 'We're going to do this again and again and again. We're going to find treasure all over the world. We're a business.'[4]

Meanwhile, there was the small problem of determining just where the wreck lay on the 41-mile-long North Riff. Haskins's researches in Spanish and English archives were aided by the drawing of the only accurate chart of the Silver Bank in existence, a chart which was based on a specially commissioned aerial mosaic. This was to prove an enormous aid both to research and to navigation. The aerial mosaic enabled all reef-heads less than two fathoms deep to be identified and it was at last

possible to see the exact shape and formation of the North Riff. What
was clear was that the North Riff was made up of three main sections of
reef separated by deep-water channels. Each reef had the unique 'lily-
pond' formation of the Silver Bank, that is to say, formed of hundreds of
individual coral towers coming up direct from the bottom, whose heads
of golden-brown, honey-combed dead coral were sometimes just below
the surface, sometimes exposed at low water and sometimes exposed at
all times. But there was no place where the reef rose more than a few feet
above sea level. There was no rock fifty feet high which 'apeares like a
boate keele up.' Relating the findings of the aerial survey to the vague in-
dications of seventeenth-century Spanish survivors and English salvors
was none too easy. All relations were quite definite that the wreck-site
was in an area where the reef-heads were exposed. Beyond this, there
was little that could be learned from the Spanish documents. The pilots
had been hopelessly lost and no survivor left a really convincing description of the reef-heads surrounding the wreck or of their position in relation to the reef as a whole. The English documents at Haskins's disposal
were more useful. The main information provided by Phips was that the
'reef was like unto a half moon' and that the wreck lay towards the eastern end of the North Riff. With the aid of the aerial survey it was clear
that this meant that the wreck lay somewhere on the easternmost of the
three main sections of reef, whose shape justified its confident labelling
on the treasure-hunters' chart as Half-Moon Reef, a judgement which
was confirmed by an intelligent reading of Hubbard's chart. Half-Moon
Reef is composed of over a thousand separate reef-heads and is six miles
long and between half a mile and three-quarters of a mile wide. This
makes a formidably large search area, but since Webber had plenty of
financial backing, he decided to do the thing in the most scientific way
possible. Every reef-head was numbered and, if necessary, every reef-
head would be surveyed, starting with the most likely areas and going on
until the whole reef had been searched. Webber knew that the
Concepción would be a weak magnetic target, since Haskins's research in
Seville had shown that she had shed her anchors before striking the reef,
carried non-magnetic bronze guns and few large metal fittings. But
Webber had the best magnetometer in existence and he knew how to use
it. He was very confident.

Webber chartered a Florida fishing-boat called the *Big G* and got together his team. They were good men for the job. His head diver was an
old school friend from Pennsylvania called Bob Coffey who had com-

bined a successful career in textile management with a wide experience in diving. Coffey gave up his career to work for Webber. He was a valuable asset, a man who describes himself as an organizer and a working diver rather than a treasure-hunter, a man who works hard himself and has the ability to organize other men and make them work hard too. Another old friend was Duke Long, a powerfully built Pennsylvania Dutchman whose many talents range from being a crack shot with rifle or spear gun to an ability to execute in the most delicate detail the old sailors' art of scrimshaw work on whalebone. Then there was Johnnie Berrier, who served twenty-seven years in the U.S. Navy before making a new life for himself in his early forties. Since then he had spent more than a decade in every variety of underwater treasure-hunting, diving for gold in the rivers of California and for sapphires in Montana between intervals of combing the sea-bed of the Caribbean and Florida for Spanish treasure. Another 'old-timer' was Henry Taylor, a wealthy eccentric in the tradition of a character from Steinbeck, who combined all the skills of the treasure-hunter with a veritable passion for the gold and silver coins of the Spanish colonial empire. These four men, together with Haskins, made up the nucleus of Webber's team, and a formidable team it was. Every one of them had that combination of skills which make up the successful treasure-hunting diver. They could all handle small boats, navigate and understand charts, mend or improve the most intricate machinery. They all understood how to use and interpret magnetometers and metal detectors and, needless to say, they were all superb divers with many years of experience behind them. In addition, they all had their own special skills. Berrier was an excellent underwater photographer and a ham radio expert. Long was a cartographer and an artist who could re-create an artifact on paper from the merest fragment brought up from the sea-bed. Taylor was also a cartographer as well as being an expert in the identification of coins and artifacts. Webber might feel confident that, if the treasure was there, he had the men who could find it.

The *Big G*, like so many hopeful ships before her, set sail from Puerto Plata for the North Riff on 20 January 1977.[5] Early days were spent in relating the chart drawn from the aerial mosaic to the reality of the reef. The weather was poor, but in a few days they were able to identify the whole of Phips's half moon, a six-mile crescent of breakers with the open sea beyond them. Now it was time to get down to business. The reef had been divided up on the chart into grid squares, each containing a varying number of reef-heads. Each day, Webber's team went out in two rubber reef-boats. The first reef-boat motored in turn to each reef-head in that day's square and buoyed them. They were followed by the other boat, which towed the magnetometer round each reef-head and then removed the buoy. When there were no more buoys, they knew that they had completed the survey of that particular grid square and they then moved on to the next one. Nothing could have been more systematic. The motivation might be the same, but the technology and organization was light-years removed from William Covill with his two Indian divers, 'peeping among the boilers'. Nevertheless, the nature of the reef was to cause many problems.

Circumnavigating a reef-head is by no means as easy as it sounds. Enormous arms of staghorn and elkhorn coral protruded from the main bulk of the heads, forcing the divers to keep a keen watch and their boats to keep a good distance and preventing the magnetometer from being towed as near to the reef as Webber would have liked. It was also impossible to survey near the bottom, which is not a conveniently level stretch of sand but is instead a rocky jungle of coral which often rises between the main heads in intermediate summits, each with its own protecting fangs of elkhorn coral. The average bottom depth was between forty and fifty feet, but it was rarely possible to tow the magnetometer at depths greater than ten to fifteen feet, and even then there was a constant danger of snagging unless a vigilant watch was kept. The survey was made even more difficult by the weather, which was as bad in the early months of 1977 as it had been during Phips's last voyage in 1688. Work was often impossible but, even when it was possible, the swell made work on the northern, seaward side of the reef very dangerous.

Problems or not, the survey went on and the magnetometer registered many 'hits' as anomalies were encountered. The six miles of Half-Moon Reef soon proved to be a ships' graveyard littered with wrecks, ranging in date from a small ship of the late seventeenth century, possibly one of the treasure-hunting sloops from the islands, to a nineteenth-century ship carrying boilers for the West Indian sugar industry. Each wreck was given its appropriate name. There was the Link wreck and the Cousteau wreck, marking the mistaken findings of recent predecessors. There was the 'brick' wreck, the 'carronade' wreck and the 'cross-staff' wreck, the last named for the single most valuable artifact discovered – a seventeenth-century cross-staff. Altogether, thirteen different wreck-sites were located. Thirteen times, spirits were raised, only to be dashed again when investigation by the divers demonstrated that what had been found was not the wreck of the *Concepción*.

Fresh hope was raised when they learned of the existence in the Institute of Jamaica of a chart drawn by the mathematician John Taylor, who had come out to the wreck-site with the *Falcon* in 1688.[6] Now it would be possible to pin-point the wreck. But when the details were radioed through, they served only to confirm what they already knew – that the wreck was somewhere on Half-Moon Reef. But could this be true? On 27 May, Webber expressed his doubts in the expedition's log. 'We are now about one survey day away from a completion of the entire Half-Moon Reef, south-east point to end. If the wreck of the *Concepción* is not found in this remaining area, the survey shall be terminated on Silver Shoals. At this point, it can only be concluded if we don't find the wreck that her remains do not present a detectable ferro-magnetic target to the magnetometer. Nevertheless this is most difficult to believe when observing the records of our other finds on this reef.' Webber shared his private doubts with his log-book, but they were shared in much more positive language by the members of his crew who were beginning to feel that there was good reason for Webber's long history of failure.

The early days of the survey had been full of hope and had been enlivened by a number of exciting incidents, such as the seeing-off of a rival American treasure-hunter with a search licence from the Turks and Caicos Islands, or the searching of what appeared to be a drug-running trawler by an armed boarding party provided by their partners in the Dominican Navy. But, as March moved into April and April into May, morale fell and tempers rose, and members of the crew slept with loaded guns beside their pillows.

There was a physical as well as a psychological reason for nerves being stretched taut. Every member of the crew was suffering, without knowing it, from a particularly nasty form of fish poisoning called ciguatera which is caused by eating fish which feed on coral reefs. The symptoms are extremely unpleasant: tingling about the lips, tongue and throat, followed by numbness, headaches, nervousness, dizziness, insomnia and muscle pains – hardly the best condition in which to conduct a physically exhausting survey of a dangerous reef. Ciguatera and failure made a cruel combination and all the men who served on this expedition recall it with horror.

Still Webber went on. His charts and documents were examined and re-examined. Arguments were met with counter-arguments. All the evidence showed that the wreck of the *Concepción* was on Half-Moon Reef. Webber would go on to the end. He did. Only after he had completed the survey of the reef, only after he had checked 1,891 coral heads and spent a quarter of a million dollars, did he give up. No treasure-hunting expedition had ever been so well equipped or so well financed, but the location of the *Concepción* remained a mystery. The partners formed a new company, Seaquest International, and began to seek licences to search for other wrecks. Operation Phips was shelved.

It was now that Webber was to have his only real stroke of luck. It was at about this time that I began research on this book. I knew nothing about Operation Phips or Seaquest International and it was by pure co-incidence that Webber and Haskins heard about my work from my research assistant in Seville. They rushed over to see me in London in April 1978, a trip which soon justified its cost when I told them the location of a document they had surprisingly overlooked. This was the log-book of the *Henry*, the ship captained by Francis Rogers which had first found the wreck of the *Concepción* in 1687. The document formed part of the papers of Admiral Narborough and had remained in a family archive until a few years before when it was deposited in the Kent Archives Office at Maidstone,[7] hardly the first place that a treasure-hunter would think of looking. Since the *Henry* was first on the scene, the log-book contained much better locational data than those of any of the other ships which were to visit the wreck-site in 1687 and 1688.

The log-book gives four vital pieces of information. First, it tells us that the *Henry* approached the North Riff from the east and that the wreck lay in the first section of reef with exposed reef-heads; in other words it confirmed that the wreck lay on Half-Moon Reef. Then it tells us that the wreck 'lyes in ye midst of reife' and that it lay between '3 large boylers [reef-heads] that the tops of them are dry att low water'. Finally, and most important, it gives the co-ordinates of the wreck. 'Shee bares from our ship E by S ½ S about 3 miles off, ye westmost end of ye reife in sight bareing west of us, & ye eastmost end SE by E ½ S.'

When Webber saw this log-book he felt certain that the treasure of the *Concepción* must be his. After months of surveying and studying his charts he had the whole picture of the reef in his mind and he felt that he could actually see the place where the wreck must lie. The only real problems were the location of the anchorage from where Rogers took his compass bearings and the variation in magnetic deviation of the compass which had taken place between 1687 and 1978. But, on reflection, these problems were fairly small ones. Whatever the variation, the angle between Rogers's bearings on the east end of the reef and on the wreck-site itself must remain the same. All that was needed was to make a two-armed pointer with the same angle, place one point on the chart at the east end of the reef, and manoeuvre the other pointer to various sites within the reef in accordance with a number of assumptions about the location of Rogers's anchorage. The total search area indicated by all the assumptions was a mere one-eighth of a square mile containing one hundred and fifty reef-heads, nothing compared with the area searched in 1977.

Small though the new search area was, it still posed one essential problem. Webber had already surveyed it. It was clear that the words he had written in his log in May 1977 were only too true. 'At this point, it can only be concluded if we don't find the wreck, that her remains do not present a detectible ferro-magnetic target for the magnetometer.' There was only one answer. If Webber wanted to raise fresh finance, he would have to design a new magnetometer, even more sensitive than the one used on the previous expedition and, most important, capable of being carried by a diver a few feet from the bottom and right up close to the reefs. Only then would it be possible to record the anomalies signalled by the small iron fittings, such as nails and hand-spikes, which must be the only magnetic targets left on the wreck. Anything much larger would have been already recorded.

This was the sort of problem that Webber, 'the world's expert in the design of housings for magnetometers for underwater use', was uniquely qualified to solve. In fact, he was so convinced that the *Concepción* must lie on the Half-Moon Reef that he had begun to solve it long before the log-book of the *Henry* gave him a fresh incentive. Webber rose to the occasion. On 17 July 1978, he reported his success in a letter to his partners in Seaquest International. 'Working with Varian Associates of Canada during the last twelve months, I have developed a completely submersible, diver-operated, hand-held cesium magnetometer that will allow a diver to position the sensor head to within inches of the base of the reefheads.' It is a very delicate instrument with a long pointed sensor head that can easily be damaged with clumsy handling. Underwater it is more easily manoeuvrable, but it needs a highly skilled man to operate it in the surging seas and swift currents between the reef-heads. Webber estimated that the new magnetometers, which cost $17,000 each, were ten times more sensitive than the towed instruments that were used on the 1977 expedition. With the new magnetometers and the log-book of the

Henry, Webber was absolutely certain that the *Concepción* was now a 'low-risk' target, a suitable target in fact to get Seaquest International off the ground as the most efficient, best equipped and best financed treasure-hunting business in the history of the game.

Webber's expedition might be better equipped than the expedition of the *James and Mary* in 1686, but there were many of the same problems to be faced. His ambition was not likely to be fulfilled without money and a good ship and the summer of 1978 was to be as busy for Webber as that of 1686 had been for Phips. A new company, Operation Phips II, L.P., was set up as a subsidiary of Seaquest to raise the $450,000 needed to meet the search and preliminary salvage costs. The offering circular is a marvellous blend of caution and optimism that would have done credit to Phips himself.[8] Potential investors are warned of the highly speculative nature of treasure-hunting, or rather of 'ocean salvage activities of the type contemplated'. 'These securities', it says, 'are only suitable for investment by persons who can assume the risk of complete loss of their investment.' The optimistic bit comes further on when an estimate is made of the potential value of the treasure. Not even Phips in his wildest dreams can have imagined that the *Concepción* carried such a fortune. First, the most optimistic assumptions were made of the silver and other goods loaded at Vera Cruz. Then this was boosted by the inclusion of an astonishingly valuable cargo reputed to have been loaded at Havana. The total cargo was said to comprise, apart from silver, a large quantity of gold in bars and worked objects, 43 chests of pearls, 21 chests of emeralds from Colombia's Muzo Mine and 436 chests of trade goods from the Far East, including a large quantity of Chinese porcelain. After Phips's takings were deducted, an estimate was made of the total value that the remaining cargo would be likely to make at auction. No account is taken of the six months of salvage operations conducted by the sloops from Jamaica and Bermuda in 1687. The result is a truly mouth-watering sum, made even more attractive by the fact that Phips recovered virtually no gold and no pearls, emeralds or porcelain. But was all this cargo really on board? Did the *Concepción* really take on a valuable extra cargo in Havana? Seaquest's estimate was based on research done by another treasure-hunter, Robert Marx, in the early 1960s. He claimed to have found the information in a bundle of documents filed as Indiferente General 2536 in the archives at Seville. But neither Jack Haskins nor myself found this information when we looked through the same bundle. Indeed, I have found no evidence that any extra cargo was taken on at

Havana. When Marx was faced by Haskins's doubts, he suggested that the papers might have been misplaced or had even been stolen.[9] This is, of course, quite possible. Whatever the truth, Marx's research and Webber's confidence made the *Concepción* look a very attractive target. The disappointments of 1977 could be forgotten in the light of the discovery of the log-book of the *Henry* and the new magnetometers. The money required was soon raised. Most of the investors were millionaires whose total personal capital was reputed to top a billion dollars. But there was at least one real gambler in the syndicate, Ray Lewandowski, a Polish-American manufacturer of custom-built golf equipment, who actually mortgaged his house in Chicago to pay his share. He had a hunch that Webber's luck was about to change.

While Stearns was raising the money, Webber was seeing to the thousands of detailed preparations necessary if the expedition was to succeed. A converted British minesweeper called the *Samala*, with an English captain and crew, was chartered at Antigua in the West Indies and fitted out at Miami. It was, it will be remembered, an expedition led by an American but with an English crew which found the *Concepción* the first time. Webber was beginning to think like that. There was nothing English about Webber's divers. Despite the frustration and unpleasantness of the 1977 expedition, Coffey, Long, Berrier and Taylor all signed on again. The new developments had given them new faith, though they all swore never to eat Silver Bank fish again. They were joined by Don Sommers, a novice diver from Missouri who had almost drowned on the first expedition and had been expertly revived by Coffey. Now he was experienced and wanted to go back. Two new divers with no experience of treasure-hunting were also signed on, Billy Fothergill, a river diver from Louisville, Kentucky, and Jim Nace, a massively built lifeguard and former football star from the Webber country in Pennsylvania. The new divers and the English crew were required by Webber to listen each evening to what they irreverently called 'Children's Hour', readings from the large file of copies of seventeenth-century documents which Webber kept in his cabin. Everyone must know exactly what they were planning to do. Everyone must know the story of the *Concepción* and of Captain Phips. This was not to be simply an exciting commercial diving operation. It was to be an expedition of world-shattering historical significance. The second Captain Phips was being born.

Seven weeks were spent in Miami fitting out. The long wait was caused by almost inevitable delays as vital equipment failed to turn up, and last-minute modifications had to be made to the magnetometers. But at last, all was ready, and early in November the *Samala* sailed from Miami to Puerto Plata and then, on 24 November, to the North Riff where she was anchored about half a mile from the Half-Moon Reef. On his first full day Webber tested the new magnetometers on one of the wreck-sites discovered the previous year. The results were 'excellent beyond belief'.[10] Now it was time to put them to work to find the wreck of the *Concepción*.

Two days later they knew they were very near. The magnetometers were recording a pattern of hits very close to the spot indicated by the log-book of the *Henry*. Pottery shards, iron straps and other metal fittings were found. A long trail of rounded ballast stones provided further dramatic evidence of the concealed presence of an ancient wreck. As if he knew that he would soon have something to guard, Webber ordered small arms practice that evening, and the reefs rang with the blast from the formidable array of rifles and machine-guns which the gun-loving Webber had brought from America. The next two days saw steadily mounting excitement as more anomalies were recorded and more pottery shards, iron fittings and ballast stones were discovered by the divers. And then, on 30 November, five days after they had arrived on the reef, the new-comer, Jim Nace, turned over a ballast stone and found the first coin. 'I tapped Burt on the shoulder. He saw what it was. He grabbed me and hugged me.'[11] Webber shot to the surface with the coin in his hand, eyes popping in a grin of success that wiped out twenty years of failure.

Nace's coin was to be the first of tens of thousands. But the first success is always the most exciting, as the expedition's log of 30 November records. 'Praise God, silver pieces of eight were recovered in great quantities plus splashes of silver, a religious holy water container, Chinese porcelain cup and portions of dish along with pottery shards.' One hears the echo from Francis Rogers's log-book of 20 January 1687. 'For which blessing wee return infinite praise and thankes to Almighty God.'

There was no doubt that they had re-discovered the remains of the *Concepción*. On that first day they found 128 pieces of eight and a few coins of smaller denomination. Some were dated and none bore a date later than 1639, the year before the arrival of the *Concepción* in Vera Cruz. Since then, coins of 1640 and 1641 have been found. The *Concepción* sailed from Vera Cruz on 23 July 1641. Most of the coins are from the Mexico City mint but there are quite a few from Potosi, which probably got to Mexico in the way of trade. The Chinese porcelain, some of which is intact, bears the marks of the late Ming period, which ended in 1644, and would have been brought from the Philippines by the 'Acapulco galleon' and then transported across Mexico for shipment to Europe.

It was not long before a second site was discovered, about one hundred and fifty yards to the north-east of the place where the first finds had been made. It was soon apparent that this was the location of the main wreck-site worked by Phips and Narborough. Here were Rogers's '3 large boylers', now suitably labelled Webber, Haskins and Coffey Reefs. Between the reefs was a long coral basin where the last resting-place of the *Concepción* could almost be seen as the magnetometer recorded its galleon-shaped pattern of anomalies. There was, of course, no visible sign of the wreck, most of whose timbers had already been 'consum'd away' in 1687, but excavation has revealed pieces of planking four feet below the sea bottom, all that now remains of the once proud galleon.

In the midst of the beautiful coral basin where the *Concepción* had lain, an intermediate coral head rises to some twenty feet below the surface. On its summit is a pile of ballast stones which are easily visible to a swimmer wearing a face-mask. Reference to the 1977 log-book showed that this section had been surveyed on 28 February. If only something had gone wrong that day, thought those who had taken part in that frustrating first expedition. If only a line had snagged and a diver had been sent overboard to clear it. He would never have missed such an obvious clue as a pile of ballast stones. But nothing did go wrong and they surveyed all three of the reef-heads which mark the last resting-place of the *Concepción* without the magnetometer recording a single anomaly.

Close inspection of Haskins Reef, on which the stern must have rested, soon demonstrated a fascinating fact. It was now obvious that the stern had never been incorporated into the reef as Narborough had assumed and that the efforts of his divers and Phips's hazardous attempt to blow up the coral had been a waste of time. Narborough had cleared the wreck from the bow to some distance beyond the foot of the mainmast and had then come up against the reef and had made the not unreasonable assumption that the reef concealed the remaining section of the ship. But looking at the reef with modern eyes, it could be seen that this was simply not possible. If the stern was not under Haskins Reef, where was it? A long trail of ballast stones leading from the main wreck-site to the first site discovered provided the most likely answer. It seemed probable that the stern had broken away from the rest of the ship and had then pin-balled through the reefs to end up on the site which they had already started working. They had already located the famous treasure-filled stern which had inspired so many men to search for the wreck of the *Concepción*. The Indian servant, Andres de la Cruz, whose evidence provides our only information on what happened when the *Concepción* finally broke up, said that part of the stern broke away before he left the wreck, but this testimony has usually been ignored in the face of Narborough's certainty that the stern was intact under the reef.[12]

If the assumption that the stern now lies one hundred and fifty yards away from the main wreck-site is correct, it is remarkable that Phips's divers never found it. Ballast stones which are clearly visible now should have been visible then. Be that as it may, neither Phips nor Narborough record finding treasure at any distance from the main site between the three boilers. Even more ironic is the fact that most of Webber's hopes of finding treasure were pinned on Narborough's statement that the whole stern section lay imprisoned in the coral. Webber saw himself breaking into something very like a cave full of treasure, which would have made salvage a comparatively simple matter with modern tools. The whole survey system of checking the coral heads had been based on this assumption. But he was wrong, and the salvage of the treasure of the *Concepción* is going to take him a long time.

The conduct of salvage operations from the *Samala* bears a distinct family resemblance to those conducted nearly three hundred years previously from the *James and Mary*. Underwater salvage is still extremely hard work. There is the same routine, the same interest of the expedition leader in the maintenance of productivity, the same feeling of near contempt for a bucketful of silver coins which is the product of familiarity. But if the divers become a little blasé about the thousands of pieces of eight which they are raising from the sea bottom, there is also a growing number of artifacts to stimulate their interest. First prize so far goes to a bronze astrolabe, dated 1619, perhaps the very one used by that incompetent pilot, Bartolomé Guillen; but the divers have also raised silver plates, spoons, candle-snuffers and a whole range of other fascinating items from sand sprinklers to cannon-balls. They have also found evidence of their predecessors, including what can only be one of Phips's crows, shaped rather like a double-headed adze, with a hole where the original forty-foot handle would have fitted, and the bases of two seventeenth-century English brandy bottles embedded in the coral, the last remains of what had once been Phips's trading cargo. No one knows what they are going to find next. No one knows whether the next day or the next minute may produce some treasure which will completely transform the whole expedition – a bucketful of emeralds, a section of the sea floor carpeted in gold escudos or the remains of a chest containing the jewellery of the Viceroy of Mexico.

The day starts early, soon after sunrise, with breakfast prepared by the Irish cook, 'Chunkie' Cardwell. Then there is a flurry of activity as divers prepare their gear and start to load the reef-boats under the watchful eye of the head diver with his checklist. The fourteen-foot reef-boats look incredibly overladen as they leave the *Samala* with four divers each, complete with personal diving gear and spare air tanks, a compressor and pumps, rolls of piping and a very heavy hydraulic rig. Work on the reef resembles nothing so much as a quarrying operation, with the important exception that no explosives are used in order to preserve the delicate artifacts. Fifty feet down, at the foot of the towering cliffs of coral, the divers excavate areas which their Aquapulse metal detectors tell them are 'hot spots'. Great rocks weighing more than a ton are lifted away by airbags. Sand is removed by suction. Then, well below the sea bottom, the divers work with hammer and chisel and with hydraulic cutting tools to locate the treasure. The final work is done with bare hands, prints worn away by the coral. A hand is inserted into a hole. Probing fingers find the edge of a coin and pull it out. But loosening one coin brings a shower of others, 'like a seventeenth-century slot machine'. Slowly, the 'goody bag' is filled up and, only too soon, the diver's decompression meter tells him it is time to come back to the surface. The divers make three or four dives a day, spending several hours underwater at their fascinating and arduous trade.

Picking up treasure is hard work. It is also dangerous. Burrowing into the foot of the coral cliffs, the divers create their own caves, which have dangerous overhangs that have to be shored up with steel plates if disaster is to be avoided. Routine diving precautions are strictly enforced, but all the same, there is a regular run of minor injuries, and the men with paramedical qualifications are kept busy treating fingers and hands ripped by the razor-sharp coral, sore ears, popping sinuses or the strained backs of men who have struggled to lift massive coral boulders fifty feet below sea level. And there have been worse accidents, much the worst being when Burt Webber himself was nearly lost because of breathing in carbon monoxide from the exhaust of the compressor. When he came to the surface he blacked out. Only very prompt action by head diver Bob Coffey enabled a helicopter lift to hospital in Puerto Rico to be organized. It was a dramatic and worrying incident. Success has made Webber careless, and this is only one of many accidents he has suffered.

Supporting the whole venture are the five members of the English crew of the *Samala*, led by the Yorkshire-born ex-submariner and gourmet chef, Captain Tony Garton, and 'the best navigator in the West Indies', Jim Blackburn, a World War II hero who has lived on boats for thirty years. The crew are busy with the non-stop maintenance required of any vessel, but they are also servicing the divers, feeding them, filling their empty air tanks, racing to the reefs with extra gear and returning at intervals with the buckets of blackened, coral-encrusted silver pieces of eight whose recovery is the object of the whole exercise. An ordinary domestic rubber bucket holds well over five hundred coins, which, tipped out on deck ready for preliminary processing, do not look particularly impressive – and certainly do not look as though they are worth the $50,000 to $100,000 which they are later expected to fetch at auction. They look a little better after they have been dipped in hydrochloric acid to remove the coral encrustation. But they still do not look like valued collectors' pieces as the representative of the Dominican Navy counts them and places them in white bags, each holding five hundred coins and labelled Banco Central de la República Dominicana.

The *Samala* stays on site for about a fortnight at a time and then returns to port in Santo Domingo where the accumulated treasure is inventoried and receipted in the offices of the naval chief of staff, a real treasure-house surrounded by armed sailors of the Dominican Navy. Inside the treasure-house, the coins and artifacts are cleaned and identified by Henry Taylor, released from diving to process the coins he loves. The cleaned treasure is then transferred to a vault in the Dominican Central Bank. Two tons of silver coins have already been raised, but there is plenty more to come and no realistic estimate can yet be made of the value of Seaquest's discovery. That will depend on how much is raised in the long months of salvage that still lie ahead, on whether there are really emeralds and gold coins lying concealed on the Silver Bank, and on how much people are prepared to pay when the treasure is sold. One thing is clear, however: a seventeenth-century treasure-hunter could only expect to realize the bullion price of his treasure, but his twentieth-century successor can expect to be paid prices ten or twenty times the bullion price by purchasers in the numismatic and souvenir markets, not to mention the vast sums which a collector can be expected to pay for unique artifacts raised from the bottom of the sea. There seems no doubt that what Seaquest have already salvaged is worth several million dollars. There also seems no doubt that Webber and Stearns and their colleagues are going to become very rich men and that Ray Lewandowski will be able to pay off the mortgage on his house in Chicago. The realization of this fortune remains in the future, but the reader of this book will already detect a nice irony in the situation that now exists: three hundred and thirty-seven years after the fiasco of Villavicencio's attempts to salvage his ship, some of the silver from the *Concepción* has returned to Santo Domingo, and half of this treasure will remain the property of the Dominican government, the heirs of the King of Spain in the Indies.

The other half will eventually be sent to the United States for sale and distribution. In the meantime, the investors were given a chance in February 1979 to fly down to Santo Domingo and see for themselves what it was that their dollars had raised from the coral-cluttered canyons of the Silver Bank. Many took this opportunity of a winter holiday in the Dominican sun. What did they think as they filed round the tastefully presented exhibition in the admiral's office? Were they disappointed? Only a small portion of the treasure was on display and it must have been difficult to believe that the small number of cleaned and labelled pieces of eight, the lumps of coral with coins embedded in them, the battered, blackened silver artifacts, the two 'Woolworth's' Ming cups, the pottery shards, the cannon-balls and the earthenware olive jars were really worth a fortune. They looked more like 'a load of junk', as one investor's wife put it. But maybe they were not too worried. They had already heard on television and read in the press that the treasure of the *Concepción* was worth a fortune, indeed, worth somewhere between $40 million and $900 million, according to the various estimates that commentators and journalists had dreamed up. And then, of course, they were buoyed by the thought of all that silver and gold, those emeralds and pearls, which Seaquest's offering circular informed them was still to come.

Nobody could have been disappointed by the party given later that day on the *Samala* herself. Here was the whole treasure-hunting business summed up in a moment on a white-painted English ship, with the palm trees of the sunny Dominican Republic in the background. Here were the polo-playing millionaires fresh from the snows of Chicago and New

York. Here were the bronzed divers and crew filling the air with stories of treasure and wrecks and pieces of eight. Here were the smartly uniformed officers of the Dominican Navy. The setting might be rather different, but it was impossible not to think back to that other great party thrown by the Duke of Albemarle and his fellow adventurers at the Swan Tavern in London. No one, least of all Burt Webber and his colleagues, could avoid being continually struck by the parallels between these two sensational rediscoveries of the wreck of the *Concepción*.

When the party was over, the *Samala* sailed back to the North Riff, to disturb the ghost of Sir John Narborough once more, to pick up a few thousand more pieces of eight. This time I was fortunate enough to sail with her, a strange experience for an author who, when he started this book, thought that it would be entirely about the seventeenth century and never hoped to see the Silver Bank for himself. It was an evocative experience to stand in the wheelhouse of the *Samala* as she crashed through the stormy seas of the Mona Passage and later to see the breakers on the six-mile crescent of coral-heads which make up Half-Moon Reef. It was very moving to swim above the last resting place of the *Concepción* and look down at the enormous growths of staghorn and elkhorn coral, which reach out below the surface from Rogers's three 'boylers'. My first image as I lay on the water and gazed down into this dramatic coral basin was of the hundreds of Indian divers from the sloops of Bermuda and Jamaica fighting and grabbing on what must have still been just recognizable as the forepart of a galleon; then I saw the more organized activity of Sir John's divers, fifty at a time working on what they mistakenly thought was the concealed stern of the vessel. And then, as I surfaced and stood uneasily on the dead coral of Haskins Reef with the sea surging over my feet, I thought of those last few days as the thirty remaining survivors of the *Concepción* searched to the south and west for their friends. As I stood there, I could see one of the reef-boats working one hundred and fifty yards away and, perhaps half a mile beyond it, the *Samala*, a comfortable, homely ship where a good meal was already being prepared. Andres de la Cruz and his friends could see nothing save the occasional whale blowing on the horizon, the green and white seas surging round the coral on the heads near to them and the long line of breakers on the Half-Moon Reef to their east and west. It is a beautiful and very desolate place.

Sources and Bibliography

ABBREVIATIONS

Add	Additional Manuscripts, British Library
ADM	Admiralty Papers, Public Record Office
AGI	Archivo General de Indias, Seville
BL	British Library
Bodl	Bodleian Library, Oxford
C	Chancery Papers, Public Record Office
C de la C	Casa de la Contratación
CO	Colonial Office Papers, Public Record Office
CSPAWI	*Calendar of State Papers, America and the West Indies*
CSPC	*Calendar of State Papers, Colonial*
CSPD	*Calendar of State Papers, Domestic*
Ct	Contratación Papers, Seville
CTB	*Calendar of Treasury Books*
DNB	*Dictionary of National Biography*
HMC	Historical Manuscripts Commission
IG	Indiferente General Papers, Seville
Jesuit	Colección de Jesuítas, ci, fos. 277–9
KAO	Kent Archives Office, Maidstone
PRO	Public Record Office
Navarrete	Colección de Navarrete, vii, fos. 144–51
NMM	National Maritime Museum
T	Treasury Papers, Public Record Office
Villavicencio	Ct 5101 6 Apr 1642
Volumbozcar	Ct 5118 31 Mar 1642

MANUSCRIPT SOURCES

The story of the shipwreck of the *Nuestra Señora de la Concepción* and the subsequent Spanish attempts to locate and salvage the wreck is very well documented. I will not pretend to have exhausted the material in the Spanish archives relating to the wreck, and I list below only those documents which I, or my research assistant, Victoria Stapells-Johnson, have actually consulted.

Sources and Bibliography

Seville: Archivo General de Indias
Ct 2900 Lib. I: Registers of the fleet of New Spain.
Ct 3053, 3054, Papeles de Armada, 1627–41: Roque Centeno and Juan de Campos.
Ct 5101, Havana, 1 Mar 1642: Francisco Diaz Pimienta to C de la C.
Ct 5101, Santo Domingo, 6 Apr 1642: Juan de Villavicencio to C de la C.
Ct 5118, Vera Cruz, 15 Jul 1641: Oficiales reales to C de la C.
Ct 5118, Santo Domingo, 31 Mar 1642: Antonio de Volumbozcar to C de la C.
IG 2525, 2699: Documents relating to private Spanish expeditions to search for the *Concepción* and to the Spanish reaction to Phips's success.
IG 2536: A very large collection of papers containing letters, reports and testimonies relating to the loss of the *Concepción*.

Madrid: Real Academia de la Historia
Colección de Jesuítas, ci, fos. 277–9: Letter dated Santo Domingo, 20 Dec 1641, describing the loss of the *Concepción* and the fate of the survivors.

Madrid: Museo Naval
Colección de documentos de Fernández de Navarrete, vii, fos. 144–51: Report of the unfortunate fate of the *almiranta* of New Spain.
There is a copy of this document in BL Sloane 2496 fos. 203–6.

The English material on the various attempts to find the wreck is also voluminous. Much of this is in standard collections, such as the Colonial Papers, Admiralty Papers and State Papers, Domestic, references to which can be found in the notes. The following documents are those which are primarily concerned with matter relevant to the subject of this book.

London: British Library
Egerton 2526: John Knepp's journal, 3 Sep 1683–2 May 1684.
Sloane 50: Journal of *James and Mary*, 11 Sep 1686–4 Jun 1687.

London: Public Record Office
ADM 51/345: Logbooks of *Falcon*, 1682–4 and 1685–8.
ADM 52/35/2. Logbook of *Foresight* kept by Captain Stanley, 1687–88.
C/10/227/63: John Smith *v*. Christopher, Duke of Albemarle *et al*.
CO 1/57 fo. 38: Deposition of T. Smith about the silver wreck.

London: National Maritime Museum
ADM/L/F/198: Logbook of *Foresight* kept by Lieut. Hubbard, 1687–8.
LBK/1: Letter-book kept by Sir John Narborough, 1687–8.
SOU/10, 11: Papers relating to wrecks belonging to Robert Southwell.

Maidstone: Kent Archives Office
U 1515/010: Journal of *Henry*, 24 Sep 1686 – 16 Mar 1687.

Sources and Bibliography

Oxford: Bodleian Library
Rawlinson A.171, fos. 204–7: Mr Smith's information . . . touching the whole processe of C. Phipps's late expedition.
Rawlinson A.300: Journal of *Bonetta*, 8 Apr 1683 – 19 Jul 1686.

Kingston, Jamaica: Institute of Jamaica
John Taylor MS, 'Multum in parvo or parvum in multo': BL M/696 is a microfilm copy of this important source for both Jamaican history and the story of the salvage of the *Concepción*. Unfortunately, the microfilm has been so poorly executed as to be virtually illegible.

PRINTED SOURCES
Edward Berwick (ed.), *The Rawdon Papers* (1819)
Richard Blome, *Description of the Island of Jamaica* (1672)
J. S. Cummins (ed.), *The Travels and Controversies of Friar Domingo Navarrete, 1618–1686* (Cambridge, 1962)
Dialogo entre un viscaino y un montañes sobre construccion de naves (1640) in C. Fernandez Duro, *Disquisiciones naúticas* (Madrid, 1895–1903) vi, 105–220
Juan Diaz de la Calle, *Memorial . . . de las Indias Occidentales* (Madrid, 1646)
John Ellis, *Correspondence* (1829)
John Esquemeling, *The Buccaneers of America* (1st Eng. ed. 1684)
An Exact and Perfect Relation of the Arrival of the Ship the James and Mary, Captain Phipps Commander (1687)
Martin Fernandez de Navarrete, *Biblioteca maritima española* (Madrid, 1851)
Thomas Gage, *The English American* (1648; reprinted 1928)
George Gardyner, *A Description of the New World* (1651)
Cristobal Gutierrez de Medina, *Viaje del Virrey Marques de Villena* (Mexico City, 1640; reprinted 1947)
Sir J. H. Lefroy, *Memorials of the Bermudas*, 2 vols (1877–9)
Joseph de Veitia Linaje, *Norte de la contratación de las Indias Occidentales* (Madrid, 1672)
London Gazette No. 2249 (6–9 June 1687)
Harcourt Malcolm, *Historical documents relating to the Bahamas* (1910)
Thomas Malthus, *Present State of Jamaica* (1683)
Cotton Mather, *Pietas in Patriam: The Life of His Excellency Sir William Phips, Knt.* (1697; reprinted New York, 1929)
José Pellicer de Ossau, *Comercio impedido* (Madrid, 1640)
N. M. Penzer (ed.), *The Voyages of Christopher Columbus* (1942)
Relacion de todo lo sucedido en estas provincias de la Nueva España desde la formación de la Armada real de Barlovento (Mexico City, 1642)
John Stevens, *The Spanish Rule of Trade to the West Indies* (1702)
Edward Maunde Thompson, *Correspondence of the Family of Hatton* (1878)

Sources and Bibliography

Sir Hans Sloane, *A Voyage to the Islands Madeira, Barbados . . . and Jamaica*, 2 vols (1707, 1725)

J. R. Tanner (ed.), *Catalogue of the Pepysian MSS*, 4 vols (1903–22)

Antonio Vázquez de Espinosa, *Compendium and Description of the West Indies* (Washington, 1942)

SECONDARY AUTHORITIES

Admiralty, *The West Indies Pilot (North Western Part)*, vol i (1971)

G. de Artiñano y Galdácano, *La arquitectura naval española en madera* (Madrid, 1920)

——, *Historia del comercio con las Indias* (Barcelona, 1917)

P. J. Bakewell, *Silver Mining and Society in Colonial Mexico: Zacatecas, 1546–1700* (Cambridge, 1971)

Viola F. Barnes, 'The Rise of Sir William Phips', *New England Quarterly*, 1 (1928)

C. R. Boxer, *The Dutch Seaborne Empire* (1965)

Carl and Roberta Bridenbaugh, *No Peace beyond the Line* (1972)

J. Cadbury, 'Conditions in Jamaica in 1687', *Jamaican Historical Review*, iii (1959)

C. D. Chandaman, *The English Public Revenue 1660–1688* (Oxford, 1975)

P.-F.-X. Charlevoix, *Histoire de L'Isle Espagnole*, 2 vols (Paris 1730–1)

Huguette et Pierre Chaunu, *Séville et l'Atlantique*, 8 vols (Paris 1955–6)

Michael Craton, *A History of the Bahamas* (1968)

Wesley Frank Craven, *The Colonies in Transition, 1660–1713* (New York, 1968)

N. M. Crouse, *French Pioneers in the West Indies, 1624–64* (1940)

E. A. Cruikshank, *Life of Sir Henry Morgan* (Toronto, 1935)

Jacques-Yves Cousteau and Philippe Diolé, *Diving for Sunken Treasure* (1971)

Frank Cundall, *The Governors of Jamaica in the Seventeenth Century* (1936)

K. G. Davies, *The Royal African Company* (1957)

G. R. de Beer, *Sir Hans Sloane and the British Museum* (Oxford, 1953)

Daniel Defoe, *Essay upon Projects* (1697)

Antonio Domínguez Ortiz, 'Los caudales de Indias y la politica exterior de Felipe IV', *Anuario de Estudios Americanos*, xiii (1956)

Florence E. Dyer, *The Life of Admiral Sir John Narborough* (1931)

J. P. W. Ehrman, *The Navy in the War of William III* (Cambridge, 1953)

Cesareo Fernandez Duro, *Armada Española*, vol. iv, (Madrid, 1898)

——, *Naufragios de la Armada Española* (Madrid, 1867)

Genaro García, *Don Juan de Palafox y Mendoza* (Mexico City, 1918)

Robert H. George, 'Treasure Trove of William Phips', *New England Quarterly*, vi (1933)

Earl J. Hamilton, *American Treasure and the Price Revolution in Spain, 1501–1650* (Harvard, 1934)

——, 'Wages and Subsistence on Spanish Treasure Ships, 1503–1660', *Journal of*

Political Economy, xxxvii (1929)

C. H. Haring, Buccaneers in the West Indies in the Seventeenth Century (New York, 1910)

—— , Trade and Navigation between Spain and the Indies (Harvard, 1918)

Dave Horner, The Treasure Galleons (1973)

R. D. Hussey, 'Spanish Reaction to Foreign Aggression in the Caribbean to about 1680', Hispanic American Historical Review, ix (1929)

J. I. Israel, Race, Class and Politics in Colonial Mexico, 1610–70 (Oxford, 1975)

C. H. Karraker, The Hispaniola Treasure (Philadelphia, 1934)

—— , 'Spanish Treasure, Casual Revenue of the Crown', Journal of Modern History, v (1933)

Pierre de Latil and Jean Rivoire, Sunken Treasure (1962)

Marion Clayton Link, Sea Diver (New York, 1958)

Alice Lounsberry, Sir William Phips (New York, 1941)

J. Lynch, Spain under the Hapsburgs; vol. ii, Spain and America, 1598–1700 (Oxford, 1969)

Robert F. Marx, Shipwrecks of the Western Hemisphere (New York, 1975)

—— , They Dared the Deep (1968)

—— , Treasure Fleets of the Spanish Main (Cleveland, 1965)

P. A. Means, The Spanish Main; Focus of Envy, 1492–1700 (New York, 1935)

W. H. Miller, 'The Colonisation of the Bahamas, 1647–70', William and Mary Quarterly, ii (1945)

A. P. Newton, The Colonizing Activities of the English Puritans (New Haven, 1914)

—— , European Nations in the West Indies (1933)

J. H. Parry, The Spanish Seaborne Empire (1966)

Michael Pawson and David Buisseret, Port Royal, Jamaica (Oxford, 1975)

Mendel Peterson, History under the Sea (Washington, 1965)

Dudley Pope, Harry Morgan's Way (1977)

John S. Potter, The Treasure Diver's Guide (1973)

W. R. Scott, The Constitution and Finance of English, Scottish, and Irish Joint-Stock Companies to 1720, 3 vols (Cambridge, 1910–12)

S. A. G. Taylor, The Western Design (1965)

A. P. Thornton, West-India Policy under the Restoration (Oxford, 1956)

Peter Throckmorton, Shipwrecks and Archaeology (1970)

William H. Tillinghast, Notes on the Historical Hydrography of the Handkerchief Shoal in the Bahamas (Harvard, 1881)

Robert Noxon Toppam, Edward Randolph (Boston, 1899)

A. P. Usher, 'Spanish Ships and Shipping' in Facts and Factors in Economic History; Essays Presented to E. F. Gay (1932)

José Wangüemert y Poggio, El Almirante D. Francisco Diaz Pimienta y su época (Madrid, 1905)

Sources and Bibliography

Estelle Frances Ward, *Christopher Monck, Duke of Albemarle* (1913)
Robert C. West, *The Mining Community in Northern New Spain: the Parral Mining District* (Berkeley, 1949)
Henry Wilkinson, *The Adventurers of Bermuda* (1933)

Notes

Works listed in the Bibliography are cited by short title

CHAPTER ONE: A Capitana for New Spain

1. John Evelyn, *Diary and Correspondence* (1906) p. 461.
2. KAO U 1515/010 20 Jan 1687.
3. The description of the organization of the silver fleets which follows is based on the following authorities: Haring, *Trade and Navigation*; Artiñano y Galdácano, *Historia*; Chaunu, *Séville*; Parry, *Spanish Seaborne Empire* (1966).
4. For a recent general study of Spanish history during this period see Lynch, *Spain*, ii. For the connection between the arrival of treasure and Spanish foreign policy see Domínguez Ortiz, 'Los caudales'.
5. Hamilton, *American Treasure*.
6. Bakewell, *Silver Mining, 1546–1700;* West, *The Mining Community*.
7. AGI Ct 3053.
8. She is described as a *nao creolla* in Ct 3053. For her age see Volumbozcar p. 4.
9. For the contract see AGI Ct 3053. For the number of guns see AGI 2699/3. She carried some cheaper copper and iron guns in addition to her main complement of bronze cannon. For her previous voyage to New Spain see Chaunu, *Séville* v, 324–5 and 350–3.
10. For Spanish shipping in this period see Haring, *Trade and Navigation*; Artiñano y Galdácano, *La arquitectura* and Usher, 'Spanish ships and Shipping'.
11. For an interesting critique of Spanish ships by a contemporary Spaniard see *Dialogo*.
12. Gutierrez de Medina, *Viaje*, pp. 5–12.
13. This brief description of silver-mining is based on Bakewell, *Silver Mining* and West, *The Mining Community*.
14. Hamilton, 'Wages and Subsistence'.
15. Gage, *The English American* p. 10.
16. Gutierrez de Medina, *Viaje* p. 42.

17. Cummins, *Travels of Navarrete* i, 19–20.
18. García, *Palafox y Mendoza* pp. 58–81 is a description of Palafox's voyage to Mexico based on Gutierrez de Medina, *Viaje*.
19. Gutierrez de Medina, *Viaje* pp. 11–16.

CHAPTER TWO: A Passage to Mexico
 1. Gutierrez de Medina, *Viaje* p. 21. This chapter is based on the account given in this book, pp. 21–49, and I will give no further references to it.
 2. Cummins, *Travels of Navarrete* p. 20.
 3. For details of all these regulations see Linaje, *Norte de la contratación* and the abridged English translation by Stevens, *The Spanish Rule of Trade*.
 4. For a complete list of the ships in the fleet see Chaunu, *Séville* v, 360–1.
 5. For a discussion of pilots see Haring, *Trade and Navigation* pp. 298–315.
 6. Gage, *The English American* p. 18.
 7. BL Egerton 2395 fo. 101.

CHAPTER THREE: Too Long in Vera Cruz
 1. Gutierrez de Medina, *Viaje* pp. 49–52.
 2. For the corsairs see Fernandez Duro, *Armada Española* iv, 31–45, 107–116, 333–355. On the Dutch see Boxer, *Dutch Seaborne Empire*.
 3. Vázquez de Espinosa, *Compendium* p. 39.
 4. Chaunu, *Séville* viii (1), ch. 9.
 5. Diaz de la Calle, *Memorial*.
 6. For the Providence Island Company see Newton, *Colonizing Activities*.
 7. *CSPC 1574–1660* p. 124.
 8. 'The Nature of the Island Catalina', *Navy Records Soc. Publns* xiv, 440–2.
 9. *CSPC* p. 216.
10. Ibid. p. 150.
11. BL Sloane 758.
12. Hussey, 'Spanish Reaction'.
13. Gutierrez de Medina, *Viaje* pp. 51–2. See also Fernandez Duro, *Armada Espannola* pp. 335–7. For the general history of the Armada de Barlovento see Hussey, 'Spanish Reaction'; Parry, *Spanish Seaborne Empire* pp. 262–4 and Israel, *Race, Class and Politics* pp. 193–8.
14. Gutierrez de Medina, *Viaje* p. 51.
15. Fernandez Duro, *Armada Española* p. 336 fn. 1 has a list of the ships in the Armada de Barlovento. For the New Spain fleet see Chaunu, *Seville*, v, 360–1.
16. Fernandez Duro, *Armada Española* p. 336.
17. Gutierrez de Medina, *Viaje* pp. 51ff. For the Viceroy's career see Israel, *Race, Class and Politics* pp. 199–212.
18. Volumbozcar pp. 1–2; AGI IG 2536 p. 374.

19. Vázquez de Espinosa, *Compendium* p. 129.
20. Irving A. Leonard, *Baroque Times in Old Mexico* (Ann Arbor, 1959) p. 3.
21. Chaunu, *Séville* v.
22. Volumbozcar p. 4.
23. Villavicencio has been described as a veteran in some accounts of the ship-wreck, but his age was clearly documented when he gave evidence later in Santo Domingo. AGI IG 2536 p. 384.
24. Fernandez de Navarrete, *Biblioteca*.
25. Unless otherwise stated the sources for the rest of the chapter are Volumbozcar pp. 1–4; Villavicencio pp. 1–2.
26. Chaunu, *Séville* viii (2), 1846.
27. For brief comments on the stowage of the treasure see Navarrete p. 146 and AGI IG 2536 pp. 207, 489. For a general discussion of the stowage of treasure in Spanish ships see Potter, *Treasure Diver's Guide* pp. 16–19.
28. AGI Ct 5118. Vera Cruz 15 Jul 1641. But note that Domínguez Ortiz, 'Los Caudales' p. 50 fn. 83, gives the much smaller figure of 770,000 pesos for the royal treasure on the two ships. On the office of *maestre de plata* see Haring, *Trade and Navigation* p. 221.
29. AGI IG 2536 p. 406.
30. Medina's statement in AGI IG 2536 p. 406. See also p. 375 for Diego Centeno's claim that he had 90,000 pesos of his own silver and jewels on board; p. 429 for a merchant with 60,000 pesos on board. Antonio Petri y Arce's statement is in AGI IG 2699/1 p. 2. The writer would like to empha-size that estimating the value and weight of the ship's cargo of silver is made even more difficult from the fact that it is never clear whether the word 'peso' means the piece of eight of 272 maravedís or the *peso ensayado* of 450 maravedís.
31. Haring, *Trade and Navigation* p. 220.
32. AGI Ct 5118. Vera Cruz 15 Jul 1641. The other man was Gaspar Gutierrez, co-owner of the *Concepción*.
33. Volumbozcar p. 14.
34. The evidence on the number on board is rather confused. The lowest figure is 400 given by Don Diego de Aldana, Captain of Infantry (IG 2536 pp. 391–4) and the highest is 514 (Navarrete letter p. 146). Several other people said there were over 500.
35. Vázquez de Espinosa, *Compendium* p. 103.
36. For a good account of the capture of Providence see Newton, *Colonizing Activities* pp. 298–304. See also Wangüemert y Poggio, *El Almirante Pimienta* pp. 107–26.
37. Chaunu, *Séville* viii (2), 1846.

CHAPTER FOUR: Shipwreck

1. Jesuit fo. 277. There are four excellent descriptions of the last voyage of the

Notes

Concepción: Villavicencio, Volumbozcar, Jesuit and Navarrete. These all agree on essentials but have varying amounts of detailed description. I will only give references when I quote from the text of these documents.

2. Jesuit fo. 277v. This letter gives much the best and most detailed description of the storm.
3. Villavicencio p. 3.
4. Ibid.
5. Jesuit fo. 278.
6. Volumbozcar p. 6.
7. Jesuit fo. 278.
8. Villavicencio p. 4.
9. Only Navarrete gives this latitude, and, in fact, the anonymous author gives 32 degrees. But this is the latitude of Bermuda and would make a nonsense of the story. I have assumed that the copyist read 32 for 22, which makes much more sense.
10. Villavicencio p. 4.
11. Ibid. p. 5.
12. AGI IG 2536 p. 61. Evidence of the *alferes* (lieutenant), Antonio de Soto.
13. The chronology of the next few days is rather confused in the documents, but the following account makes the best sense of the conflicting evidence.
14. Jesuit fos. 278v–9.

CHAPTER FIVE: Sauve Qui Peut
1. AGI IG 2699/3 p. 5. The sources for the rest of the chapter are the same as for the previous chapter, with the addition of AGI IG 2536, the record of the enquiry held later at Santo Domingo, which has much information on the last days spent on the wreck and the adventures of the survivors.
2. The best source for the controversy over the latitude is AGI IG 2536, especially pp. 34 and 54–5, the evidence of the gunner, Juan de Guebara, and the Constable, Diego de Castro. See also Villavicencio p. 6.
3. Villavicencio p. 6.
4. Gardyner, *Description* pp. 70–1.
5. Villavicencio p. 7.
6. IG 2536 pp. 499–500. Evidence of Gaspar Guttoes.
7. Villavicencio p. 7; Navarrete fo. 146; IG 2536 pp. 235–7, 400–1, 409, 415–18 give conflicting descriptions of this incident.
8. Villavicencio p. 8. This account of the adventures of the long-boat party is based on Villavicencio p. 8; Volumbozcar pp. 9–10 and IG 2536 pp. 385–7 (evidence of Villavicencio); pp. 391–4 (evidence of Diego de Aldana); ibid. pp. 534–65 (evidence of people from the towns of Cotuy, La Vega and Santiago).

9. Gardyner *Description* p. 61.
10. Villavicencio p. 8.
11. Ibid.
12. Penzer (ed.), *Voyages of Columbus* p. 227.
13. Villavicencio p. 8.
14. Navarrete fo. 146v; Jesuit fo. 279; IG 2536 pp. 53, 64, 68.
15. Navarrete fo. 146 v.
16. IG 2536 pp. 562–8.
17. For the adventures of this party see Jesuit fo. 279; Navarrete fo. 147; IG 2536 especially pp. 40, 45–6, 64, 71, 111, 117, 324, 385–7, 435, 436, 483–4.
18. IG 2536 p. 71. Evidence of Vicente de Guzman.
19. Navarrete fo. 147v.
20. IG 2536 p. 40. Evidence of Castro.
21. Jesuit fo. 279.
22. Jesuit fo. 279v.
23. IG 2536 pp. 477–8. Evidence of Andres de la Cruz. See also *ibid.* pp. 479–84 for the evidence of three friars and Don Diego Centeno who had discussed the Indian's story with him, and Navarrete fo. 147.
24. Navarrete fo. 147.
25. Villavicencio p. 12; Navarrete fo. 150v; Volumbozcar p.14; Navarrete fo. 151 has a list of 57 survivors, including one woman, the only mention of a woman on board. Another fifty names could be added to this list from survivors of the wreck who gave evidence in the enquiry held at Santo Domingo (IG 2536).

CHAPTER SIX: Santo Domingo
1. AGI IG 2536 pp. 99–111, 419–27; Volumbozcar p. 10. This chapter is based mainly on IG 2536.
2. IG 2536 pp. 101–3, 109–11.
3. Ibid. pp. 151, 304–12.
4. Ibid pp. 25–31, 116–18, 151–2, 266–7; Villavicencio pp. 7–9; Volumbozcar p. 11.
5. Villavicencio p. 7.
6. It is just possible that Villavicencio did go out for a short while, but the evidence is very confused. Here I am following Volumbozcar p. 11 who has the clearest account of the change of plan. One account (IG 2536 p. 118 – evidence of Don Juan de Retverta, *oydor* of the Audiencia of Santo Domingo) said that Villavicencio went out for fifteen days, recognized the shoals where the ship was lost and even picked up some survivors, but this must be nonsense. Villavicencio does not mention it in his own account, nor does anybody else, and the Almirante was definitely in Santo Domingo on 3 December (six days after the meeting) when he gave evidence before Retverta himself about the wreck. (IG 2536 pp. 384–7).

7. IG 2536 pp. 142–8.
8. Ibid. pp. 118–19; Villavicencio p. 8; Volumbozcar pp. 11–12.
9. Ibid. pp. 119, 203; Villavicencio pp. 10–11.
10. Ibid. pp. 150–72.
11. Ibid. pp. 441–4.
12. Ibid. pp. 384–429, 534–67, etc.
13. Ibid. pp. 460–2.
14. AGI IG 2699/1 pp. 1–2; see also IG 2699/3 p. 1 where Maldonado confirms Granillo's statement.
15. IG 2536 pp. 454–5, 463–75.
16. Ibid. pp. 34–55.
17. Ibid. pp. 59–91, 316–32, 479–500.
18. Ibid. pp. 502–3, 513–28.
19. Ibid. pp. 94–5, 99–100, 529–31.
20. Ibid. pp. 568–9.
21. Ibid. pp. 477–8.
22. Ibid. p. 119.
23. Ibid. p. 123. Evidence of Retverta. This witness wrote a report which includes quite a few things not mentioned by anyone else, and I have treated it with suspicion. See above, note 6. Neither Villavicencio nor Volumbozcar mention this expedition.
24. Ibid. pp. 100–1.
25. Ibid. pp. 276–301.
26. Ibid. pp. 202, 257–9, 266–8.
27. Ibid. p. 122.
28. Ibid. pp. 188–250. Quotations from pp. 207, 232.
29. Ibid. pp. 257–73. Quotation on pp. 262–3.
30. Ibid. pp. 130–1.
31. Ibid. pp. 175–81.
32. Ibid. pp. 184–5.
33. Ibid. p. 381.
34. Navarrete pp. 147–8; Jesuit fo. 279v; AGI Ct 2900 Lib I fo. 241v.
35. Villavicencio p. 2.
36. Domínguez Ortiz, *op. cit* 'Los Caudales' p. 50.

CHAPTER SEVEN: Sea Change
1. AGI IG 2699/6 and 7.
2. AGI IG 2699/2, 17, 19, 21 and 25. For the wreck of the *Nuestra Señora de las Maravillas* see Horner, *Treasure Galleons* ch. 12 and Potter, *The Treasure Divers Guide* pp. 219–20. In 1972 the treasure-hunting firm, Sea Finders Inc., claimed to have rediscovered the lost Almiranta under twenty feet of sand;

International Journal of Nautical Archaeology and Underwater Exploration ii
(1973) p. 209.

3. AGI IG 2699/1, 2 and 17.

4. AGI IG 2699/5, 17 and 21.

5. AGI IG 2525/1, 2 and 3; IG 2699/4 and 17 for Villegas; IG 2699/17 for
García.

6. This section on the disintegration of wrecks is based on Throckmorton,
Shipwrecks and Archaeology; Peterson, *History under the Sea* and Potter, *Treasure Divers Guide.*

7. This discussion of change in the West Indies is based on the works by Parry,
Lynch and Hussey already cited and Bridenbaugh, *No Peace Beyond the Line;*
Newton, *European Nations in the West Indies* (1933); Crouse, *French Pioneers;*
Haring, *Buccaneers;* Means, *Spanish Main.*

8. *The Buccaneers of America* (1st Eng. ed. 1684).

9. On Morgan see Cruikshank, *Life of Sir Henry Morgan;* Dudley Pope, *Harry Morgan's Way.*

10. Newton, *European Nations* p. 270.

11. For a useful general discussion of the navy's role on the Jamaica station see
Pawson and Buisseret, *Port Royal* pp. 42–62.

12. *CSPD* 29 Aug 1682.

CHAPTER EIGHT: The Wreckers

1. Quoted in Wilkinson, *Adventures of Bermuda* p. 53.

2. *CSPC* 6 Feb 1622.

3. Massachusetts Historical Society, *Winthrop Papers* (Boston, 1947) v, 232–3.

4. On the early history of the Bahamas see Craton, *History of the Bahamas;* Malcolm, *Historical Documents;* Miller, 'Colonisation of the Bahamas'.

5. *CSPAWI* 23 Aug 1672. John Wentworth, Governor of New Providence to
Sir Thomas Lynch.

6. BL Egerton 2395 fos. 472–6.

7. Ibid. fo. 558.

8. *CSPAWI* 23 Aug 1672.

9. *CSPAWI* 29 Aug 1682.

10. *CSPAWI* 15 Mar 1684.

11. Potter, *Treasure Diver's Guide* pp. 28–40.

12. Marx, *They Dared the Deep* p. 21.

13. Ibid. pp. 24–5.

14. Ibid. p. 35.

15. John Winthrop, *Journal* (ed. J. K. Hosner, 1908) ii, 67.

16. *CSPAWI* 29 Aug 1682.

17. John Taylor, 'Multum in parvo . . .', MS at the Institute of Jamaica, iii, 785.

18. Pope, *Harry Morgan's Way* p. 296.

19. AGI IG 2699/1.
20. BL Egerton 3984 fo. 191.

CHAPTER NINE: The Captains and the King

1. *CSPAWI* 29 Aug 1682. Sir Thomas Lynch to Lords of Trade and Plantations.
2. Bodl. Rawlinson A. 189 fo. 76. For a useful general discussion of the laws relating to treasure-hunting see Karraker, *Hispaniola Treasure* ch. 1.
3. PRO ADM 106/52. 10 Oct 1682.
4. PRO ADM 1/3553 pp. 59–60.
5. PRO ADM 106/52. 9 Nov and 5 Dec 1682.
6. Dyer, *Life of Narborough*; for Narborough's early interest in the wreck see AGI IG 2699/4 pp. 4–5.
7. PRO CO 1/57 fos. 34–5, 311v; Bodl. Rawlinson A. 300, entries for 25 May 1684, 3 May and 11 Oct 1685.
8. For scraps of information on Sir Richard White see *CSPD* 14 Sep 1685; PRO C.7/366/54; C.7/366/69; C.7/599/115; C.8/562/101; Davies, *Royal African Company* p. 328. For the family background of the Whites see R. G. Maunsell, *History of Maunsell, or Mansel, and of some related families* (Cork, 1903) pp. 144–6 and G. E. Cockayne, *Complete Baronetage* (1904) iv, 86. White is often referred to as Don Ricardo de Vite or similar hispanic interpretations of his name.
9. For Harmon's connection with the pilot see AGI IG 2699/9 p. 4; see also PRO ADM 51/345 9 Jul 1683.
10. PRO CO 1/57 fo. 34v.
11. Information on the size, manning and location of royal ships is taken from the Admiralty List Book, 1673–89. PRO ADM 8/1.
12. PRO ADM 2/1726 p. 420; ADM 51/345. 9 Jul 1683.
13. Sharpe's orders are in PRO ADM 2/1726 p. 396. For Sharpe's career as a buccaneer see Haring, *Buccaneers* pp. 223–9.
14. Brief information on the careers of all naval officers can be found in PRO ADM 10/10.
15. See the two log-books, PRO ADM 51/345 for the *Falcon* and Bodl. Rawlinson A.300 for the *Bonetta*.
16. PRO ADM 51/345. 3 May 1683.
17. The only source for the early career of Phips is the contemporary biography by Mather, *Pietas in Patriam*: my quotations are taken from the 1929 New York edition.
18. AGI IG 2699/12 p. 1.
19. PRO ADM 1/3554 p. 449.
20. BL Egerton 2526, 3 Sep 1683.
21. PRO ADM 1/3554 p. 469.
22. BL Egerton 2526 is the source for the rest of the chapter.

CHAPTER TEN: The Stanley Brothers at Sea
1. Most of this chapter is based on Bodl. Rawlinson A.300, Captain Stanley's journal, supplemented by PRO ADM 51/345, the journal of the *Falcon*. For a discussion of the cartography of the area see Tillinghast, *Hydrography of the Handkerchief Shoal*. See also, for general information, *The West Indies Pilot (North Western Part)* vol. i (1971).
2. AGI IG 2699/19 p. 3.
3. *CSPAWI* 28 Feb 1684. Lynch to Lords of Trade and Plantations.
4. *CSPAWI* 17 Sep 1684.
5. For this business see Davies, *Royal African Company* pp. 326–35 and F. J. Osborne, s. J., 'James Castillo-Asiento Agent', *Jamaican Historical Review* viii (1971).
6. The crew list is in PRO CO 1/55 fos. 105–6.
7. *CSPAWI* 28 Feb 1683/4. Lynch to Lords of Trade and Plantations.
8. *CSPAWI* 15 Nov 1684. Molesworth to William Blathwayt.
9. Pawson and Buisseret, *Port Royal*, provide the most detailed description of Jamaica at this time and make clear the sources on which they draw.
10. PRO CO 1/57 fo. 34v.
11. PRO CO 1/57 fo. 38. 'Deposition of T. Smith about the Silver Wreck'.
12. CO 1/57 fo. 34. Molesworth to Blathwayt. 3 Feb 1684/5.
13. Ibid. See also 'The Articles of Agreement between Hender Molesworth, Lieutenant-Governor of Jamaica on behalf of His Majesty and Thomas Smith'. CO 1/57 fo. 40v.
14. See the muster and pay-book of the *Bonetta*. PRO ADM 33/126 and ADM 39/261.
15. CO 1/57 fo. 40.
16. CO 1/57 fo. 35; Bodl. Rawlinson A.300 31 Jan 1684/85.
17. CO 1/57 fos. 311v–12v and 407. Molesworth to Blathwayt. 15 May 1685 and Captain Stanley's instructions, dated 24 Jun 1685.
18. CO 138/5. Molesworth to Blathwayt. 27 Nov 1685.
19. Ibid.

CHAPTER ELEVEN: The Cruise of the Rose of Algeree
1. BL Egerton 2526. 5 Sep 1683. The first eight pages of this chapter are based on this document and I will give no further references.
2. Toppam, *Edward Randolph* iii, 251–2, 262, 265.
3. Ibid. pp. 251–2.
4. *CSPAWI* 6 Jun 1684.
5. Toppam, *Edward Randolph* p. 265.
6. *CSPAWI*, 18 Nov 1684. Molesworth to Blathwayt.
7. *CTB* 12 Apr 1686 and 24 Nov 1686; BL Sloane 45 fo. 72.

8. Mather, *Pietas in Patriam* pp. 20–1.
9. Ibid. pp. 21–4.
10. *CSPAWI* 18 Nov 1684.
11. Bodl. Rawlinson A.300. Stanley was engaged on various tasks for the Governor in the winter of 1684, but was in Port Royal 1–11 Oct and 13 Nov–9 Dec. He does not mention Phips in his journal.
12. AGI IG 2699/30 p. 3. For more about White's claim see below pp. 197–8.
13. Mather, *Pietas in Patriam* pp. 24–5.
14. Bodl. Rawlinson A.171 fo. 205.
15. Mather, *Pietas in Patriam* p. 25.
16. See above p. 140 PRO CO 1/57 fo. 312v. 15 May 1685.
17. Mather, *Pietas in Patriam* p. 25.
18. *CSPAWI* 4 Jun 1685. Cony to Sunderland.
19. *CSPAWI* 3 Aug 1685. Phips to Sunderland.
20. *CSPAWI* 4 Aug 1685. Blathwayt to Graham.
21. *CSPAWI* 27 Feb and 6 Jun 1684. The King to Joseph Dudley and William Stoughton and their reply.
22. PRO ADM 1/3554 p. 449.
23. George, 'Treasure Trove'.

CHAPTER TWELVE: Captain Phips's Wreck Project
1. HMC *12th Report* Appendix ix (1891) p. 90. Duke of Beaufort to his Duchess, 16 Jun 1687.
2. Defoe, *Essay upon Projects* p. 16.
3. Mather, *Pietas in Patriam* p. 26.
4. HMC *12th Report* Appendix ix (1891) p. 90.
5. AGI IG 2699/9 p. 6.
6. Bodl. Rawlinson A.171 fo. 205.
7. PRO CO 138/5 fos. 120–1. Molesworth to Blathwayt 27 Nov 1685. 'You shall have his journal by next ship'. Letters from Jamaica took about two and a half months.
8. PRO C/10/227/63. All the details relating to the business side of the project and the fitting out of the ships come from this document, and I shall give no further references.
9. Bodl. Rawlinson A.171 fo. 205.
10. BL Sloane 3984 fo. 282. Most of the information on Albemarle is from Ward, *Christopher Monck*.
11. Ward, *Christopher Monck* pp. 217–18.
12. PRO C/107/25. Anthony Parker to Mr Croft. 1 Feb 1686/7.
13. Dyer, *Life of Narborough*.
14. PRO C/8/427/84.
15. For Smith see PRO C/10/227/63.

16. On Falkland see *DNB* and Ehrman, *Navy in the War of William III* p. 643. For Hayes's revenue farm see *CTB* viii, 1423–5 and other references in the same volume.
17. PRO ADM 2/1741 p. 263. Royal order countersigned by Pepys.
18. HMC, *Calendar of letters . . . sent to Christopher Monck, 2nd. Duke of Albemarle* (1976) p. 118; ADM 2/1741 p. 378. The new grant was dated 4 Mar 1687, six months after Phips had sailed.
19. The articles of agreement have not survived, but they are summarized in PRO C/10/227/63 (Smith's Bill of Complaint) and in C/8/540/85.
20. They are appended to PRO C/10/227/63.
21. Defoe, *Essay upon Projects* p. 16.
22. The accounts are in the log-book of the *James and Mary*. BL Sloane 50.
23. Bodl. Rawlinson A.171 fo. 205 says there were six divers, but the log-book and accounts of the *James and Mary* refer on several occasions to the four dyvers'.
24. See above p. 151.
25. Berwick, *Rawdon Papers* pp. 388–91.
26. Mather, *Pietas in Patriam* p. 26.

CHAPTER THIRTEEN: Shipwreck Refound
1. Journal of *James and Mary* is BL Sloane 50. Journal of *Henry* is KAO U1515/010. I will only give references for quotations, using just the name of the ship.
2. *Henry* 11 Dec 1686.
3. *Henry* 29 Nov 1686.
4. *CSPD* 4 Sep 1686. For Bannister's career see Pawson and Buisseret, *Port Royal* pp. 52–5.
5. *CSPAWI* 9 Feb 1687.
6. BL Sloane 50 fo. 61. The accounts relating to the disposal of the ship's cargo are scattered through this journal.
7. *James and Mary* 28 Dec 1686.
8. PRO C/10/227/63. 'Wm. Phipps' Answer'.
9. *James and Mary* 12 Jan 1687.
10. *James and Mary* 13 Jan 1687.
11. Taylor, 'Multum in parvo', MS at the Institute of Jamaica, iii, 705 and 808. I am indebted to Burt D. Webber, Jr., for my quotations from Taylor's MS.
12. *Henry* 18 Jan 1687. All the following quotations are from this journal.
13. Sloane to Sir Arthur Rawdon in Berwick, *Rawdon Papers* pp. 388–91 quoted by G. R. de Beer, *Sir Hans Sloane and the British Museum* (Oxford, 1953) p. 29.
14. Mather, *Pietas in Patriam* pp. 27–8.
15. Bodl. Rawlinson A.171 fo. 206v. This is a summary of the discovery of the

wreck, reputedly based on the journal of the *Henry*. But whether the writer, a Mr Smith, had really seen the journal is doubtful as he makes quite a few errors, including attributing the first discovery to Rogers.

16. This is very well described in Taylor, 'Multum in parvo' ii, 412 and iii, 759 and 805.
17. *Henry* 22 Jan 1687.
18. Taylor, 'Multum in parvo' iii, 705, 808.
19. *Henry* 23 Jan 1687.
20. *James and Mary* 25 Jan 1687.
21. Bodl. Rawlinson A.171 fo. 206v.
22. Mather, *Pietas in Patriam* pp. 28–9.
23. His name appears in the accounts of the *James and Mary*. Sloane 50 fos. 43 and 44. My speculation that he was a diver rests on the fact that his name, and that of Francis Anderson, appear together with the two men we know were divers, Jonas Abimeleck and John Pasqua.
24. Bodl. Rawlinson A.300. 9 Jul 1683.
25. Ibid. 15 May 1684.
26. The last three paragraphs owe much to a long conversation which the author had with Messrs Webber and Haskins.

CHAPTER FOURTEEN: Salvage
1. *James and Mary* and *Henry* 9–17 Feb 1687. Most of this chapter rests on these two journals and I will give no further references to them.
2. Quoted by Link, *Sea Diver* p. 279.
3. Quoted by Lounsberry, *Sir William Phips* p. 158.
4. 17–21 Mar.
5. Link, *Sea Diver* pp. 256–7.
6. Quoted by Link, *Sea Diver* pp. 276–7.
7. E.g. Kip Wagner, *Pieces of Eight* (1967) pp. 103, 130.
8. Mather, *Pietas in Patriam* pp. 31–2.
9. Ibid. p. 30.
10. HMC *Downshire* i (1924) p. 245.

CHAPTER FIFTEEN: Good News for the Mint
1. HMC *12th Report* App. v (1889) p. 114.
2. Thompson, *Correspondence of the Family of Hatton* ii, 67; see also Ellis, *Correspondence* i, 294–7; HMC *12th Report* App. ix (1891) p. 90; HMC *Downshire* i (1924) p. 245 for other letters.
3. *London Gazette* No. 2249 (6–9 June 1687). There is also a good account in the broadside *An Exact and Perfect Relation*.
4. BL Add. 25, 374 fo. 157. Correspondence of Francesco Terriesi.
5. For a detailed account of what follows see George, 'Treasure Trove'.

Notes

6. PRO T 52/12 p. 345.
7. PRO T 27/11 p. 434; HMC *Downshire* i, 300; George, 'Treasure Trove'.
8. PRO T 52/12 p. 345.
9. PRO C/10/227/63.
10. Same sources as notes 8 and 9. For the guns see the letter of the Spanish ambassador in AGI IG 2699/12.
11. Morgan shared 400,000 pieces of eight at Panama (£100,000); 250,000 at Porto Bello and 250,000 at Maracaibo, making a total haul from the three raids of £225,000. Pope, *Harry Morgan's Way* pp. 154, 184, 246.
12. Chandaman, *English Public Revenue* pp. 360–1.
13. Mather, *Pietas in Patriam* p. 38.
14. Ibid. p. 33.
15. No record says exactly what Phips received, but it is clear that he did get one-sixteenth from the figures in the table on p. 201.
16. PRO C/10/227/63.
17. HMC *Downshire* i, 256.
18. Quoted in de Beer, *Sir Hans Sloane* p. 29.
19. AGI IG 2699/10; BL Add. 25,374 fo. 143v; ibid. fos. 145–6 are a copy of the Spanish Memorial.
20. IG 2699/9 and 12. See also IG 2699/13. Ronquillo to King of Spain, 27 Jun 1687.
21. IG 2699/9 p. 6.
22. IG 2699 passim.
23. IG 2699/29 p. 1.
24. BL Add. 25,374 fo. 143v.
25. IG 2699/3. Dated Madrid 6/16 Aug 1687.
26. His name appears neither in IG 2536 nor in Navarrete fo. 151, but, since these only cover about half the survivors, this is by no means conclusive.
27. IG 2699/30.
28. IG 2699/30 p. 3.
29. *CTB* viii, 1534.
30. The following is based on PRO C/10/227/63.
31. Smith's petition is in the *Acts of the Privy Council, Colonial Series* 16 Jul 1687.
32. Quoted by George, 'Treasure Trove' pp. 313–14.
33. Quoted in de Beer, *Sir Hans Sloane* p. 29.
34. Bodl. Rawlinson A.189 fos. 370–2.
35. BL Add. 25,374 fo. 186.
36. PRO C/8/540/85. The indenture was dated 20 Oct 1687.
37. BL Add. 25,374 fo. 258v.
38. Ibid. fo. 186v.
39. NMM ADM/L/F/198. Log-book of *Foresight*; PRO ADM 51/68/3. Log-book of *Assistance*.

40. NMM SOU/11 fo. 25.
41. Chandaman, *English Public Revenue* pp. 348–61.
42. NMM SOU/11 fo. 29.
43. *CSPD* 23 Jul 1687.
44. PRO C/105/35 No. 22. This document relates to the assignment of a share in this company.
45. Gilbert Burnet, *History of his own Times* (Oxford, 1823) iii, 262.

CHAPTER SIXTEEN: Unhappy Return

 1. The voyage of the *Foresight* in 1687–8 is very well documented. We have the log-book kept by Captain Edward Stanley (PRO ADM 52/35/2); the log-book kept by Lieut. John Hubbard (NMM ADM/L/F/198); and a letter-book kept by Sir John Narborough (NMM LBK/1). I will only give references for quotations.
 2. NMM ADM/L/R/198 24 Nov 1687; PRO ADM 2/1742 p. 43.
 3. NMM LBK/1 fo. 3.
 4. PRO ADM 52/35/2 26 Nov 1687.
 5. PRO CO 1/64 fos. 24–5; NMM SOU/10. Declaration by Hender Molesworth dated 17 Dec 1687.
 6. *CSPAWI* 19 Dec 1687. Albemarle to Lords of Trade and Plantations.
 7. NMM LBK/1 14 Apr 1688.
 8. Mather, *Pietas in Patriam* pp. 32–3.
 9. *CSPAWI* 28 Feb 1687/8. See also ibid. 6 Jul, 17 Nov, 7 Dec 1687.
10. *CSPAWI* 26 Dec 1687; NMM SOU/10 n.p; NMM SOU/11 fo. 53; BL Sloane 3984 fos. 200–9.
11. NMM SOU/11 fo. 55.
12. *CSPAWI* 11 Jul, 10 Aug, 21 Oct 1687; PRO CO 1/64 fos. 24–5.
13. *CSPAWI* 28 Jan 1688; PRO CO 1/64 fos. 24–5. See also Karraker, 'Spanish Treasure'.
14. *CSPAWI* 19 Mar 1688. Horzdesnell to Lords of Trade and Plantations; PRO ADM 51/3987. Log of *Swan* 15 Jan to 27 Mar 1688.
15. PRO T.27/11 p. 430; *CSPAWI* 30 Apr 1688. Molesworth to Lords of Treasury. For more on Constable's activities see Karraker, 'Spanish Treasure' p. 318.
16. NMM LBK/1 fo. 14.
17. For the 200 divers see NMM LBK/1 fo. 19. For the rest of the chapter the sources are the same as in Note 1.
18. NMM LBK/1 fo. 5v.
19. PRO ADM 51/68/3. Log of *Assistance*. She stayed at Samaná till 14 March.
20. The *Drake* was at Jamaica and the *Maryrose* at Barbados. PRO ADM 8/1.
21. *DNB* Charles Mordaunt, 3rd Earl of Peterborough, 1658–1755.
22. Taylor, 'Multum in parvo' iii, 759.

23. NMM LBK/1 fo. 16. 14 Apr 1688.
24. Taylor, 'Multum in parvo' iii, 805.
25. NMM LBK/1 fo. 10.
26. See Captain Stanley's log-book (PRO ADM 52/35/2) for 9 Apr 1688.
27. PRO ADM 51/3987. 13 Apr 1688.
28. NMM LBK/1 fo. 19.
29. Ibid. fo.19. 4 May 1688.
30. Mather, *Pietas in Patriam* p. 40.
31. NMM ADM/L/F/198. 20 May 1688.
32. NMM LBK/1 fo. 23.
33. PRO ADM 52/35/2 and NMM ADM/L/F/198 26–27 May 1688; NMM LBK/1 n.p.; Bodl. Rawlinson A.179 fo. 270. Letter to Pepys from his nephew, Samuel Jackson, who had served on the *Foresight*, 20 Jul 1688.
34. NMM ADM/L/F/198 14 Jul 1688.
35. Ibid. 24 Jul.
36. Ibid. 2 Aug.

CHAPTER SEVENTEEN: The Treasure-Hunters
1. The evidence for the third expedition is in the records of the lawsuit discussed below. See in particular PRO C/8/540/85; C/24/1177/30; C/8/365/31 and HMC *House of Lords MSS* n.s. vi, 59–60.
2. PRO C/24/1177/30; C/8/540/85 fo. 4, 'account of the charge of the three voyages made to the wreck'.
3. BL Sloane 3984 fo. 284v.
4. See refs in Note 1 and *Appeals to the House of Lords, 1717–21*.
5. Ehrman, *Navy in the War of William III* pp. 506–7; *DNB* Anthony Cary, fifth Viscount Falkland.
6. PRO C/8/365/31.
7. Mather, *Pietas in Patriam* p. 204.
8. *CSPAWI* 12 Oct 1692. Phips to Blathwayt. For what follows I have relied on Marion L. Starkey, *The Devil in Massachusetts* (New York, 1950); Lounsberry, *Sir William Phips*; *DNB* and *Dictionary of American Biography*.
9. *CSPAWI* 12 Oct 1692. Phips to Blathwayt.
10. On the treasure-hunting boom see Karraker, *Hispaniola Treasure* pp. 81–91; Scott, *Constitution and Finance of Joint-Stock Companies* ii, 485–8; Defoe, *Essay upon Projects*; Bennet Woodcroft, *Titles of Patents of Invention, 1617–1823* (1854) pp. 51–63.
11. Potter, *Treasure Diver's Guide* p. 281.
12. Wagner, *Pieces of Eight*.
13. Wagner, *Pieces of Eight* p. 190.
14. For Korganoff see Latil and Rivoire, *Sunken Treasure* ch. 2; see also Link, *Sea Diver* ch. 2 and Cousteau and Diolé, *Diving for Sunken Treasure*.

Cousteau's book has some superb underwater photographs of the coral on Silver Bank.

15. Cousteau and Diolé, *Diving for Sunken Treasure* p. 64.
16. S. Wignall in *International Journal of Nautical Archaeology and Underwater Exploration* iii (1974) p. 181.
17. NMM LBK/1 fo. 19.

CHAPTER EIGHTEEN: The Second Captain Phips

1. This chapter is based mainly on conversations with Burt Webber and his colleagues in Seaquest International, and on a number of documents pertaining to Operation Phips and Seaquest International kindly lent to me by Webber.
2. The *Maravillas* was found in 1972 by Robert Marx, and the *Atocha* in 1975 by Melvin Fisher.
3. A translation of this agreement is appended to the offering circular of Operation Phips II, L.P.
4. Quoted by *The Miami Herald*, 7 February 1979.
5. This section is based on conversations with members of Webber's team and on the Daily Activity Log of Operation Phips.
6. This chart forms part of Taylor's MS 'Multum in parvo or parvum in multo.'
7. Its reference is U1515/0 10.
8. This offering circular is dated 1 August 1978.
9. Letter from Marx to Webber dated 28 September 1976.
10. This and other quotations from the Daily Activity Log of Operation Phips II.
11. As quoted in *The Miami Herald*, 7 February 1979.
12. AGI IG2536 pp. 477–8.

Index

(names of ships in italics)

Index

Index

Guillen, Bartolomé, 48–9, 60–1, 64–5, 71–2, 77–8, 86, 91, 120, 122

Haddock, Sir Richard, 119, 158
Haiti, 229
Half-Moon Reef, 230, 233, 234, 238
Handkerchief (Handkercher) Bank *see* Abrojos
Harmon (or Hermans), Captain Isaac, 121–3, 129–32, 140, 142, 160–1, 179–80, 213
Haskins, Jack, 223, 227, 229–30
Haskins Reef, 239
Havana, 16, 42, 45, 49–52, 54–5, 62, 91, 98, 100, 104, 106, 110
Hayes, Sir James, 164, 201, 203, 207, 218
Henry, 164–82, 184, 187, 189–90, 192, 198, 203, 234
Heyn, Piet, 37
Hispaniola, 33, 95, 107, 114, 116, 123, 133, 136–7, 164–5, 188, 202, 213; buccaneers in, 38–9, 59, 96, 99, 115; survivors of shipwreck in, 68, 72–6; Spanish attempts to launch expedition to find *Concepción* from, 77–91; English wreck hunters in, 129, 131, 139–41, 155, 168–72, 177–9, 188, 207
Horzdesnell, Henry, 210–11
Howard, Sir Philip, 163
Hubbard, John, 207, 209, 212, 214–15, 223

international relations, 16–17, 31, 36–42, 96–104, 133–4, 194–6, 205
Ireland, 104, 121, 145
Isabella, 38, 68, 72, 80

Jamaica (*see also* Port Royal), 33, 41, 108, 110–11, 114–15, 126, 129, 151, 156, 160, 185; English conquest of, 96–7; buccaneers in, 99–104, 120; Stanley in, 131, 133–41, 154; Phips in, 153–5; Albemarle and, 163, 202–3, 206–7, 212–13, 218; attempt to collect royalty on wreck silver in, 208–9, 211
James and Mary, 164–72, 177–91, 194, 198, 203, 206–7, 220, 240
James II, King of England, 156–60, 164–5, 191–8, 202–5, 213, 215–16
Jenner, Captain, 147
Joll, Admiral, 37

Karraker, Cyrus H., 223
Kelly, Charles, 167, 188
Key West, 54, 222
King, Sir Edmund, 191
Knepp, John, 126–7, 144–52, 159, 166
Korganoff, Alexandre, 222–3

La Cruse, John de, 178
La Cruz, Andres de, 75, 86, 178, 244
La Feria, Juan de, 48
La Garca, 55–6
La Nouvelle Trompeuse, 134
La Plaza, Don Antonio de, 43, 52, 83, 88–90
La Rodo, Don Geronimo de, 73
La Santissima Trinidad, 88
La Vega de Concepción, 170
Larco, Juan de, 110–11
Lesser Antilles (*see also* individual islands), 31–2, 37, 96, 97
Lewandowski, Ray, 237

270

Index

Index